FAIR WAYS

• •

NUMBER 103
Centennial Series of the Association
of Former Students,
Texas A&M University

FAIR WAYS

How Six Black Golfers

Won Civil Rights

in Beaumont, Texas

Robert J. Robertson

TEXAS A&M UNIVERSITY PRESS   COLLEGE STATION

Library of Congress Cataloging-in-Publication Data

Robertson, Robert J.
  Fair ways : how six black golfers won civil rights in Beaumont, Texas /
  Robert J. Robertson.— 1st ed.
     p. cm. — (Centennial series of the Association of Former
     Students, Texas A&M University ; no. 103)
  Includes bibliographical references and index.
  ISBN 1-58544-442-1 (cloth : alk. paper)
I. African American golfers—Civil rights—Texas—Beaumont—History—
20th century.   2. Discrimination in sports—Law and legislation—Texas—
Beaumont—History—20th century.
I. Title. II. Series.
  KFX1123.B3482C567 2005
  342.764'1450873—dc22
                    2005000435

The four golfers pictured on this book's jacket are *(left to right)* J. P. Griffin,
Jr., son of Joseph P. Griffin; and officers of the Tri-City Golf Association,
James Clark, tournament director; Royal W. Thomas, sergeant at arms; and
Harold Nelson, president.

For

June, Christine, and Colleen

Adin, Alyssa, Colin, Christian, and Charlotte

Lou, Christopher, Nicholas, and Emma

• • • • • • • • • • • • • • • • • • •

CONTENTS

· ·

ILLUSTRATIONS

• •

Beginning in the late nineteenth century, white Americans in southern states instituted the Jim Crow caste system; they established laws and customs that codified longtime racial prejudices against African Americans and relegated them to segregated and subservient positions in society. African Americans opposed this racial discrimination from the beginning and over the years have struggled to overcome the caste system and win their share of the American dream. During the last half of the twentieth century, they achieved considerable progress, through their own efforts, the activities of the National Association for the Advancement of Colored People (NAACP) and other civil rights organizations, and by the actions of presidents, Congress, and the federal courts. The courts became "vehicles of social transformation," in the words of Thurgood Marshall, the black NAACP attorney who won *Brown v. Board of Education* and other landmark civil rights cases.[1]

Marshall, later a Supreme Court justice, spoke on occasion about four elements necessary for producing this judicial transformation: crusading lawyers, receptive federal judges, a progressive Supreme Court, and, last but not least, the "Joe Doakeses"—ordinary citizens who "believed in the promise of justice and equality, [and] never gave up the fight against the relics of slavery."[2] In Beaumont, Texas, all the necessary elements came together: three black lawyers, one white federal judge, the Supreme Court of Chief Justice Earl Warren, and a half dozen Joe Doakeses—six black golfers who wanted to play the local municipal golf course on the same basis as white golfers.

In June, 1955, early in the modern civil rights era, Booker T. Fayson and five other African American golfers became "Joe Doakes" plaintiffs. They sued the city of Beaumont in federal court for the right to play the Tyrrell Park municipal golf course. Fayson and his friends Joseph P. Griffin, William Narcisse, Thomas A. Parker,

Johnnie R. Ware, and Earl V. White were avid golfers; they had learned the game as youths while working as caddies at Central Park, Tyrrell Park, and the Beaumont Country Club. They loved golf but because of Jim Crow segregation were not permitted to play their hometown public course. They could play the Tyrrell and other local courses on "caddy days" when the courses were closed to white patrons, or they could drive to Houston, where African Americans had recently gained access to municipal golf courses.

Beaumont, where Fayson and his golfing friends resided, was a southern town of 110,000 persons, with whites making up about 70 percent of the population and blacks, about 30 percent. White citizens enforced the Jim Crow caste system against black citizens, denying them entry as equals to hotels, restaurants, and theaters, as well as libraries, parks, swimming pools, and golf courses. Black Beaumonters wanted access to these facilities; they wanted to change the caste system, but the black community had almost no power. African Americans had little wealth, no elected officials, few lawyers, and no judges. The white majority had most of the power—economic, political, and judicial. The city government, its park system, and its golf course were controlled entirely by white officials, a group that included Elmo Beard, the mayor; Mrs. Willie Brockman, city manager; Reese Martin, parks commissioner; golf professional and course manager Henry Homberg; and assistant golf professional Johnnie Barlow.

But Booker Fayson and his Joe Doakes friends were not helpless. They had the advantages of education and military experience. Five of their number had served in the armed forces, and four had attended college, experiences that gave them the vision and ambition to assert their rights and improve their lives. In terms of occupational status, the group was mixed. William Narcisse was a railroad laborer and Earl White, a restaurant worker, but the other four men had middle-class jobs. Fayson was an insurance agent while Joe Griffin, Tom Parker, and Johnnie Ware were postal employees. All six men were courageous, willing to challenge the status quo of the southern caste system.

Fayson found the crusading lawyers needed to challenge the caste system. In Beaumont he met Theodore R. Johns and then Elmo Willard III, two young black lawyers just graduated from

Howard University's law school, then the national center for civil rights litigation. At Howard University Johns and Willard had studied constitutional law, were influenced by Thurgood Marshall, and became fired with the crusading spirit of civil rights reform. Johns and Willard in turn recruited a third black lawyer, U. Simpson Tate, NAACP regional counsel in Dallas. The NAACP, through its regional and national offices, orchestrated a nationwide legal campaign attacking the Jim Crow caste system, bringing class-action lawsuits to desegregate colleges, schools, and other public entities. Marshall, the lead NAACP attorney, had just won a momentous victory in *Brown v. Board of Education,* a ruling that outlawed segregation in public schools. The *Brown* decision showed that the Supreme Court of Chief Justice Warren was progressive, that it was amenable to changing the caste system.

With the progressive Warren court, and with Johns and the other crusading lawyers, Booker Fayson and his Joe Doakes friends had three out of four elements necessary for attacking the caste system and gaining access to the local municipal golf course. But they still needed a receptive federal judge, a judge who would hear their complaints and, hopefully, interpret the law in their favor. In this way Fayson and other black Beaumonters hoped to find new power for themselves, the power of the federal judicial system that they could use to attack the caste system in Beaumont.

A new federal judge appeared in the person of Lamar J. R. Cecil, a white lawyer recently appointed to the bench by President Eisenhower. But would Judge Cecil be a "receptive" judge? Would he apply the new legal principles of the *Brown* school case to questions pertaining to a municipal golf course in Beaumont? Would he use federal power to override state laws and outlaw local customs? Judge Cecil had handled no civil rights cases and had no track record on such questions. By way of his profession and personal life, he could be identified as a conservative, one inclined to defend the status quo. The son of a Houston railroad executive, Cecil had graduated from the Rice Institute and the University of Texas law school. He married into a wealthy Beaumont family, prospered as an insurance lawyer, and became a leader among the local elite, spending much of his spare time golfing, playing cards, and socializing with friends at the Beaumont Country Club. But Lamar Cecil was more than a wealthy attorney: He was a professional lawyer who believed in the rule of law and respected the U.S. Constitution. In addition, he was a proven politician and a leader in the newly emerging Texas Republican Party. He helped General Eisenhower win the presidency and parlayed that achievement into an appointment as federal judge in the Eastern District of Texas. In this way, Lamar Cecil worked politics to get judicial power for himself. So the question loomed. How would Judge Cecil wield that power? Would he be receptive to the new Supreme Court ruling and the desires of the black golfers, or would he be conservative, interpreting the law to sustain the caste system and reserving Tyrrell Park golf course for the exclusive use of white players?

ACKNOWLEDGMENTS

• •

This history of golf course desegregation in Beaumont, Texas, features ten key persons: six black golfers, Booker Fayson, Joe Griffin, Bill Narcisse, Tom Parker, Johnnie Ware, and Earl White; three black lawyers, Theodore Johns, Elmo Willard, and U. Simpson Tate; and one white judge, Lamar Cecil. All these men have passed away except for Theodore Johns, who lives in Beaumont and serves as magistrate judge of the municipal court. I congratulate Judge Johns and the others for their leadership in the desegregation of the Tyrrell Park municipal golf course, when they worked the rule of law to initiate positive and peaceful changes in race relations in Beaumont and southeast Texas. The desegregation of the golf course led directly to the desegregation of the local state college, another important development in which the same three lawyers, Johns, Willard, and Tate, and the same judge, Cecil, played prominent roles.

I thank Judge Johns for helping me gather material for this history and for providing his insights about the desegregation story. For sharing memories, photographs, and other materials, I thank family members and friends of the other key players, among them Mary Bell Fayson, Anthony Griffin, J. P. Griffin, Jr., Charles Narcisse, Laura Narcisse, Albertine Parker Simpson Simon, Thomas Parker, Jr., Linda Ware Kyle, Geraldine White, Ruby White Harris, Louis White, Pat Willard, Grayson Cecil, Lamar Cecil, Jr., Edith Cecil Flynn, and Mary Reed Cecil, who passed away August 10, 2003.

To Judge Johns and to the families and friends of the other key persons, I apologize for any errors in fact and interpretation, especially in the matter of giving credit for accomplishments, where I may have paid too much attention to one person or group and not enough to another. I have tried to tell this story accurately, but of course mine is just one version of the story. Judge Johns, and the others if they were alive, could present different and valid versions of the story.

Other Beaumonters played significant roles in this early desegregation story: African American leaders such as Pauline Brackeen, Rev. G. W. Daniels, O. C. Hebert, Marion Lewis, Rev. W. N. McCarty, Archie L. Price, and Dr. Ed D. Sprott, Jr.; and white leaders, including the mayor, Elmo Beard, city council member Jimmie P. Cokinos, city manager Mrs. Willie Brockman, city attorneys George Murphy and John D. Rienstra, civic committee chair Charles D. Smith, and journalist Robert Akers. I applaud these citizens and others, black and white, who helped the people of Beaumont and southeast Texas deal peacefully with changes in race relations.

Friends and fellow citizens contributed valuable information as well as interesting anecdotes. For these I am grateful to Johnnie Antoine, Johnnie B. Barlow, Leonard Bruno, Rhoda Carter, Andrew Cokinos, Jimmie P. Cokinos, Bobby T. Cowart, Myrtle Sprott DePlanter, Rhew Dooley, Woodson E. Dryden, Henry Durham William T. Faucett, Benny H. Hughes, Jr., Tanner T. Hunt, Jr., Ednita Lane, Clarence Lartigue, James D. McNicholas, Elizabeth Mouton, Nancy Brooks Neild, Dora Nisby, Maudry Plummer, Mike Porter, Richard Price, Kenneth E. Ruddy, John Terry Smith, Lynn Walker, Jerry C. White, Robert Williams, Mildred Yates, and especially Ed Moore and Cleveland Nisby, longtime African American leaders who read parts of the manuscript and provided critical first-hand information about Beaumont during the days of the Jim Crow caste system.

Professional librarians and archivists who provided critical assistance and furnished essential materials include Kun-Woo Choi, Beaumont Public Library; David Montgomery, Penny Clark, Ednita Lane, and Elizabeth Mouton, Tyrrell Historical Library, Beaumont; Charlotte Holliman and Theresa Storey, Lamar University Library, Beaumont; Doug Stark, United States Golf Association; Judy Thompson, National Golf Foundation; Bill Penn, Texas Golf Association; Robert Haynes, African American Museum, Dallas; Clifford L. Muse, Jr., Moorland Spingarn Research Center, Howard University; Norma B. Leftwich, Howard University; Katherine Fox and Stephanie Malmros, Center for American History, Austin; Adrienne Cannon and Patrick Kerwin, Manuscript Division,

ACKNOWLEDGMENTS

Library of Congress; Keith Andreucci, Government Services Administration; Jeffrey C. Adams, State Bar of Texas; Father William Huette, Saint Charles College, Grand Coteau, Louisiana; Father John Lynch, Saint Paul's College, Washington, D.C.; Mike Widener, Tarlton Law Library, University of Texas at Austin; Kinga Perzynska, Special Collections, Fondren Library, Rice University; Barbara Constable, Dwight D. Eisenhower Presidential Library; Barbara Rust, National Archives and Records Administration, Fort Worth; William H. Davis, National Archives and Records Administration, Washington, D.C.; Bruce Ragsdale, Federal Judicial Center, Washington, D.C.; Sammie T. Lee, Dallas Public Library; and Dave Maland and Mike Lantz, Office of the Clerk, United States District Court, Tyler, Texas.

I am thankful to professional historians who read all or parts of the manuscript, made suggestions, and supplied encouragement. These scholars include John W. Storey and Ralph A. Wooster, Lamar University; Randolph B. Campbell, University of North Texas; Kristin M. Szylvian, Western Michigan University; and Francelle Pruitt, Ira D. Gruber, and John B. Boles, Rice University. I am deeply grateful to John Boles, managing editor of the *Journal of Southern History,* who arranged for me to present my manuscript at a meeting of the Houston Area Southern History Seminar and who read and marked the entire manuscript on two occasions. I regret that Barry A. Crouch, Gallaudet University, has passed away, as he helped me in the beginning and would have enjoyed seeing me complete this history. Crouch was an ardent admirer of Clio, the Muse of History, and so are the others—Storey, Wooster, Campbell, Szylvian, Pruitt, Gruber, and Boles.

FAIR WAYS

· ·

Prologue

On the morning of Tuesday, June 14, 1955, five black men hurried up the wide front steps of city hall in Beaumont, Texas. They passed beneath the tall fluted columns of the neoclassical building and pulled open heavy double doors. Dressed in Sunday clothes, the men were on their way to a regular meeting of city council. People who saw the men might have guessed something unusual was happening because of the way they carried themselves: respectful as always but now with a new sense of determination. Generally, African Americans came to city hall as individuals, with hat in hand, to render taxes, pay water bills, or apply for labor jobs, but almost never as a delegation of full-fledged citizens wanting to discuss official business with city council. These were the days of Jim Crow segregation, when black Americans suffered widespread discrimination and were forced to live a humiliating second-class existence.

Inside city hall the men climbed a double flight of stairs to the second story and headed for council chambers. They knew which way to go; they had been there a year earlier. Booker T. Fayson, an insurance agent, probably led the way, followed by Joseph P. Griffin, Thomas A. Parker, and Johnnie R. Ware, all letter carriers for the U.S. Postal Service, and Theodore R. Johns, a lawyer. Fayson was the group's leader, Johns their official spokesman. The black men entered council chambers and found seats in the audience, just in time to see the all-white city officials take their places on the dais. In the center was the mayor, Elmo Beard, president of Tyrrell Hardware Company, and on either side were the four council members: Paul Anger, refinery worker; Jimmie P. Cokinos, insurance agent; Harry Mason, pharmacist; and J. R. Venza, dentist. At adjoining tables were key staff members: Mrs. Willie Brockman, city manager; George Murphy, city attorney; and Jim Mulligan, police chief.[1]

After a reading of the minutes, Mayor Beard called for agenda item number one—the Fayson group. Attorney Johns got to his feet and introduced himself, chairman of the Legal Redress Committee of the local NAACP, then the others: Fayson, Griffin, Parker, and Ware, all members of the Beaumont Golfers Club. The delegation was there on behalf of black golfers and the NAACP, Johns said, asking for access to Tyrrell and Central Parks. Both parks, including the Tyrrell municipal golf course, were strictly off limits to African Americans because of racial segregation. Fayson, president of the Beaumont Golfers Club, explained the situation of black golfers. He and fellow club members had to travel one hundred miles to Houston to play eighteen holes of golf. Since Beaumont had its own municipal golf course, Fayson reasoned, there should be no need to go elsewhere.[2]

Council member Cokinos spoke up quickly, noting this request was not a new one. Indeed, Fayson and the other black golfers had begun their campaign in June, 1954, when they first asked city officials for permission to play the Tyrrell Park course. Cokinos recalled that an interracial committee had been appointed to study the issue of public parks. In those days Beaumont had various public parks, including Tyrrell, from which blacks were excluded, and several "colored parks," which offered no golfing facilities. Mayor Beard chimed in, explaining that the interracial committee had been studying the problem but had made no recommendation, and consequently the council had taken no action. The mayor went on to assure everyone that "this Council would always act . . . for the best of all the people of the city—both colored and white." But, he declared, he "would not vote to do anything that might cause strife for the people who . . . live here."[3]

Attorney Johns responded politely but firmly. "We are not seeking strife," he said, "but will be in accord with any action of good faith with regard to the use of the parks." Johns went on, explaining that black Beaumonters were determined, that they considered use of Tyrrell and other parks as their right. Mayor

Beard urged patience, saying that "the people of this town are not quite ready to accept this thing." Johns countered again. Fayson and his golfing friends should not have to wait for approval by the whole white community, he argued, as there might always be individuals who would oppose use of the parks by African Americans.[4]

Council member Cokinos asked Johns if his delegation was affiliated with the national NAACP, a group that many white people thought was becoming too aggressive, even radical, in demanding an end to segregation and discrimination all across the nation. Johns temporized, explaining his group was not in league with NAACP groups in New York or Mississippi but was working only from a local point of view. Johns had to be cautious. He and his black clients were walking a fine line, demanding their rights but not wanting to provoke retaliation, even violence, against themselves and their families. Beaumont was a southern town, where many white citizens harbored racist attitudes against their fellow black citizens. Just a dozen years ago the town had suffered a terrible race riot.[5]

Mayor Beard closed the discussion, repeating his opinion that most Beaumonters were not ready for desegregation of the parks but promising that the question would be given further study. Of course he was correct: Most Beaumonters, meaning the majority white population, favored the status quo and opposed integration. But not so for the thirty thousand black Beaumonters; they wanted an end to segregation in all public facilities, including the golf course at Tyrrell Park. Some, including Booker Fayson and his fellow golfers, were determined to force the matter by issuing a challenge in federal court.[6]

. . . .

Beaumont, Texas, 1955

Booker Fayson lived in "the Pear Orchard," a "colored" section of Beaumont, while Mayor Elmo Beard resided in South Park, an area reserved for white people. Likewise for Judge Lamar Cecil and all the others, white and black, involved in the Tyrrell Park golf course lawsuit: They lived in single-race neighborhoods. The separation of blacks and whites into different neighborhoods was one manifestation of the Jim Crow caste system that prevailed in Beaumont in 1955. At that time the city had a population of 110,000 persons, 78,000 white and 32,000 black. The two races lived in the same town, but their perceptions of the place were markedly different. In the eyes of Mayor Beard and other white city officials, Beaumont was a good town, prosperous and growing, with plenty of opportunity for everyone. But Booker Fayson and his black friends saw another Beaumont: a typical southern town where African Americans of all economic and social classes suffered the discriminations and restrictions of the caste system.[1]

Mayor Beard and other civic leaders were proud of their town. Beaumont was "the keystone of prosperous Southeast Texas" and the "hub of the Sabine-Neches industrial district," boasted Chamber of Commerce publications. Indeed, Beaumont was a bustling industrial town. The seat of Jefferson County, largest city in the area, and thriving seaport, Beaumont benefited greatly from the continuing development of area refineries and chemical plants. At the southeastern city limits was Magnolia Petroleum Company, a gigantic refinery with tank farms, loading docks, and more than two thousand employees. Nearby at Nederland, Port Neches, and Port Arthur were other huge facilities—the plants of Atlantic Refining, Gulf Refining, Sun Oil, Pure Oil, Stanolind Oil, and Texas Company—where thousands of workers processed and transported vast quantities of petroleum. Taken together, plants in the Beaumont area refined more than 800,000 barrels per day, 10 percent of the nation's needs. Chamber advertising touted the benefits of the local petroleum industry: "Beaumont: Where Oil Flows and Industry Grows."[2]

Mayor Beard had strong connections to local business and industry. He was president of Tyrrell Hardware, a company that sold paint and supplies to Magnolia Petroleum and other local plants; he also was a director of Norvell-Wilder, another industrial supply company. An able and veteran politician, he had served several terms on city council before winning the mayor's office. By way of business and politics, he was a proven member of the Beaumont establishment, an all-white group of business and industry men who exercised strong leadership in local affairs during the 1950s. Often these men worked their leadership through the Beaumont Chamber of Commerce, an all-white organization dedicated to promoting tourism and advancing the interests of business and industry.[3]

Chamber leaders bragged about Beaumont's natural environment. It was a thoroughly southern town with surroundings much akin to the nearby bayou country of Louisiana. Situated on the banks of the wide, slow-moving Neches River, forty miles above the Gulf of Mexico, Beaumont was noted for mild temperatures, abundant rain, and a profuse assortment of towering trees, tangled vegetation, and lush grasses. Some visitors raved about the beautiful Saint Augustine lawns, brilliant azalea bushes, and magnificent oaks and pines; others complained about the heat, humidity, and mosquitoes. The countryside to the north and east was thickly wooded, harboring bogs and swamps, but the land to the south and west was open and fertile, well suited for cattle ranching and rice farming. Bayous, lakes, marshes, and the nearby Gulf abounded with fish and wild game, especially migratory ducks and geese. Beaumont, as the chamber said, was a paradise for hunters and fishermen.[4]

At chamber meetings, Beard associated regularly with an all-white group of establishment leaders: Roy Nelson, president, Gulf States Utilities; Donelson Caffery, district manager, Sun Oil; Frank Betts, president, American National Bank; John Newton, plant manager, Magnolia Petroleum; and E. C. Rechtin, general manager, Bethlehem Steel. Beard also worked with Howard Hicks, the chamber general manager who helped orchestrate civic and political affairs behind the scenes. Other key civic leaders were John Gray, executive vice president, First National Bank; Robert Akers, editor, *Beaumont Enterprise* newspaper; and Tanner T. Hunt, editor, *Beaumont Journal* newspaper. First National, the largest bank, and the two newspapers were intimately connected: The bank controlled the Mapes Trust that owned and published both newspapers. Working together, the bank and the two newspapers exerted great influence on local business and politics.[5]

Other whites wielded power in Beaumont because of their public offices. Judge James A. Kirkland presided over Jefferson County Commissioners Court, while Sheriff C. H. "Charley" Meyer and Constable Reagan Baker had responsibility for county-wide law enforcement. State judges included Lewis B. Hightower III, William S. Nichols, Harold B. Clayton, and Melvin M. Combs. At city hall day-to-day operations were directed by Mrs. Willie Brockman, the only female city manager in the state of Texas, while policy decisions were made by Mayor Beard and the four council members: Paul Anger, Jimmie Cokinos, Harry Mason, and J. R. Venza. Venza and Cokinos were political veterans, each having the experience of several terms on the council. Cokinos, an energetic and outspoken council member, would soon win the mayor's office and serve multiple terms.[6]

Mayor Beard and the other establishment men were solid business people; they labored to build their companies, improve their profits, and earn money for themselves. But they also assumed the mantle of city fathers, working to create jobs, keep taxes low, promote tourism, and build churches, hospitals, and schools. Charged with a spirit of boosterism, they longed for the day when Beaumont would become "Big B," in the same way that Dallas was known as "Big D." Often they touted Beaumont's assets: mild climate, strategic location, good transportation, abundant fresh water and natural gas, low electric rates, ample labor, and "excellent living conditions." Sometimes they bragged about "good race relations," but on this issue Beard and the others seemed blinded by racial ideas and practices inherited from earlier generations.[7] Like most other southern leaders, they could not imagine the real aspirations of their black fellow citizens.

The city fathers could recount a broad outline of local history, at least from the perspective of white citizens. Organized in 1838, Beaumont was a budding railroad and sawmill town at the time of the Civil War, a conflict in which most local white people sided with the South and suffered the consequences of defeat and Reconstruction. After the war, the town recovered slowly, but by the end of the nineteenth century it had developed into a prosperous lumber town with 9,500 people. With the 1901 discovery of the phenomenal Spindletop oil field, Beaumont was transformed. First it became a boomtown, then a refinery town, and finally an industrial city. A "second Spindletop" discovery at Beaumont in 1925 and two world wars pushed the expansion of local refineries, shipyards, and railroads, as well as related industrial companies. Thousands of jobs were created and the population increased dramatically, rising from 20,640 in 1920 to 94,041 in 1950. This was a dynamic and positive history, of which white leaders were justly proud. But they were largely ignorant of the history of the local African American population, a group that made up almost 30 percent of their town.[8]

Black history was different and often disheartening; it derived from the dark story of human slavery. On the eve of the Civil War, Beaumont was a slaveholding town. Black slaves, which then made up 18 percent of the town's population, were owned by white citizens and employed by them in a variety of occupations: farming, ranching, sawmilling, railroad construction, and domestic service. Slaves were advertised for sale in the local newspaper. They were subject to flogging by the town constable for violations of slave codes, ordinances that restricted their movement and activities. With the defeat of the Confederacy, black Beaumonters gained their freedom and commenced a long and still unfinished struggle to gain their share of the American dream. During Reconstruction they voted, held minor public offices, and made some progress in terms of jobs and economics. But during the 1890s and early decades of the next century, local blacks suffered the same fate as African Americans throughout the South. They were turned back, their progress thwarted by white citizens who created the Jim Crow laws and practices that relegated African Americans to the bottom rungs of society. Blacks lost the right to vote, were denied public office, and were subjected to discrimination and segregation in virtually every aspect of life.[9]

Based on twin theories of white supremacy and black subordination, the Jim Crow laws and customs evolved over time into a complex and pervasive caste system. Historians have documented the development of this caste system in the various southern states. In the Lone Star State the all-white legislature passed a law in 1891 requiring racial segregation in railroad cars and then extended the practice to railroad stations with laws ratified during the 1909–11 legislative session. From these beginnings in public transportation, the segregation codes and practices spread to towns and cities throughout Texas. The state legislature broadened and strengthened the system in 1927, passing a law that authorized municipalities to promulgate ordinances formalizing segregation in housing and other venues. Ultimately the laws and customs of the caste system separated the races in most private and public places, including hotels, restaurants, theaters, schools, parks, libraries, and courthouses, even restrooms and drinking fountains. White Beaumonters adopted their own version of the caste system. In 1904 the all-white city council passed an ordinance requiring segregation on streetcars, a segregation that was extended in subsequent years throughout all parts of the community. By the early 1950s the Jim Crow caste system was a basic fact of life for all Beaumonters, white and black.[10]

In Beaumont and other southern cities, the caste system included an etiquette of race, a collection of customs and rituals that dictated behavior for all citizens, black and white, and of every social and economic class. In part the etiquette derived from age-old relationships that developed in Europe and arose from economic and social classes, as between medieval lords and peasants, or between aristocrats and servants; an example is portrayed in *Upstairs, Downstairs,* a British television series in which white Victorian aristocrats ruled over white servants. But in a larger part, the southern etiquette derived from racism, a belief common among Caucasian Americans that the black race was not equal to the white. Handed down through many generations, the caste system and its race etiquette were common features of everyday life, so rooted in tradition that they were taken for granted by whites and rarely challenged publicly by blacks. Most whites and blacks followed the race etiquette with great care and usually with southern civility, being courteous to one another and avoiding sharp confrontations or harsh words.[11]

Generally blacks were deferential and respectful to whites—nodding and smiling, averting eyes, saying "sir" and "ma'am"—not presumptuous or insolent. Black men yielded right-of-way to whites, stepping off the sidewalk, holding open the door, and doffing the hat. Black women working in white households entered by the back door, used the most out-of-the-way toilet, and seldom drank or ate from the better glasses or dishes. At the same time, white men and women played their parts in the southern etiquette of race. Assuming their superiority, they lorded over blacks, mostly calling them by their first names, often declining to shake their hands, and in a thousand other ways reminding them of their inferior position. Many whites, however, treated blacks with kindness and consideration, and some shared genuine friendships with them. Frequently whites extended a helping hand to blacks, by lending money, helping someone find a job, or arranging medical care, but often these gestures were tinged with paternalism, where care was linked with control.[12]

Americans born after 1960 may wonder how earlier generations, both white and black, could have tolerated the southern caste system that so grossly violated the democratic ideals and principles of the United States. The French historian Marguerite Yourcenar recounted the story of Louise of Lorraine, a sixteenth-century queen who was famous for her piety and her works of mercy and charity. In the company of her husband, Henri III, the young queen attended the execution of the traitor Salcève, where the man was chained hand and foot to four stallions and ripped asunder. Louise watched the horrific scene calmly, apparently finding it reasonable and natural, so utterly does custom govern our sentiment, Yourcenar remarked.[13]

In Beaumont the southern caste system created "two towns," one white and one black. The "white town" was the main town, the one advertised by the Chamber of Commerce, the one controlled by Mayor Beard and the local establishment. Here whites held most of the economic power. They owned almost all the land, buildings, shops, stores, and factories. They had most of the political power, controlling entirely the city, school, and county governments, occupying all the elected offices, and holding all the better jobs. They had almost all the judicial power, having most of the lawyers and all the judges. Blacks on the other hand had little power—economic, political, or judicial. They had little wealth, no elected officials, few lawyers, and no judges. Black citizens worked, shopped, and traveled in the "white town," but they paid strict attention to the caste system, being careful not to cross the invisible line that zigzagged throughout society. Booker Fayson and his friends refrained from entering the front doors of hotels and cafes; they shopped in department stores but avoided the "whites only" lunch counters; and they sought out the restrooms and drinking fountains marked "colored." For the most part, they adhered to the racial etiquette, deferring and giving way to white persons.[14]

The black town, really a handful of "colored" districts, was a dim shadow of the main town, but it was owned and run by black citizens. In these residential and business districts, African Americans lived freely, with little or no interference from whites. Black citizens owned real estate, operated stores, practiced professions, and managed churches, clubs, and fraternal groups. Booker Fayson and his wife Johnnie lived and worked in the Pear Orchard. They owned a home on Harriot Street and an office building on Washington Boulevard, where they operated an insurance agency and rented office space to others. White citizens, including Mayor Beard and other establishment members, were free to enter the residential and business districts of the black town; there was no color line restricting their movements in the black community. Often whites drove along the main streets of the "colored" sections, but they rarely stopped. Generally whites did not visit in black homes or shop in black stores.[15]

The two towns, white and black, sometimes exclusive and other times overlapping, presented an agonizing dilemma for African Americans in Beaumont and towns across the nation. "One world or two?" pondered historian John Hope Franklin, an African American himself. The African American "was compelled to live in a world apart from the dominant in the community," Franklin wrote, "and therefore developed institutions of his own in order to preserve his identity and individuality. At the same time . . . he participated to some limited extent in the affairs of the larger community. . . . The two processes went on simultaneously and imposed on the Negro a most difficult task: that of trying to live in two worlds at the same time."[16]

During the 1950s the Chamber of Commerce map depicted the city as a half circle spreading west from its historical core near the river. As there were no superhighways or shopping malls, Beaumont, the "white town," thrived in the central business district, along century-old streets: Main, Pearl, and Orleans running north and south; Forsythe, Fannin, Bowie, and Crockett going east and west. U.S. Highway 90, the main route from California to Florida, went right through the town center, following along College and Main Streets before crossing the river. The skyline was marked by the twenty-two-story Edson Hotel (for a while the tallest hotel west of the Mississippi), the San Jacinto office tower, with its stately clock visible for miles around, and the Jefferson County Courthouse, a soaring structure where jail inmates peered out on the surrounding countryside. Other notable buildings included Hotel Beaumont, the Goodhue Building, the LaSalle Hotel, the Crosby Hotel, and American National Bank, as well as city hall, the Tyrrell Public Library, and the federal building. The central business district was vibrant day and night. Stores, restaurants, and movie theaters lined the downtown blocks. Shoppers and office workers thronged the sidewalks. Autos trailed slowly along the crowded streets.[17]

White men of the Beaumont establishment controlled the central business district; they ran the businesses and presided over governmental councils. They enforced the segregation practices inherited from earlier generations, practices that greatly restricted the lives of Booker Fayson, his golfing friends, and their local attorneys. The Graham brothers, Will and Fletcher, owned and operated the fashionable White House department store; they welcomed African American shoppers, people such as Thomas and Bobbie Gene Parker, but refused them access to the popular luncheon counter and the chilled-water drinking fountains. American National Bank president Frank Betts gladly accepted deposits from black customers, perhaps Joe and Elizabeth Griffin, but sent them to a "colored" restroom in the basement if they needed to relieve themselves. Bob Akers, editor of the *Enterprise,* happily collected subscription and advertising monies from black citizens, such as Johnnie and Ruth Ware, but would not publish their wedding photographs or obituaries in the newspaper.[18]

Downtown retailers included the Rexall and Sommers drugstores, as well as variety stores such as Kress, Woolworth's, and Neisner's. In all these establishments white managers and employees enforced a version of the "color line." African Americans were invited to shop and spend their money but not permitted to enjoy soda fountains or restrooms. But there were exceptions and variations in racial practices, in some instances class related, where white business people afforded equal or even preferential treatment to wealthy black patrons. The Fashion, an upscale women's clothing store owned by the Weiss brothers and managed by Henry C. Brooks, catered to the wives and daughters of the white Beaumont establishment, but the store also gave attentive and friendly service to Bessie Knighton, the affluent African American owner of Knighton Funeral Home. Another example of white businesses catering to certain black customers was seen at Ener & White Tire Store, where the white salesman Billy King gave preferential treatment to Ocie Jackson, the oil-rich African American rancher who habitually drove a late model Cadillac. Making an exception to discriminatory customs of the caste system, salesman King always treated the rancher with great courtesy and addressed him as "Mr. Jackson."[19]

Sometimes the color line produced confusing and humiliating situations. Mildred Campbell Yates, a white Beaumonter, remembered an afternoon in 1955 when she and her four-year-old daughter Mary were giving a ride home to Charlotte Allen, her fifty-year-old black domestic servant. In those days many African American women found employment in white homes, working as maids, cooks, and babysitters; generally they depended for transportation on their employers or the city bus lines. En route from the Campbell residence to Charlotte Allen's home, the threesome stopped to buy popcorn at the Sears store on Magnolia Street; they all liked the little bags of hot popcorn. While Yates waited in the car, Allen and the toddler Mary went hand-in-hand into the store to buy the treats. Time passed and they did not return. Becoming worried, Yates left her car and hurried into the store. At the popcorn booth, she observed a situation that angered her. The white sales clerk was serving one white customer after another, while at the same time ignoring Allen, the would-be black customer. "What's the trouble?" Yates inquired impatiently. "Oh," the clerk said, peering over the side of the high counter, "I didn't see the little white child."[20]

The wealthy Waldo Wilson operated Hotel Beaumont, a modern upscale hotel that featured two restaurants, the Black Cat and the Kitten, and two ballrooms, the Rose Room and the Sky Room. On most days well-groomed business leaders and stylish women shoppers waited in line to lunch at the Black Cat; on Wednesdays two hundred Rotarians in business suits filed into the Rose Room for their luncheon meeting. At the hotel Wilson and his staff enforced the southern color line, declining entry to African Americans as guests and customers but welcoming them as kitchen help, janitors, and waiters. Elmo Willard, one of the black lawyers in the Fayson lawsuit, worked there as a youth; he began in the kitchen and later became a "roll boy," circulating among white diners and serving hot rolls from a silver tray.[21]

Three blocks away were other "hotels," the brothels on Crockett Street. During the 1940s and 1950s, Beaumont was both famous and infamous for its whorehouses: the Boston, Copeland, Dixie, Marine, and Maryland, right there in the center of town. Technically illegal, the brothels operated openly, peacefully, and within the framework of the southern caste system. Sexual relations between the two races were against Texas law, as was marriage, so black prostitutes did not work at the white brothels, and neither were black male patrons admitted to such establishments. Of course African Americans worked in these places as maids and porters. Nearby in the black Forsythe business district were several African American brothels, establishments that operated casually and without official names and that catered to both black and white patrons.[22]

Julius Gordon directed Jefferson Amusement, a company that operated movie theaters in Beaumont and southeast Texas. During the early 1950s, before the blossoming of television, Beaumonters flocked to the movie houses, enjoying the films and relaxing in the air-conditioned comfort of the theaters. Especially popular was the Jefferson Theater, a multimillion dollar movie palace that ran the latest Hollywood films. Gordon and his white employees enforced the color line, refusing entry to African Americans at downtown theaters such as the Jefferson and the Liberty. Films at the two theaters during June, 1955, included *The Americano,* starring Glenn Ford and Ursula Thiess, and *Love Me or Leave Me,* featuring Doris Day and James Cagney. If the black insurance agent Booker Fayson and his wife Johnnie tried to purchase tickets to see the Glenn Ford film, they were refused. But Julius Gordon made accommodations for black customers; he operated the Star Theater, advertised as "exclusively colored," and the Peoples Theater, a segregated cinema where white patrons sat downstairs and blacks were sent to the balcony. With this arrangement, whites could hear but not see the black patrons.[23]

Segregation in the white theaters was not airtight, as shown by an experience of Pat Willard, wife of the young lawyer Elmo Willard. A stylish African American woman, Mrs. Willard was born and reared in Chicago, where blacks suffered discrimination but not the segregation practices of the South. Sometime during the middle or late 1950s, she and Bobbie Johns, wife of lawyer Theo Johns, decided to test the segregation barrier at the Liberty Theater in downtown Beaumont. One afternoon they walked up to the theater box office, offered their money, and ordered two tickets. The white cashier peered at them, hesitating, and then slowly pushed forward their tickets. "You're Mexicans, right?" the woman said. Willard and Johns said nothing but picked up their tickets and hurried into the welcome darkness of the theater.[24]

Hospitals were another venue where white Beaumonters required segregation of the races but nevertheless made arrangements for African Americans. Baptist Hospital, the newest institution, accepted black patients and assigned them to special rooms or wards. But Baptist did not admit black physicians; they had to practice in "colored" establishments. Black doctors were also barred from Saint Therese and Hotel Dieu, two large and prestigious hospitals operated by the Sisters of Charity of the Incarnate Word. Saint Therese Hospital refused service to African American patients, but Hotel Dieu welcomed them for treatment, assigning them to the Martin de Porres wing, a modern brick facility operated exclusively for black patients. On one occasion, however, the de Porres wing was pressed into service as an integrated facility. John Terry Smith, a longtime Beaumont physician, remembered the polio epidemic of the early 1950s, when for a time the entire first floor of de Porres was taken up by iron lung patients, blacks and whites lined up together.[25]

Sometimes segregation in medical care posed awkward and serious problems. Mildred Campbell Yates, a previously mentioned white Beaumonter, recalled a night in 1944 when she was single and had a date with a white U.S. Army captain. Together they were driving back to Beaumont after an evening of dancing at the Southern Club, a roadhouse in Orange County. Along the way, they happened upon a highway accident in which a black truck driver had suffered a severe arm injury, an injury they feared might cause the loss of the limb. Yates and her date picked up the driver and sped back into Beaumont, driving directly to the nearest hospital, Saint Therese. While the army captain waited in the car with the injured man, Yates hurried up the hospital steps and into the lobby. Quickly she told the white nuns of Saint Therese about the accident, the injured black man, and the severity of his injury; just as quickly, they told her they could not, would not treat the black man, that they must take him across town to Martin de Porres, the facility for blacks at Hotel Dieu. Yates and her date delivered the man to Martin de Porres, where he was well treated and his arm was saved.[26]

Jefferson County had two tuberculosis hospitals, the main one on French Road and the "Negro Unit" on Sarah Street in "colored town." The city operated one charity hospital, Beaumont Municipal, an institution on Washington Boulevard that treated whites and blacks alike, though in separate wards. Directed by Dr. William A. Smith, the hospital was staffed by both white *and* black physicians who volunteered their time. In this institution, and generally elsewhere, black doctors limited their practice to black patients, while white doctors treated patients of both races. Dr. E. D. Sprott, Jr., for example, was a black general practitioner who operated a clinic exclusively for African Americans. On the other hand, although many white doctors did treat both whites and blacks, they generally did so within the framework of the southern caste system. At the Calder Street clinic of Dr. Hugh

Alexander, Sr., black patients entered through a back door and sat in a separate waiting room. At the offices of Dr. Stuart Wier in the Goodhue Building, white and black patients entered through the same door, signed one registration book but waited in separate rooms, and then were treated in order of arrival, without priority as to race. Dr. Leonard Toomin, a pediatrician, had still another procedure, where he treated white and black mothers and their children with complete equality; they made appointments by telephone and upon arrival were escorted without discrimination directly into examining rooms.[27]

The caste system produced segregation of the races in many other venues: schools and churches, as well as fraternal, housing, and governmental organizations. The two local school districts, Beaumont Independent School District and South Park Independent School District, were controlled by white trustees and directed by white superintendents, Fred Hunter and Joe Vincent. They assigned all African American students to "colored" schools, institutions operated by black administrators and teachers. At the high-school level, white students attended Beaumont, French, and South Park high schools, while blacks were sent to Charlton-Pollard and Hebert high schools. In the environment of Jim Crow, the school superintendents probably allocated the "colored schools" proportionately fewer funds for facilities and teacher salaries. There was also a "color line" at the college level. At Lamar State College of Technology, a four-year institution with an enrollment of forty-six hundred, President F. L. McDonald and the white board of regents registered only white students and hired only white faculty. Any African Americans seen on campus would have been service workers such cooks, janitors, or gardeners.[28]

Religion was an area where both whites and blacks favored segregation of the races. During the days of Reconstruction, African Americans in the South avoided white churches and formed congregations of their own. Likewise in Beaumont, the two races went their separate ways, each developing their own versions of the Baptist, Methodist, Catholic, and other denominations. As the Chamber of Commerce proudly noted, the town had "60 churches for white people . . . [and] over 60 churches for Negroes." Prominent white congregations in the downtown area included First Baptist, First Methodist, Westminister Presbyterian, Saint

Mark's Episcopal, Saint Anthony's Catholic, and Temple Emanuel. Among the suburban congregations were First Christian, Saint Michael's Orthodox, Calder Baptist, Roberts Avenue Methodist, South Park Baptist, and Trinity Methodist. Generally black Beaumonters were not members of these congregations nor did they attend their worship services, but they were invited on special occasions. Often black domestic workers were seen at funerals of their late employers, sometimes sitting in a reserved pew, other times with white family members.[29]

As with churches, whites and blacks in Beaumont separated themselves voluntarily in fraternal groups such as the Masons, Odd Fellows, Elks, and Knights of Pythias. Both races operated lodges with similar fraternal missions: fellowship, life insurance, and public service. Rarely if ever did blacks attend meetings of white lodges, and vice versa. Also, the color line was strictly observed in white service and civic clubs, where no African Americans were accepted as members or guests. Included here were women's groups such as the Pilot Club and Sertoma, and men's groups such as the Lions, Kiwanis, Jaycees, Exchange, and Rotary, the largest and most prestigious.[30]

Rotary, a weekly forum for the Beaumont establishment, was composed exclusively of white men: doctors, lawyers, bankers, plant managers, insurance agents, real estate brokers, and others, mostly from the upper echelons of their particular business or profession. On occasion wives of members or other white women were invited as guests to the Wednesday luncheons in Hotel Beaumont. African Americans were not admitted as members or guests, but many Rotarians enjoyed friendly relations with black waiters in the Rose Room. In 1955, for example, Rotary president Ewell Strong, an insurance lawyer, and club executive secretary Lorice Buelar worked closely every week with Hughes Murdock, the veteran black headwaiter who managed the setting of the banquet hall and serving of the meal. Among Murdock's staff were Johnnie Antoine, Floyd "Buffalo" Loeb, and Earl White, one of the plaintiffs in the Fayson suit.[31]

The special relationship between black waiters and white Rotarians was played out in other settings, especially private clubs such as the Beaumont Club, Town Club, and Beaumont Country Club. The clubs were popular with many members of the Beaumont establishment, including men and women of the Beaumont elite, a smaller and more exclusive group distinguished by wealth, social connections, cultural affiliations, and family heritage. Always among the elite were representatives of Beaumont's "first" families: Broussard, Kyle, McFaddin, Phelan, Reed, Stedman, Steinhagen, Tyrrell, and others. During the 1950s, for example, Randolph C. Reed, president of the Reed Company, and his brother-in-law, U.S. District Judge Lamar Cecil, were members of all three clubs. They and their families went to the clubs frequently, enjoying their society, privacy, activities, food, and drink, especially the drink. Texas laws at that time prohibited the sale of liquor by the drink in public restaurants and saloons, so private clubs were the only legal venue where a person could buy a mixed drink. The clubs attracted members for an additional reason: Under federal income tax laws, monthly dues for the private clubs were deductible as a business expense.[32]

White men dominated the Beaumont Club, Town Club, and Beaumont Country Club. During the 1950s, men held almost all the memberships and most of the director and officer positions. Every club president was a man. The clubs discriminated against all women, female members as well as the wives, daughters, and mothers of male members. With policies and practices inherited from earlier generations, the clubs excluded women from various rooms and denied them certain privileges. At the Beaumont Club, for example, women were excluded entirely from the card room and denied entry to the main dining room until after four in the afternoon. At the same time, black waiters, male *and* female, moved freely in areas from which white women were barred. At the Beaumont Country Club, women golfers were barred from the course on Saturdays all day, but given exclusive use of the links on Wednesday mornings. In this way, the private clubs presented a microcosm of racial and gender hierarchies that pervaded and complicated the larger community.[33]

Within the confines of the private clubs, Randolph Reed, Judge Cecil, and other white male members often developed personal relationships with black male waiters and also with black male caddies who worked the country club golf course. Among the waiters and caddies were Joe Griffin, Johnnie Ware, and Earl White, all of whom became parties to the Fayson lawsuit. Of course the men in these white/black relationships were not equals. The white men were employers; the black men were employees. One was master, the other servant. Additionally, there was a wide disparity between them in terms of education, diction, clothing, wealth, and other factors that determined economic and social class. Nevertheless, white members and black waiters often enjoyed friendly relations and sometimes more than casual banter.[34]

Black waiters played essential roles in every club activity, setting and serving the business luncheon, afternoon cocktail, weekly card game, formal dance, and wedding party. On club premises, Johnnie Ware and other black waiters witnessed every scene. They saw Randolph Reed, Lamar Cecil, and other white members at their best and worst, when they were courteous, charming, and eloquent, and when they were intoxicated, crude, and irreverent. With their proximity, the white members and black waiters developed friendships that were authentic, yet circumscribed by the customs of the southern caste system. In a sense the white member/black waiter relationships were symbiotic. Clearly many blacks needed their waiter jobs because white society barred them from many better positions. At the same time white members needed the services of black waiters in order to enjoy the pleasures of club life. Also, perhaps white members needed black waiters to witness their achievements, to confirm their high status as compared to all persons, both white and black.[35]

Chamber of Commerce literature touted various leisure-time activities in Beaumont, public events such as the South Texas State Fair and the games of the local baseball club, the Exporters; in both these venues, racial segregation was strictly enforced. Staged every October by the Young Men's Business League, the fair featured a livestock show, sideshows with dancing girls, and a midway with Ferris wheel and other rides. The annual event was an "an outstanding affair," the chamber said. It attracted "more than 225,000 persons" each year, but African Americans were denied entry to the fair except for one "Negro day." The Exporters, a Texas League team and farm club for the New York Yankees, played its home games at Stuart Stadium, "a magnificent park with new lighting fixtures." Black baseball fans were restricted to a separate section. Tanner T. Hunt, Jr., remembers attending a major league exhibition game at Stuart Stadium, when the black superstar Jackie Robinson was playing. The baseball player drew a huge turnout of African American fans, who overflowed from the "colored" section and stood shoulder-to-shoulder along the foul lines, applauding and cheering Robinson's every move.[36]

As indicated earlier, the southern caste system resulted in segregated housing. Black Beaumonters were confined to specific areas, while white citizens had the choice of various neighborhoods, sections that varied in age and convenience, as well as in the affluence and status of the homeowners. During the early 1950s the older additions in South Park and the North End remained popular with white citizens; Mayor Beard and council members Harry Mason and J. R. Venza resided in the South Park area, while council member Paul Anger lived in the North End. But the older sections were losing favor as more affluent residents moved to newer areas west of downtown. Council member Jimmie Cokinos had a home on Hazel Street, not too far from the residences of various Beaumont elites: Anthony M. "Mickey" Phelan, E. Harvey Steinhagen, J. L. C. McFaddin, and C. Fletcher Graham III as well as previously mentioned Randolph Reed and Judge Lamar Cecil.[37]

Farther to the west, Calder Place, Calder Terrace, Caldwood, and other newer developments attracted more and more residents, including many doctors, lawyers, and additional members of the Beaumont establishment. Other affluent white families made their homes on Thomas Road, a tree-lined street noted for large houses, stately grounds, and winding driveways. Here resided close friends of Judge Cecil: James W. Mehaffy, lawyer; L. W. Pitts, architect; Mose Sampson, steel wholesaler; and Julian Fertitta, physician. In all these white sections, old and new, African Americans worked as maids, cooks, and gardeners, and sometimes they might stay in servants' quarters, but they could never rent or buy a home of their own in that neighborhood. They were excluded from white neighborhoods by state segregation laws, "whites-only" real estate covenants, and customs of the caste system.[38]

In the field of public transportation, African Americans were confronted with a variety of racial rules and customs. Eastern Airlines, Delta Airlines, and Trans-Texas Airways, serving Jefferson County Airport, posted no barriers to black citizens, but few if any African Americans opted for air transportation. Greyhound, Continental Trailways, and other regional bus companies, on the other hand, enforced typical Jim Crow rules, segregating black and white customers in their buses and terminals. Yellow Cab Company carried white passengers only, but black citizens had ready access to "colored" taxis. Both Southern Pacific Railroad and Kansas City Southern Railroad operated passenger stations, each with segregated waiting rooms. Beaumont City Lines, Inc., a private company, operated city buses that every day carried thousands of white and black citizens. Licensed by the city and paying an annual street rental, the company charged a fifteen-cent fare and served all parts of the town. No doubt with the blessing of the city administration, the company enforced segregation on their buses. Their white drivers used the notorious "White/Colored" sign that was suspended on an overhead track running the length of the passenger section. Depending upon the number of white passengers, the driver moved the sign forward or backward, always confining and sometimes crowding African Americans in the back of the bus.[39]

The city hall building, where Mayor Beard presided over council, was a handsome two-story structure, fronted by tall Greek columns and surrounded by expansive lawns and stately oak trees. Situated in the center of town at Pearl and Forsythe Streets, the building contained a large auditorium as well as council chambers and offices of many city departments. The three-thousand-seat auditorium was popular with white citizens; every spring it was the site of high-school graduations and year-round the stage for musical and theatrical shows. Graduating classes from the three white high schools conducted their ceremonies there, while seniors from the two black high schools had to find other accommodations. A local symphony orchestra and ballet company drew crowds to the auditorium, as did performing artists brought to town by the Beaumont Music Commission and other groups. During the 1940s and 1950s, classical music fans jammed the hall to see the world's finest performers: Isaac Stern, José Iturbi, Jascha Heifetz, Yehudi Menuhin, Risë Stevens, Van Cliburn, and others. Probably no black citizens bought tickets and attended these events, but certainly African American workers took care of janitorial duties for the auditorium.[40]

In Beaumont's city manager form of government, Mrs. Brockman, the chief executive officer, earned $1,000 per month.

Mayor Beard and each council member received monthly stipends of $150 and $100, respectively. Deferring to the mayor and council for policy decisions, Mrs. Brockman directed a work force of six hundred employees and managed an annual budget $2.2 million. About one half of revenues were derived from general property taxes, while the balance was raised by an assortment of rentals, fees, and service charges. No doubt white people and white-controlled companies contributed most of this income, because they owned most of the valuable property and operated all the large businesses. But of course Booker Fayson and other African Americans paid taxes too, on their homes and businesses in the "colored" sections of town.[41]

In terms of city expenditures and employee head count, the police, fire, street, and sanitation departments were largest, together taking up at least 70 percent of the totals, while administration, public health, libraries, recreation, and others made up the balance. Of the six hundred city jobs, whites held about 75 percent, including all the higher-paying and more desirable positions, from department managers to secretaries. Almost without exception, blacks occupied the lowest-paying jobs. In the waste collection department, for instance, the white superintendent earned $475 per month, while the black drivers and helpers collected about $225 for the same period. At the charity hospital, the white supervisor received $460 per month and the black porters took home $165 for an equal time. Of course these large pay discrepancies between whites and blacks resulted mainly from differences in job responsibility, but blacks had no chance of getting the better jobs. Because of the southern caste system, they were confined to certain types of jobs, and often to the most menial assignments.[42]

The city's relegation of African Americans to the lowest-paying jobs was common throughout the Lone Star State, in government as well as business and industry. Among Texas non-farm workers in 1950, more than 90 percent of all black males were employed in domestic service, labor, and service jobs, while few worked as business owners or professionals, a very small group that included doctors, lawyers, dentists, teachers, and ministers. The same was true for black females in Texas: Most worked as maids, cooks, and other domestic servants. Black Texans earned low incomes as compared to whites; their median income amounted to only about 50 percent of incomes collected by white Texans. The numbers were similar in Beaumont, where the median income for black workers amounted to 53 percent of all workers. Reasons for these low levels of employment and income were various, some perhaps derived from lack of education, experience, or expectations. But certainly the main reason was the southern caste system, as devised, handed down, and enforced by white citizens. For generations white Texans would not hire or promote black Texans for the better jobs. This discrimination in hiring must have been the most damaging of all the hardships that blacks suffered under the caste system. Without good jobs, without adequate money, African Americans had little chance to make meaningful progress in society.[43]

But the plight of African American workers in Texas was not completely static or hopeless. During the 1940s and 1950s, and especially beginning with the entry of the United States into World War II, blacks made gradual progress in terms of occupations. While most still worked in agricultural, labor, and service jobs, small numbers of black Texans found better jobs in construction, manufacturing, trucking, warehousing, retailing, government, and health care. In part these improvements were brought about by the actions of the federal government and labor unions. Presidents Roosevelt, Truman, and Eisenhower all issued executive orders aimed at ending racial discrimination in industrial plants holding government contracts. The executive orders, while important symbolically, often met stiff resistance from white workers and were not strictly enforced. In 1955, the AFL-CIO followed the federal government's lead, setting up a civil rights committee and calling at least theoretically for an end to discrimination nationwide. In Texas, the Oil Chemical & Atomic Workers (OCAW) union signed new contracts during 1955–56 with the Gulf and Shell refineries in Houston and with Magnolia Refining Company in Beaumont; these contracts included provisions aimed at reducing racial discrimination. At the Beaumont refinery about seventy members of the black OCAW Local 229 benefited by new "line of progression" rules that prohibited the confinement of black workers to segregated departments and provided them with plant-wide seniority and in-plant training.[44]

In terms of living conditions, African Americans in Beaumont were making slow but steady progress. For several decades the local NAACP, Negro Goodwill Council, Black Ministerial Alliance, and other groups had worked to ameliorate the conditions of black citizens. African American leaders such as Pauline Brackeen, Rev. G. W. Daniels, Rev. Charles Graham, O. C. Hebert, Rev. William N. McCarty, Dr. Laddie L. Melton, Edward C. Moore, Cleveland Nisby, Maudry Plummer, Leantha Redd, Dr. E. D. Sprott, Jr., and others lobbied white governmental officials for better schools, improved streets, and more public services such as parks and libraries. In some instances white officials answered their pleas, granting changes and improvements, but always within the context of the southern caste system. In June, 1954, Mayor Beard boasted in a *Beaumont Enterprise* article about the "good relations" between the city government and the black community. "For several years," he noted, "city officials have been meeting regularly with a Negro goodwill council to discuss current matters of mutual concern." These words may sound empty, but they were genuine, at least within the customs of the time. Funds from a recent bond issue were in fact being spent for extension of water and sewer lines into "all parts of the city, bringing more conveniences to Negro as well as white residents."[45]

In the *Enterprise* story Mayor Beard went on to enumerate other improvements bestowed on the black community by the white city government. "During recent years," the mayor explained, "the city has built two new Negro parks, . . . established a Negro library, [and] . . . employed four Negro police officers. The city late last year also placed in operation the first Negro scout car." The city was remodeling the swimming pool at Liberia Park and also providing a summer recreation program "directed and staffed by Negro supervisors." The new parks, library, police officers, and recreation program were significant advancements for the black community, but ironically they worked to enforce segregation and perpetuate the southern caste system. African American police officers would patrol only in the "colored" sections of town. Black families would picnic at "Negro parks." Black students would read books in the "Negro library" on Wall Street. The library was new, opened with much interracial fanfare in 1950, but it was strictly third rate compared to the whites-only Tyrrell Public Library in terms of facilities, collections, and budget. For the year 1955, when library salaries amounted to forty-nine thousand dollars, a sum of only two thousand dollars was allocated for the Wall Street branch.[46]

Mayor Beard's upbeat comments about good race relations probably carried a second and more subtle meaning. In recent years there had been no significant incidents of race violence: no riots, no killings, no cross burnings. This was good news, because violence was an ever-present danger in the southern caste system. Only a few days before the mayor had made those comments there were ugly incidents just twenty-five miles away in Orange, Texas. According to a story in the Beaumont newspaper, the "Moonlight Gang," a white supremacy group, burned a cross in "a Negro section of Orange" and posted "anti-Negro" signs around town. White city officials in Orange strongly condemned the racist actions, vowing to arrest and jail the perpetrators. No doubt Mayor Beard breathed a sigh of relief, thankful that this time his town had escaped the contagion of violence.[47]

Earlier Beaumont had not been so fortunate. During the boom days of World War II, the town suffered a horrible race riot. On the afternoon of June 15, 1943, white workers at Pennsylvania Ship Yard heard a rumor that a black man had raped the wife of one of their fellow workers. Enraged and bent on revenge, several thousand white workers marched out of the shipyard, paraded through downtown streets, and invaded the police station. Unable to get satisfaction there, the mob broke into smaller groups and rioted through the night, roaming wildly and terrorizing the area of black-owned businesses along Forsythe and Gladys Streets. Armed with guns, axes, hammers, and other tools, the rioters burned automobiles, destroyed shops and stores, and assaulted black citizens. The next day Beaumont police officers along with Texas Rangers and Texas state guard troops restored order, but great harm had been done. Much property was damaged and several hundred persons were injured. Three people—two black and one white—lost their lives.[48]

But the 1943 riot was an aberration, an exception to the normally "good relations" between the races that Mayor Beard liked to mention as a community asset. Generally the two races coexisted quietly in Beaumont, with both groups adhering to the laws and customs of the southern caste system. Each group had its own territory, the white majority reigning supreme in the "white town" and the African American minority keeping to its place and practices in the "black town."

CHAPTER I

Black Beaumont

Forsythe, Gladys, and Irving Streets and Washington Boulevard formed the backbones of four districts that thrived with businesses owned and operated by African Americans. These districts were the home territories of Beaumont's black middle class, a small group of business and professional people who evolved out of the southern caste system. The caste system that produced black communities also created economic opportunities for a limited number of African Americans who prospered moderately by providing goods and services to their fellow black citizens. These sales and professional people, along with certain other workers, qualified as members of the middle class or bourgeoisie, a group distinguished by education, income, occupation, and social position. All in all, about 10 percent of African American workers in the South held middle-class jobs and positions.[1]

In Beaumont and many other southern cities, the black middle class included doctors, lawyers, dentists, pharmacists, and undertakers as well as preachers, schoolteachers, realtors, insurance agents, and property owners. Others were business people who operated bars, cafes, cleaners, tailor shops, barbershops, beauty parlors, and service stations. Also included were clerical workers and other white-collar employees, such as postal clerks and letter carriers of the United States Postal Service. Many members of the black middle class had attended colleges such as Fisk, Hampton Institute, and Prairie View A&M. Having advantages of education, they provided leadership in the black communities, helping develop churches, fraternal organizations, social groups, and civic associations. In some instances they worked to foster racial pride and racial solidarity, urging fellow African Americans to read black newspapers and favor black merchants. On occasion they provided tactical connections with the white establishment, working quietly to resolve racial problems or lobbying discreetly for improvements in the black community. Also, some middle-class blacks joined the NAACP and pushed openly to defeat the southern caste system.[2]

Forsythe was the premier black business district in Beaumont, having the greatest concentration of commercial and professional activities. The district's main thoroughfare was Forsythe Street, which came directly from the white central business district and thus tied the two areas together. After passing City Hall, Tyrrell Public Library, and the White House department store, drivers heading down Forsythe Street would cross Park Street and then be in the "colored" portion of Forsythe Street, which led to and formed the center of a six-block commercial district. Other streets in the black section were Wall and College, also running east and west, as well as Neches, Trinity, and Jefferson, going north and south. There were some white-owned businesses in the area, however, such as the Texas Storage Company at the corner of Forsythe and Neches; also, some Forsythe area landlords were white, among them Carliss Lombardo Carey.[3]

The Forsythe district featured no tall office buildings, modern hotels, or grand stores. But Forsythe was still a vibrant commercial and civic district, with more than fifty business and professional establishments operated by African Americans, many of whom qualified as members of the middle class. Mike Gant had a photography studio; Everett Johnson, a men's clothing store; Allen Fowler, a pharmacy; and Joseph White, a fish market. Both Willie Gaines and R. V. Hebert operated dry cleaners, and Hebert also ran a barbershop. Others engaged in barber and beauty businesses, as well as related shoeshine activities, were Ruth Minix, Cherry Edwards, George Washington, Helen Sorrell, and Elmo Maple. Two men, Allen Hawkins and Charles Wilson, managed liquor stores in the area, and Wilson had multiple interests with locations elsewhere in town. Using the name Chaney, Wilson operated three liquor stores, one lounge, and Chaney's Auditorium on

Irving Street in the South End. Chaney's Auditorium was a popular nightclub that often featured shows by traveling bands.[4]

Everett Johnson, the haberdasher mentioned above, had multiple businesses interests; he and his wife Marguerita operated two other enterprises: Marguerita's Coffee Shop and Marguerita's Tap Room. Other eating and drinking establishments included Harrison Joseph's Shorty's Tavern, Alphonse Conner's Eagle Rock Bar & Café, and Maurice Simpson's Barbeque & Steakhouse. Another was Ed Long's Café & Barbecue, a well-known restaurant founded by the late Ed Long and carried on by his widow, Georgia Long. Hotel accommodations in the Forsythe district were very limited, with no facilities comparable in any way to Hotel Beaumont and the finer white establishments. Several individuals, such as James Oliver and Pearl Starks, rented out furnished rooms, but only two operated facilities that might qualify as hotels. Hannah Phillips had the Phillips Hotel & Restaurant, a two-story frame building, while R. Nelson Whitney managed the Hotel Theresa, also a two-story wooden structure.

Nelson Whitney, obviously an ambitious and energetic man, had a second job that demonstrated white and black connections in the world of business. He worked as a radio announcer for KJET, a broadcast station that targeted African American audiences. Owned by white investors and directed by a white manager, KJET advertised its special niche: "Sabine Area's Only Station Programming to Over 184,000 Negroes." Probably Whitney and other KJET disc jockeys filled the airwaves of southeast Texas with rock-and-roll music, in 1955 a relatively new style combining rhythm and blues, hillbilly, and "race" music and in which African Americans soared to stardom. La Verne Baker, Ruth Brown, Chuck Berry, Fats Domino, and Little Richard were among the black artists whose soulful and earthy music was heard on the radios and record players of many young Beaumonters, both black and white.[5]

Ray Pike was another African American who worked for a white-owned business that catered to black patrons. He was manager of the Star Theater, a cinema operated by Julius Gordon's Jefferson Amusement Company. Advertisements for the Star carried the words "Air-Conditioned" and featured a cartoon-like frosting of snow, the comforts of modern air-conditioning being important to all movie patrons, black and white. The movies shown at the

Star were similar to those offered at the white theaters: white films starring white people produced by white people for white audiences. In June, 1955, the fare included John Ireland in *Combat Squad* (1953) and John Wayne in two films, *The Cowboy and the Girl* (1943) and *The High and the Mighty* (1954).[6]

At the corner of Forsythe and Neches, Frank Lea and Felix Normand operated a service station where they pumped gas, fixed flats, and washed cars. Nearby were dispatch offices for two taxi companies: Busy Bee, owned by Welton Hawthorne, and Sunbeam, operated by Rufus Kempt. Sunbeam advertisements promised "Convenient, prompt taxi service to any place in Beaumont and Jefferson County [with] courteous, careful drivers." Also providing transportation services was Willard & Willard, Inc., a funeral home that operated a fleet of hearses. Elmo Willard, Jr., was a prominent black business leader and property owner; he managed the undertaking company profitably for many years but died suddenly in 1954. This event prompted his son, Elmo Willard III, a recent law school graduate, to return to Beaumont the next year to oversee the family business and, coincidentally, to take part in the Tyrrell Park desegregation lawsuit.[7]

Social service organizations in the Forsythe district demonstrated interaction between the white and black communities. The white-controlled city government operated the Beaumont Venereal Disease Control Clinic, directed by the white physician, William A. Smith, as well as the Wall Street branch library that was managed by the black librarian, Dorothy Robinson. The YMCA and YWCA had separate branches catering to African American youths. Funded in part by donations from white community members, the well-known Frances Morris branch of the YWCA was directed by Exie Clement, an African American woman. The Dorcas Community Center provided a home for needy children. Managed by its African American president, Roberta L. Smith, the Dorcas Center received partial funding from the Community Chest and was governed by a board composed of black and white citizens.[8]

The YMCA building on Neches Street provided meeting space for black organizations, including the Dorie E. Miller American Legion Post 817. Composed of African American military veterans, Post 817 raised funds to construct a lodge building on Fourth

Street. During June, 1954, Dr. Laddie L. Melton, Terry Charlton, and Wheeler Middleton canvassed the black community and sold special one-dollar tickets for admission to Stuart Stadium on June 19, when the local Beaumont Exporters played a regularly scheduled doubleheader against the Dallas Eagles. This fundraising event demonstrated how blacks accommodated themselves to the caste system: Even though they were relegated to "colored" seating in the stadium, they were avid baseball fans and proud of African American ball players who were making their way in the game. They readily purchased the one-dollar tickets and attended the "Juneteenth" event, June 19 being the day that black Texans annually celebrated the official end of slavery in 1865. During intermission of the second game, Dr. Melton spoke to the large but segregated audience, praising two World War II African American veterans: the late Dorie Miller, who won the Navy Cross for heroism at Pearl Harbor, and James Buster "Buzz" Clarkson, a wartime stevedore who was playing ball for the Exporters in 1955. A former star at Wilberforce College, a school for blacks in Ohio, Clarkson was described by the local newspaper as "Beaumont's heavy-hitting infielder" and praised for his .336 batting average. The Dallas Eagles had broken the color line in the Texas League in 1952 when they hired the black pitcher Dave Hoskins, five years after Jackie Robinson played his first game for the Brooklyn Dodgers.[9]

During October, 1954, American Legion Post 817 conducted another fundraising event, this time in conjunction with "Negro Day" at the South Texas State Fair. Co-sponsored by the Young Men's Business League, an all-white civic group that produced the fair, this event highlighted working relationships between black and white groups. Directed by post commander O. V. Williams, the African American program included an hour-long "Patriotism" parade of bands, cars, and floats, as well as a contest to select a queen for the fair. Young African American women were nominated for queen and underwritten by local black businesses, with the girl raising the most money being crowned queen. Booker Fayson's nominee, Mary Alice Williams, finished as first runner-up, while Olivia Guather, sponsored by James Armstrong Café, won the queen's title. Winners in the parade contests included the Blessed Sacrament School band, the Charlton-Pollard High

School majorettes, and the Blanchette Junior High School drill team.[10]

"Negro Day" at the fair culminated in the evening with a speech by Jack Brooks, the white U.S. Congress representative from Beaumont. Having entered Congress in 1953, Brooks was facing his first reelection bid in the coming month. A staunch Democrat aligned closely with Rep. Sam Rayburn and Sen. Lyndon Johnson, Brooks cultivated the support of labor union members and welcomed the votes of African American citizens. Introduced by black legionnaire Harvey Thomas to "a record-smashing Negro day crowd," Brooks declared, "Negroes are Americans first." They are not interested in "special privileges," he said, but in "equal opportunities to participate in the American economic life guaranteed under the Constitution of the United States." He continued, "You are devoted to our democratic principles . . . but like the Democratic Party, you are dedicated to raising our standard of living . . . so that all Americans can have better jobs, better homes, and better schools."[11]

The Forsythe district featured a number of black churches, institutions that were very important in the African American community. In Beaumont and throughout the South, the churches were the exclusive property of black people—created, owned, and managed by African Americans, without any interference from white people. They were centers of religious and social life, sponsors for education, assemblies for civic and political action, training grounds for leaders, and forums for fundraising. Most of the black congregations were Baptist or Methodist, with these groups accounting for more than 90 percent of the total in Texas. But in coastal towns with significant migration from Louisiana, including Beaumont, Port Arthur, Ames, Galveston, and Houston, black Catholics built viable congregations.[12]

On Forsythe Street near Park, at the very entry to the black business district, was Antioch Baptist Church, an imposing three-story masonry building that featured a monumental brick façade with cast stone finials and a triumphal stairway ascending to double entries at the second story. Led by the Reverend Richard E. King, Antioch Baptist traced it beginnings to 1894. Other important congregations in the downtown neighborhood were Rev. G. W. Daniels's Sunlight Baptist, Rev. Mason Pinkney's East Mount

Olive Baptist, Rev. Clarence Davis's Ebenezer Baptist, Rev. Allen M. Mayes's Saint James Methodist, and Rev. William Carr's Saint Paul's African Methodist Episcopal. Saint Paul's AME on Wall Street was the granddaddy of all local black congregations, having been founded in 1868 during the days of Reconstruction.[13]

Leaders in the Forsythe community included doctors, lawyers, dentists, pharmacists, undertakers, and insurance agents. These were men of the middle class, mostly college-educated, well dressed, owning automobiles, and living with their families in comfortable homes. They and others in the town made up a "black establishment," a group that exerted influence on social, civic, and political affairs. Dr. James C. Wallace and his son, Dr. Charles R. Wallace, rendered medical care to African Americans at their Central Hospital Clinic, an institution that also offered the dental services of Dr. Joseph W. Smith. Thomas Brackeen, M.D., had offices that included two dentists, Dr. Charles B. Charlton and Dr. Henry Jones, Jr., as well as life insurance agent Horace Chatman, a representative of Watchtower Life. Other life insurance agents in the neighborhood were Sam Clarence, Golden State Mutual; P. H. Willard, Atlanta Life; and Elton Davis, Excelsior Life. The number and apparent success of insurance agents testified to the viability of life insurance companies founded and operated by African Americans. Across the South, and throughout the nation, life insurance companies were the largest and most successful of black enterprises.[14]

Pauline Brackeen, Dr. Brackeen's wife, was a leader in the black community who, during the 1950s, served as secretary of the local NAACP. Another African American leader was the already mentioned Laddie L. Melton, a dentist who had offices on Trinity Street. Born in Louisiana and educated at Howard University, Dr. Melton began his dentistry practice in Beaumont in 1926. Active in the black community long before the modern civil rights era, Melton worked "within the system," observing the rules of the southern caste system and avoiding harsh confrontations with white leaders. "You had to push without upsetting the applecart, without creating a scene," he once said. "You didn't irritate anybody and you had to be careful about your remarks or you'd be branded a 'smart nigger.'" The efficacy of his tactics was proven during the aftermath of the 1943 race riot, when he emerged as a leader on a biracial restitution committee that appraised property damage and raised money to pay for black properties that had been burned and otherwise damaged by rioters.[15]

Sol White and his brother, George White, Jr., were prominent members of the Forsythe "establishment." Perhaps also they qualified as members of the black elite. They practiced professions, owned property, and resided with wives and children in comfortable homes on Houston Street in Beaumont's most prestigious black neighborhood. Sol White was a pharmacist and real estate owner, while George White was an attorney, in all likelihood the first African American lawyer in town. A native of Beaumont and a World War I army veteran, George attended Prairie View Normal and Industrial College before enrolling in Howard University, where he took his law degree. He earned an additional law degree from New York University and in 1930 returned to his hometown to commence a long legal career.[16]

Sol White owned the White Professional Building, no doubt the largest commercial property in the Forsythe district owned by an African American. Standing at the corner of Forsythe and Trinity, the two-story red brick building comprised almost six thousand square feet. High in the air, facing both streets, engraved signs tastefully displayed the property owner's name: WHITE. On the ground floor White presided over the Sol White Pharmacy and rented office space to Recordall, a fire and casualty insurance agency run by Samuel Berry. Upstairs White collected rents from various professional and business tenants: his brother, George White, lawyer; Dr. Peter Byrd, physician; Dr. Mitchell Normand and Dr. Sonnie Pernetter, dentists; John Carter of National Health & Accident and Betty Nichols with Standard Benefit Life, insurance agents.[17]

A leading professional in the black community, Sol White helped host a convention in Beaumont for black physicians, dentists, and pharmacists from across the Lone Star State. Meeting June 9–10, 1954, the group honored a number of doctors who had practiced for more than forty years, including Dr. G. P. A. Ford, Houston; Dr. Arthur K. Shirley, San Angelo; and Dr. Peter G. Byrd and Dr. E. S. Craven, both of Beaumont; another was Dr. Lawrence Nixon, the El Paso physician who earlier sued the Democratic Party of Texas for the right to vote in all-white primary elections.

Because African Americans were not welcome at local hotels and other such gathering places, the group conducted its meetings at Hebert High, a black school. Dr. Melton was in charge of convention arrangements, while Sol White offered a welcoming address. In a program that demonstrated a measure of interaction among black and white professionals, an otherwise all-black luncheon featured a white speaker: Dr. Grant Taylor, dean of the University of Texas Graduate Medical School from nearby Galveston.[18]

Obviously Sol White and George White were successful citizens. They earned money and lived well, if within the confines of the southern caste system. Exactly how they accommodated to the system is not known. Did Sol deposit his money in Frank Betts's American National Bank? Did George buy his suits from Fletcher and Will Graham's prestigious White House department store? Did they patronize white businesses and yet risk the indignities of the caste system? Imagine George White, army veteran, New York University graduate, and lawyer, going into the White House to buy dress shirts. How would he deal with the white sales clerk? Would he experience slights and insults? Would the white floor-walker ask him not to sit at the whites-only lunch counter? Probably Sol and George found ways of accommodation, the means of getting what they wanted and at the same time avoiding racial confrontations. Probably they worked "within the system," in the same way that Dr. Melton did.[19]

Margaret Phillips, an African American, knew Sol and George White and remembered them fondly. "They were the kindest people I've ever worked for. They were really concerned about black people," she said. Phillips also had good memories of Forsythe, an area called "the heart of the black community" by Albert Harrison, a black citizen who studied local history. Forsythe "provided a safe, happy meeting place for families," Phillips recalled. "It was the kind of place where people could meet and forget their problems. Especially on weekends, it was wall-to-wall people. People from communities like Cheek and China would come to town and do their marketing and take in a western movie." Loretta Oliver, another African American, had similar recollections. "The area was full of life," she said. "I have fond memories of spending hours at the [Wall Street] library. I remember my mother telling me to wait right there. I felt safe and comfortable."[20]

Margaret Phillips recalled some unsavory aspects of Forsythe, mentioning "the usual taverns and hoodlums," but concluded that "the area was safe or my family would not have allowed me down there." Having worked a stint as librarian at the Wall Street branch, Phillips recollected some of the realities of the southern caste system. "When we needed reference books, we would have them sent over [from the white Tyrrell Public Library]. You must understand," she said emphatically, "blacks were limited, you weren't allowed to go to the white businesses." Phillips's memories are partially correct. Black citizens were indeed excluded from the main public library, but they were welcome at many white businesses, so long as they observed the rules of the caste system. Whites wanted their money, but many would not grant African Americans the courtesy of equal treatment.[21]

Dorothy James, a black Beaumonter, recalled the crowded scenes of the Forsythe district. "It was just the place everybody went," she said. "Kids could walk to town at night and they were safe." When James said "everybody," she meant African Americans only. Generally white people did not frequent Forsythe nor did they patronize the businesses there; they did not buy medications from Sol White, seek legal advice from George White, purchase insurance from Sam Clarence, see a movie at the Star Theater, or stop for lunch at Alphonse Conner's Eagle Rock Bar & Café. In many cases whites would have been welcome, but Forsythe was a black district almost exclusively. No doubt white firefighters worked the area, as did white police officers, though probably in the company of one of the four black officers. White business leaders might stop from time to time at Simpson's Barbeque & Steakhouse or Ed Long's Café & Barbecue to pick up orders of brisket, chicken, and sausage, all items popular with both whites and blacks. Or white hunters might bring in their freshly killed ducks and geese to be barbecued. While awaiting their orders in the smoky cafes, the white men might have a beer or soda water and exchange pleasantries with the black proprietors and workers. Probably the black business people were happy to have their business and eager to please them.[22]

Gladys Street, Irving Street, and Washington Boulevard formed the centers of the three other primarily black business districts. All were smaller than the Forsythe district in numbers of business and professional establishments. They were also different; whereas Forsythe was a mostly commercial area with relatively few residential inhabitants, the other three districts were associated closely with large and well-known residential neighborhoods. Each commercial district served a different neighborhood: the Gladys district, the North End; the Irving district, the South End, and the Washington Boulevard district, the neighborhood known to African Americans as the Pear Orchard.[23]

The Gladys commercial district, about fifteen blocks north of downtown, boasted approximately twenty-five black-owned businesses and professional establishments. Among these were barbershops, beauty salons, bars, and cafes. Others were the dental offices of Joseph Herbert, D.D.S.; Copasetic Newsstand, owned by Lige Rogers; and Fleming's Funeral Home, owned by Mack Hannah, a black entrepreneur who resided in nearby Port Arthur, Texas. Not all business in the immediate area was conducted by African Americans. Two grocery stores were operated by Italian Americans: Sunset Grocery & Market by W. M. Angelo, and Crescent Market by A. S. Fertitta and Sam Maida. The presence of Italian American grocers in this and other black neighborhoods represented a significant violation of the southern segregation system. Mostly second-generation immigrants from southern Italy and Sicily, they operated stores and some even resided in areas considered off-limits by most white southerners. In many instances, they had good relations with their black customers, often extending them credit for grocery purchases.[24]

Served by the Gladys commercial district, the North End neighborhood was a large residential area for blacks. It included streets such as Evalon, Ashley, and Long, as well as Pine Street, a curving road that ran north for more than twenty-five blocks. Noted for its tall sycamore trees and gently rolling terrain, Pine was a historic thoroughfare that served both the white and black communities. White funeral-goers traveled the street to attend burial services at the century-old Magnolia Cemetery, and white business leaders used the route to get from their downtown offices to the Beaumont Country Club. But really Pine was a "colored" street, lined with homes of African Americans and intersecting with many other "colored" streets, including Isla, Plum, Simmons, Lethia, and Pollard. During the 1950s, thousands of African Americans lived along these streets, many in modest brick or frame cottages, others in simple shanties. Among North End residents were three of the black golfers who joined the Booker Fayson lawsuit. Joe Griffin and Earl White resided on Plum Street, while Johnnie Ware lived on Simmons Street.[25]

In the North End and the other predominantly African American neighborhoods, housing was different from and often inferior to housing for whites in the city. In terms of home ownership, for example, 55 percent of white householders owned their dwellings, while only 43 percent of black residents were homeowners. Racial differences were also seen in property values. The median value for all Beaumont houses was $6,791, while the median value of houses occupied by blacks was only $3,273. The same was true for household conveniences such as private toilets and hot and cold running water. Of all Beaumont residences, 93 percent featured these modern conveniences, but only 75 percent of black-occupied houses were so equipped. Some African Americans lived in so-called "shotgun" dwellings: small frame houses, frequently identical, usually painted green, sometimes single-family and other times duplexes, and often owned by white landlords.[26]

Irving Street formed the backbone of the South End, a large and historic black neighborhood located about fifteen blocks south of downtown Beaumont. Sometimes the area was known as the Lower Woods. Containing more than ten square city blocks, the area was home to thousands of black Beaumonters, including William Narcisse, one of Fayson's fellow plaintiffs, and Theo Johns, the young lawyer who worked on the Fayson suit. Irving Street, starting at Buford Street near the Port of Beaumont, ran about a dozen blocks to the south, along the way providing spaces for more than forty businesses that made up the Irving commercial district. Among the black enterprises were barbershops, beauty salons, shoe repair shops, cleaners, and liquor stores. Others were Flanagan's Taxi, Knighton Funeral Home, and Hotel Gilbert, an establishment that advertised "Air Conditioned Comfort," "Private Shower Baths," and "Reasonable Rates." Two Italian Americans, Coley Saleme and Leonard Bruno, operated grocery stores in the center of this African American district.[27]

Leonard Bruno ran Bruno's Food Store in a building that doubled as his residence. In the front section he sold groceries, and in the rear he lived with his wife, two children, his mother, and his father, the elder Bruno having immigrated to America from Sicily. On Irving Street, Bruno worked and lived in the midst of a black community. He knew many of the South End residents and was known by them. He purchased advertisements in the Charlton-Pollard High School annual and hired a black youth, Russell Sutton, to work as a butcher. But his friendly business relations with black neighbors did not extend to religious or social settings; for example, he and his family did not worship at the nearby Blessed Sacrament Catholic Church but traveled across Railroad Avenue to attend mass at Saint Joseph's Catholic Church, an Italian American parish. Bruno's store was profitable; he had many customers and extended them credit when needed. "Giving credit was the only way I could compete with the big stores," Bruno recalled. He enjoyed good relations with his black customers. "They were good neighbors, good people," he said. "We treated each other with respect."[28]

Aaron Jefferson had offices on Irving Street where he handled real estate sales and acted as distributor for the Beaumont *Informer,* a local edition of the Houston *Informer* newspaper. Carter Wesley, an African American lawyer and NAACP leader, published the weekly *Informer* in Houston and distributed customized editions for black readers and advertisers in Austin, Galveston, Beaumont, and other Texas towns. Readers in Beaumont saw a standard fare of state and national news supplemented by a handful of local stories. Also publishing the *Dallas Express,* Wesley used that newspaper and the *Informer* chain to advance the interests of black Texans, promoting African American businesses and spreading the news about the NAACP and its activities.[29]

The South End was home to Charlton-Pollard High School, one of Beaumont's two high schools for black students. Though controlled and funded by an all-white school board, Charlton-Pollard was an all-black establishment with African American administrators, teachers, coaches, and students. Like black churches, Charlton-Pollard and other such schools were important institutions in the black community. Charlton-Pollard was also a province of the black middle class, an institution where college-educated African Americans found dignified employment and where black Beaumonters embraced middle-class American values. The principal, Harvey C. Johnson, had a faculty of twenty-two women and eight men, all with bachelor's degrees and a few with advanced certificates. The administration and faculty dressed professionally: men in coats and ties, women in dresses. Charlton-Pollard's yearbook, the *Rice Shock,* in 1955 indicated a conventional high-school program: academic courses, including English, history, algebra, science, and Spanish; vocational courses such as cosmetology and homemaking; athletic teams, including girls' basketball; marching band; class favorites; student council; honor society; and parent-teacher association. Underwriters for the yearbook included both black and white advertisers: black businesses such as Willard & Willard Funeral Home, Fowler's Pharmacy, and Busy Bee Taxi, joined by white-run operations, including the Fashion, Gem Jewelry, Gulf States Utilities, and Coca-Cola. During the academic year, Principal Johnson hosted an American Education Week program: "Good Schools Are Your Responsibility." The program panel included Mrs. Willie Brockman, the white city manager; Mildred Sprott White, a black teacher; Father Edward Bowes, a white priest from Blessed Sacrament; and Elmo Willard III, the black lawyer.[30]

Obviously parts of the South End were laid out to attract black citizens. Some of the residential streets were named for national leaders dear to the hearts of African Americans: Lincoln, Grant, Sherman, Porter, and Stanton. Porter, named for the Union admiral at Vicksburg, was an important street, being the site of Blessed Sacrament, one of Beaumont's two black Catholic parishes. Founded in 1915, Blessed Sacrament forty years later was led by the Reverend Joseph M. Schmirtz, a white priest. Blessed Sacrament carried out its mission from impressive facilities; the church, convent, and school were housed in handsome masonry buildings, all well laid out and situated on ample grounds. The school, staffed by white nuns and black lay teachers, demonstrated a strong commitment by the Catholic Church to serve the needs of its parishioners and the local black community. The church itself featured handsome stained-glass windows, some bearing names of donor groups such as "South End People," "North End People," and "Pear Orchard People," names that evidenced a marked sense of neighborhood identity. Congregation members included two of Booker Fayson's golfing associates: Joe Griffin and Thomas Parker.[31]

Washington Boulevard was the main east-west thoroughfare in the southern part of Beaumont. Beginning at Railroad Avenue, the broad street ran west for about thirty city blocks. Half of Washington Boulevard was exclusively "white," serving the white neighborhoods of South Park. But after fifteen blocks, past the Southern Pacific railroad tracks, Washington became a "mixed" street, where white and black business people operated in proximity to one another. Five Italian Americans—Frank Barranco, Cecil Fontana, Dominic Gallo, Paul Lucia, and Frank Pavia—managed grocery stores in the same area where a dozen African American business owners and professionals had their offices. Among the black establishments were a barbershop, beauty salon, liquor store, dry cleaner, drugstore, auto repair shop, tavern, and nightclub. Others were James E. Powell, a physician; Marie Nelson, a music teacher; and Beatrice Moore, who operated a nursery school. There were also four insurance agents: Alvin Daniels, Marion Lewis, Alvin Randolph, and Booker Fayson. With offices at 2370 Washington, Fayson rented office space to Theo Johns and Elmo Willard, Beaumont's newest black lawyers. Willard and his wife Pat lived in the next block in a four-unit brick apartment building. Other tenants in the apartment building were a high-school teacher, Louise Taylor; Texas Company seaman Joseph Paige and his wife Agnes; and a Baptist minister, the Reverend T. F. Simmons and his wife Ethel.[32]

Washington Boulevard formed the northern boundary of the Pear Orchard, a large neighborhood that dated back to the nineteenth century. Comprising more than ten square city blocks, the Pear Orchard was home to thousands of black Beaumonters. Booker Fayson and his wife Johnnie lived on Harriot Street, as did Dr. and Mrs. Brackeen. Not far from the Fayson and Brackeen homes was Liberia Park, a city facility named for the African nation founded in 1821 by American abolitionists; the park included a swimming pool managed during summer months by Clifton Ozen, a black teacher at nearby Hebert High, Beaumont's other black high school. The Hebert High principal, Archie Price, also served as pastor of West Tabernacle Baptist Church, one of the area's older congregations. Close by was Our Mother of Mercy Catholic Church, with adjoining convent and school, headed by the Reverend Charles Hanks, a white priest.[33]

The Appomattox Club, a men's social and civic club, was located in the Pear Orchard. Founded in 1923 and consisting mostly of business and professional men, the club held weekly meetings that were occasions for fellowship and as well as civic and political discussion. Other civic and fraternal groups operated by black Beaumonters included men's groups such as Elks Lodge Number 593, Masonic Lodge Number 291, Omega Psi Phi, and the Knights of Peter Claver, as well as women's sororities: Alpha Kappa Alpha, Delta Sigma Theta, and Sigma Delta Rho. In Beaumont and throughout the South, these civic, fraternal, and social groups, like black churches and black schools, provided means for African Americans to enjoy life and otherwise accommodate to the caste system; they also furnished venues for the development of the middle class and the exercise of black leadership. Dr. Melton, for example, served many years as leader of Masonic Lodge Number 291.[34]

Just across Washington Boulevard from the Pear Orchard was another black residential area, the Cartwright Addition. A small area of only about eight city blocks, it contained many of Beaumont's better black-owned residences. Often the houses were well designed and set back on roomy, landscaped lots. The Cartwright Addition was situated in between and immediately adjoining white neighborhoods. On the east side of the Cartwright Addition, the tracks of Southern Pacific Railroad provided clear separation from a white neighborhood; in this case, the blacks lived literally "across the tracks" from the whites. But on the west side of the Cartwright Addition, black and white neighborhoods were contiguous, distinguished only by an alley that separated the backyards of black-occupied houses on Houston Street and white-occupied houses on Amarillo Street. Here black and white families, mostly middle class, lived in proximity and on apparently peaceful terms with one another.[35]

Sol White and George White, the Forsythe business leaders, lived in comfortable homes in the Cartwright Addition on Houston Street. Other middle- and lower-middle-class residents of the area included James C. Wallace, physician; David Baker, pharmacist; and R. V. Hebert, dry cleaner; as well as schoolteachers Carrie Clark and Hugh Fowler; and U.S. Postal Service letter carriers Harold Goodman, James McGovern, and Oliver Sprott.

Members of the Sprott family were among the most prominent of the neighborhood residents. Dr. Ed D. Sprott, Jr., and his two brothers, Dr. Curtis Sprott and Dr. Maxie Sprott all resided in the area and operated a modern medical clinic exclusively for black patients. Situated on Cartwright Street near Houston Street, the Sprott clinic was housed in a spacious brick building fronted by shade trees and manicured lawns.[36]

Dr. Ed Sprott, Jr., emerged as one of Beaumont's most effective leaders in the early stages of the modern civil rights struggle. In 1952 he was elected president of the local chapter of the National Association for the Advancement of Colored People, a group that was leading black people away from long-standing policies of accommodation and into newer tactics of confrontation. Sprott energized the local NAACP, building its membership, establishing chapters in Orange and Port Arthur, and helping orchestrate the federal lawsuits that desegregated Tyrrell Park golf course and Lamar College. Other local officers were Marion Lewis, Mrs. Wesley Cormier, and Pauline Brackeen, the branch secretary who handled voluminous correspondence with NAACP offices in New York City and Dallas, Texas. Sprott and his fellow officers worked hard to strengthen the local chapter, distributing manuals, placards, and pins; touting *The Crisis* magazine; and soliciting memberships and donations.[37]

Minimum annual dues for the NAACP were $3.50, but many contributed more. Dr. L. L. Melton, Dr. James Wallace, and others paid $25, while Ocie Jackson, the wealthy rancher, bought a life membership for $200. Also among the contributors were a number of organizations, such as Delta Sigma Theta sorority, Omega Psi Phi fraternity, Starlight Baptist Church, and Letter Carriers Local 842. Members and contributors included a handful of white Beaumonters, all business leaders of the Jewish faith. Ben Rogers and I. B. "Butch" Hoffer each donated $25, as did the Fair Store, Inc., a company owned by Sheldon Greenberg, Sigmund Greenberg, and Albert Klein. Rogers and the others received formal acknowledgments from Lucille Black, membership secretary in the NAACP New York office. "We are happy to include you," she wrote to Rogers, "among those who believe in our cause and who want to help in the fight for full democracy for all Americans."[38]

Dr. Sprott and Pauline Brackeen pushed constantly for new members. Mrs. Brackeen, an able and energetic worker, believed fervently in the cause. "We need a strong branch in Beaumont," she said. "The opportunities for its services are many." Their efforts yielded impressive results. Membership approached three hundred, and new leaders emerged. Especially noteworthy was Joseph Griffin, the thirty-eight-year-old letter carrier who single-handedly recruited more than one hundred new members. Gloster B. Current of the New York NAACP office recognized Griffin as "one of the outstanding membership workers in the Beaumont branch" and arranged for his photograph to be published in the April, 1955, issue of *The Crisis* national magazine.[39]

Joe Griffin was indeed outstanding. He worked to build the local NAACP, pushed to dismantle the southern caste system, and became a leader in the campaign to desegregate the municipal golf course. He joined with five other black golfers and filed a federal lawsuit to break the color line at Tyrrell Park. In this way Griffin became one of the "Joe Doakes" plaintiffs.

Booker Fayson in his Beaumont insurance office. Courtesy Mary Bell Fayson

Joseph Griffin (*left*) and Robert Williams (*right*) at golf tournament awards ceremony at the Appomattox Club, 1987. Courtesy Linda Kyle

Joseph Griffin and Elizabeth Griffin. Courtesy Joseph P. Griffin, Jr.

William Narcisse.
Courtesy Charles Narcisse

Thomas A. Parker and
Bobbie Gene Parker.
Courtesy Thomas Parker

Johnnie Ware at golf tournament awards ceremony at the Appomattox Club, 1987.
Courtesy Linda Kyle

Earl White. Courtesy
Ruby White Harris

Young lawyers Theodore Johns (*left*) and Elmo Willard (*right*) in their first office.
Courtesy Mary Bell Fayson

Theodore Johns (*left*) and Elmo Willard (*right*) at the Beaumont federal courthouse, 1989. Photo by Brad Horn, courtesy *Port Arthur News*

Elmo Willard (*left*), Judge John Paul Davis (*center*), and Theodore Johns (*right*) at a banquet in Beaumont. Courtesy Elmo Willard III Collection, Tyrrell Historical Library, Beaumont, Texas

NAACP lawyers Thurgood Marshall (*left*), Louis L. Redding (*center*), and U. Simpson Tate (*right*). Courtesy *The CRISIS Magazine*

NAACP leaders in Dallas, Texas. From left to right: U. Simpson Tate, Merrill Booker, W. J. Durham, and Carter Wesley. Courtesy Center for American History, University of Texas at Austin (CN no. 08524), Craft (Juanita Jewel Shanks) Papers

Lamar Cecil (*left*) and Jack Porter (*right*) campaigning for Dwight Eisenhower. Courtesy Grayson R. Cecil

Lamar Cecil (*left*) taking the oath given by Judge Joseph W. Sheehy.
Courtesy Grayson R. Cecil

Judge Lamar Cecil.
Courtesy Grayson R.
Cecil

TYRRELL PARK
MUNICIPAL GOLF COURSE

Henry Homberg, Pro.

City of Beaumont — Golf Department

BEAUMONT, TEXAS

Tyrrell Park Municipal Golf Course score card, ca. 1955. Courtesy Ed Campbell, Golf Professional, Babe Zaharias Golf Course, Port Arthur, Texas

• •

CHAPTER 3

"Joe Doakes" in Beaumont

"Joe Doakes" is a figure well known in American culture: He is "the ordinary Joe," "Joe Blow," and "GI Joe." He (or she) is the hard hat in the factory, the lineman on the football team, the dogface in the army—generally he does the hardest work and receives the smallest paycheck. During World War II, "Willy and Joe" of the Bill Mauldin cartoons were typical Joe Doakes characters—unsung heroes who went in harm's way. They did the fighting, won the victory, and then, receiving little but grim satisfaction, passed away with scarcely a mention in the pages of history. From the 1940s through the 1960s, Joe Doakes characters played essential roles in the NAACP campaign to dismantle the Jim Crow caste system: They served as plaintiffs in the desegregation lawsuits. Thurgood Marshall, the leading NAACP lawyer, praised these people, describing them as ordinary citizens who "believed in the promises of justice and equality, [and] never gave up the fight against the relics of slavery."[1]

Among Marshall's Joe Doakes plaintiffs were Dr. Lonnie Smith, who won the right to vote in 1944 in the Texas Democratic primary; Heman M. Sweatt, who gained admission in 1949 to the University of Texas law school; George W. McLaurin, who desegregated the University of Oklahoma graduate school in 1950; and of course Oliver Brown and his daughter Linda, the lead plaintiffs in *Brown v. Board of Education of Topeka, Kansas,* the famous Supreme Court case of 1954 that led to the desegregation of the nation's public schools. Others were Booker Fayson, Joe Griffin, Bill Narcisse, Thomas Parker, Johnnie Ware, and Earl White, all of whom played the role of Joe Doakes plaintiffs in Beaumont, Texas.[2]

Certainly Fayson, Griffin, and the others qualified as classic Joe Doakes plaintiffs: They believed in the American dream and wanted better lives for themselves and their fellow African Americans. They were courageous people, willing to stand up and challenge the racial status quo in Beaumont. They attended public meetings, signed their names on public documents, and saw their home addresses published in the local newspaper. Going public with their challenge, Fayson and the other black plaintiffs went in harm's way: They risked their jobs and their property; they exposed themselves and their families to ridicule, harassment, and even violence.[3]

Fayson and the others emerged as Joe Doakes plaintiffs by way of experiences common to generations of African Americans. Sons of the southern caste system, they were born and reared in humble households, destined for careers as laborers and service workers, and fated to be second-class citizens. But they had advantages of timing. Fayson and his fellows lived during the days of the New Deal, World War II, and the postwar economic boom, a twenty-year era when African Americans benefited from changes sweeping the nation. During the New Deal years, from 1933 to 1938, President Franklin Roosevelt, his wife Eleanor Roosevelt, and administrators such as Harold Ickes and Harry Hopkins were sympathetic to the plight of African Americans and from time to time used the power of the federal government to advance their interests. A number of the New Deal relief and economic programs provided financial assistance to some African American workers and farmers. On occasion President Roosevelt wielded his executive authority on their behalf, ordering the desegregation of cafeterias and restrooms in federal government buildings and directing the employment and promotion of more African Americans in various government departments. Many black Americans, for example, found decent employment with the U.S. Postal Department, an institution that later provided good jobs for Beaumonters Joe Griffin, Thomas Parker, and Johnnie Ware.[4]

If the New Deal represented a dawning for African Americans, then World War II and the associated economic boom amounted to a rising sun. Between 1940 and 1955, the American economy and society were transformed, providing new opportunities for all citizens, including African Americans. Waging war required large numbers of new workers and soldiers. Aided by President Roosevelt's Executive Order 8802 establishing the Fair Employment Practices Committee, which outlawed racial discrimination in hiring by defense contractors receiving federal funds, more than two million black Americans found new employment in war industries. For example, African Americans won new jobs in Texas shipyards in Orange, Beaumont, Houston, and Galveston. But in these venues many of the black workers faced indifference from white managers and stiff resistance from white union members who sometimes threatened them with violence. Booker Fayson, for one, worked for a time at Beaumont's Pennsylvania Ship Yard, a major defense facility.[5]

More African Americans went to work in federal civil service, more joined labor unions, and more moved to the cities, where they found regular employment. Thousands of black Americans served in the various branches of the military service. In the army, for example, the number of African Americans increased significantly, rising from 100,000 in 1941 to 700,000 in 1944. Even though black service members suffered traditional racial discrimination and were often relegated to support roles and segregated units, military service was an eye-opening experience, providing education, travel, and a look at the outside world. Many black soldiers—among them Booker Fayson, Joe Griffin, William Narcisse, and Johnnie Ware—returned to their homes after the war with aspirations for a better life. Some, perhaps Fayson, who served in Germany and witnessed the horrors of Nazi racism, came home with new courage to fight racism in America.[6]

The economic expansion associated with World War II was tremendous, with the gross national product jumping from $206 billion in 1940, to $285 billion in 1950 and $400 billion in 1955. The economic growth produced rapid industrialization that created more jobs and educational opportunities for all Americans, including black citizens. President Harry Truman, who succeeded Roosevelt in 1945, carried forward and multiplied his predecessor's anti-discrimination programs. Recommending increased authority for FDR's Fair Employment Practices Committee, Truman reached even further, urging the elimination of the poll tax and suggesting the termination of segregation on interstate transportation. He established the President's Commission on Civil Rights and gave support to the NAACP litigation campaign. In 1948 Truman ordered the end of all racial discrimination in the armed forces, an action that eventually led to the complete integration of the U.S. Army, Navy, and Air Force. During the Korean War, many African Americans served as combat soldiers, with some suffering injuries and death. Earl White, one of the Beaumont Joe Doakes, saw action in Korea and was severely wounded by an enemy land mine.[7]

In the Tyrrell Park desegregation campaign, the six Joe Doakes plaintiffs fell into two groups: the original four—Fayson, Griffin, Parker, and Ware—who had initiated the action in 1954, and two—Narcisse and White—who joined the team in 1955. As noted in the following biographical sketches, each man had lived a different kind of life and each brought something special to the desegregation effort.

Booker T. Fayson

Probably Booker T. Fayson was named for Booker T. Washington, the famous African American educator. Borrowing the name would have been a natural thing to do because the leader of Tuskegee Institute was a hero to millions of black Americans during the early twentieth century. Booker Fayson was born November 15, 1916, in Alexandria, Louisiana, but at an early age he was sent to Beaumont to live with an older sister, Laura Anthony. Anthony and her husband resided in small frame house on West Crockett Street, in a segregated neighborhood not far from the central business district. Just two blocks south of Anthony's house was Central Park, where the city operated a nine-hole public golf course. Young Fayson often walked from his sister's house to the nearby municipal golf course. Managed by white golf professional Henry Homberg, the course was reserved for white golfers, but white and black youths were welcomed as caddies. Fayson worked there with Johnnie Barlow, a white youth who later became a golf professional. They and others carried bags and shagged practice balls for white golfers. They picked up discarded golf clubs, found lost golf balls, and learned the fundamentals of the game. On some occasions Fayson and other boys returned to the golf course under the cover of night, wading into the lake to retrieve errant golf balls.[8]

Laura Anthony must have done a good job rearing young Fayson, preparing him for life and encouraging him to use his energy and ambition. He attended school regularly and graduated as an honor student from Hebert High School in 1935. In graduation ceremonies on the night of May 22, the Reverend U. S. Patterson delivered the invocation and school principal U. S. Blanks introduced the guest speaker: George W. Reeves, professor of education from Prairie View Normal and Industrial College. In an otherwise exclusively African American program, C. W. Bingman, the white superintendent of the school district, spoke briefly. Two students, one girl and one boy, probably class valedictorians, were honored with speaking parts, reading papers they had written for the occasion. Mildred Riggs delivered her composition, "Citizenship as Promoted in Our School," and then Booker Fayson presented his essay, "What I, As an Ideal Citizen, Owe My Community."[9]

Young Fayson may have espoused ideals of good citizenship, but leaders in the white establishment offered nothing in return except indifference. On the same day as the Hebert High School graduation, the prestigious Rotary Club of Beaumont held its regular weekly meeting and conducted annual ceremonies recognizing honor students from city high schools. Dr. Samuel Rossinger, rabbi of Temple Emanuel, made the introductory remarks. Often a speaker on moral and ethical issues at the businessmen's club, Rossinger praised the cerebral achievements of local high-school scholars, saying it will take brains "to rescue the country" from problems created by "the brainless trust," apparently referring with disdain to FDR and his New Deal advisors. Rossinger passed out engraved certificates to boys and girls from four white high schools: French, South Park, Beaumont High, and Saint Anthony's, the local Catholic institution. But Rossinger offered no certificates for Mildred Riggs and Booker Fayson, nor did he mention Hebert High or Charlton-Pollard, the other local black high school.[10]

After graduating from high school, Fayson worked as a laborer, probably for Texas & New Orleans Railroad or its successor, the Southern Pacific Railroad. In 1939 he married Audrey Mae Patterson, but that relationship soon ended. On November 29, 1941, Fayson married again, this time to Johnnie Mae Phillips. In ceremonies conducted by the Reverend J. S. Bagneris at Saint James AME church, Booker and Johnnie Fayson commenced a relationship that proved beneficial and productive for both parties. Johnnie was energetic and hardworking; under her influence Booker thrived. After the outbreak of World War II and with FDR's directives about nondiscrimination in defense industries, Fayson got a good job at Pennsylvania Ship Yard (PSY), a huge facility that employed ten thousand men and women in round-the-clock shipbuilding operations. During 1942–43 he worked about eighteen months in the PSY warehouse, sorting nuts and bolts, storing oil drums in racks, and unloading trucks and freight cars with handcarts. The heavy work must have suited Fayson just fine; he was a short and powerful man and the hard labor only made him stronger. Apparently he was working at PSY at the time of the 1943 race riot, when on the night of June 15 several thousand white workers stormed out of the shipyard and rampaged through nearby black neighborhoods.[11]

Just two weeks later, on July 2, 1943, Fayson was drafted into the U.S. Army. After basic training, he was sent to Fort Francis Warren at Cheyenne, Wyoming, a center for quartermaster services. His wife Johnnie accompanied him to Wyoming, a long journey that testified to their close relationship and that afforded them the adventure of traveling together in the American West. How Johnnie supported herself in Cheyenne or when she returned to Beaumont is not known. At Fort Warren, Fayson was assigned to a quartermaster company, a unit probably composed entirely of black troops and commanded by white officers. This situation was typical for the times when most African Americans belonged to segregated service units attached to white outfits. During December, 1944, when approximately 691,000 blacks were serving in the armed forces, about 69 percent were overseas and 31 percent in the United States. Among the 477,000 black troops overseas, more than 345,000, or 73 percent, were assigned to support and service units such as transportation, engineers, and quartermaster.[12]

In the summer of 1944, Fayson shipped out for the European theater of operations. Here race relations had already received attention from Gen. Dwight D. Eisenhower, Supreme Allied

Commander. In England, during the build-up for the Normandy invasion, Eisenhower had issued orders governing the behavior of American troops in the British Isles and subsequently in France, Belgium, and Germany. While he made no efforts to desegregate American forces, he did direct all officers to refrain from racist actions and to minimize "causes of friction between White and Colored Troops." Further, he ordered that "Negro troops . . . be accorded the same leaves and furlough privileges as other troops." Noting that interracial relationships in England were "much different from that in the United States," Eisenhower warned white American troops that there would be "a considerable association of colored troops with British white population, both men and women . . . on a basis mutually acceptable to the individuals concerned," and that "any attempt to curtail such associations . . . must not be attempted." He also ordered that all American officers and troops refrain from making "statements of a derogatory nature concerning racial groups in the United States." There were occasional racial incidents, fights, and other confrontations between black and white troops, but generally Eisenhower's race management policies were effective; according to one historian, "relations between white and Negro troops . . . were more often good than poor."[13]

Fayson landed in Europe at Cherbourg on August 6, 1944. This was sixty days after the Normandy invasion but at the same time as the "Saint Lo Breakout," when American and British forces finally overwhelmed German troops in Normandy and commenced a rapid advance across France. Fayson was a member of the 867th Quartermaster Fumigation and Bath Company, a mobile unit that followed combat outfits across the French countryside, providing bathing and delousing services to fighting troops as they took breaks from front-line action. Some might have looked with disdain on such menial tasks, but military historian Erna Risch reported that "the shower facilities . . . were tremendously effective morale builders [and] . . . were extremely popular." Fayson had charge of one of the fumigation units, a portable chamber in which he used methyl bromide to delouse and otherwise sanitize uniforms, bedrolls, and blankets. Actual use of the fumigation units was limited in the early stages of the campaign, when American soldiers suffered little from the torments of lice. But later, when American and British forces began to liberate Allied prisoner of war camps in Germany, where the prisoners suffered greatly from malnutrition, assorted illnesses, and infestations of lice, the work of the fumigation and bath outfits was much appreciated.[14]

Fayson spent ten months in Europe, seeing service in four army campaigns: northern France, Ardennes, Rhineland, and central Europe. His unit was attached to Courtney Hodges's First Army or George Patton's Third Army, forces that spearheaded the fighting in those campaigns. Exactly where Fayson and his unit traveled is not known, but it is certain they provided services to thousands of grateful American soldiers; later his contributions were recognized with a European service medal with four bronze service stars. In France, Belgium, and Germany, Fayson and his comrades must have visited many villages and towns, seen beautiful churches and cathedrals, and witnessed in various places the death and destruction of war. Maybe they met French, Belgian, or German civilians who treated them decently and fairly, without regard for the color of their skin. Truly, for Fayson and thousands of other black troops, serving in the European theater must have been an eye-opening experience.[15]

The war in Europe ended in the spring of 1945, after German armies surrendered on May 7. Six weeks later Fayson and others boarded a troopship and headed home on a two-week voyage, arriving in the United States on July 2. He remained in the army five months more, spending at least the final weeks at the quartermaster base at Fort Warren in Wyoming. As with all enlisted personnel, Fayson served at the "convenience of the government," meaning the army could hold or release him as needed. On December 3, 1945, the army discharged him at Fort Warren, giving him $61.95 travel pay and $100 cash for mustering out. With money in his pockets, Booker traveled back to Texas, going home to Beaumont and resuming his life with Johnnie.[16]

In the immediate postwar years, Booker and Johnnie worked hard and saved money. She worked as a fountain clerk at Bill Thames Pharmacy on Calder Avenue, a store popular with members of the Beaumont establishment. Racial practices at the pharmacy luncheon counter presented the maddening complications of the southern caste system: Johnnie and other African Americans were welcome to work behind the narrow counter, serving food and drink, collecting money, and visiting casually with white customers, but their fellow African Americans could not take a seat at the front of the counter. Because of their race, they would not be served. Later Johnnie worked as a cook at the Shamrock Shanty, a popular drive-in restaurant on Eleventh Street.[17]

Fayson worked several years for Southern Pacific Railroad as a laborer, but during this time he and Johnnie started their climb to the middle class. In 1947 they bought a lot for five hundred dollars on Harriot Street in the Pear Orchard and soon built themselves an attractive and comfortable dwelling. In 1950 Fayson was employed as a salesman, but the next year he attended Texas Southern University in nearby Houston. In all likelihood he studied at TSU under the "GI Bill of Rights," a government program that provided college tuition and other financial benefits for World War II veterans, benefits that were available to whites and blacks without racial discrimination. Probably Fayson took classes in business and insurance, because he soon obtained a local recording agent's license, a Texas permit that authorized him to sell fire and casualty insurance. He contracted with one or more insurance companies that authorized him to sell their policies covering automobiles, houses, and businesses.[18]

Fayson Insurance Agency was a joint operation for Booker and Johnnie. At first they operated the business out of their home on Harriot Street, and she worked there as secretary. Later, in 1952, they bought land for a thousand dollars on nearby Washington Boulevard and constructed a small commercial building; there they rented out office spaces and operated the insurance agency. Theirs was a bona fide business office, complete with glass-covered desk, swivel chair, telephone, dictating machine, typewriter, rate books, calendars, and business cards. "Play Safe with Insurance" was the slogan on their business card. In city directory advertisements and elsewhere, they offered real estate loans in addition to insurance and bonds. The agency business suited Fayson just fine. It produced a nice income, allowed him plenty of free time, and matched his personality. He was an energetic and sociable person. He liked to know people and to be known by them.[19]

"Booker was a flamboyant person," Cleveland Nisby recalled, adding that "he liked to smoke big cigars and hang out with Charlie Wilson, the man who operated Chaney's Auditorium night club." Mary Bell Fayson, Booker's third wife and widow, remembered him the same way. "Booker was real gutsy," she said, recalling her husband of twenty-two years. "One time we were at Travis Brothers [a hardware store owned by white people] and we couldn't get anyone to wait on us. Booker reached across the counter and hit a key on the cash register, opening the cash drawer and ringing a loud bell. The people came running and helped us fast." "He was a real people person," Mrs. Fayson remembered. "He knew everybody up and down Forsythe Street, Irving Street, everywhere, black and white, and everybody knew him." Booker was a member of several men's groups: Elks, Masons, and the Appomattox Club. He was an avid golfer and an energetic member of the NAACP, two activities that enabled him to become friends with Joe Griffin and others who participated in the campaign to desegregate the Tyrrell Park golf course.[20]

Joseph P. Griffin

Like Booker Fayson, Joe Griffin was in the U.S. Army during World War II. Drafted in June, 1942, he served more than three years, being discharged in December, 1945. Griffin was a member of the 1863rd Engineer Aviation Battalion, probably an all-black outfit, which did construction and maintenance work on airfields and related facilities. He spent much of 1942 and 1943 in the Texas Panhandle at Dalhart Army Air Base, where he performed well, earning the job of administrative specialist and rising through the ranks from private first class to staff sergeant. In February, 1943, while on a three-day pass, he drove to Bastrop, Texas, and married Elizabeth Hunter, a young Catholic woman he had met and courted while working in Galveston. It was a classic spur-of-the-moment wartime wedding, with Joe and Elizabeth and their families rushing in from all directions and converging on Bastrop, where the eager young couple were married by 1st Lt. John A. McGonegle, a chaplain from the army base at nearby Camp Swift.[21]

At Dalhart the army selected Griffin for special assignments, on one occasion sending him for chemical warfare training at Tucson,

Arizona; there he studied the nature of and defenses for poison gases and also learned to teach the chemical warfare program to fellow squad members. Later he traveled on another educational assignment, this time to Tuskegee, Alabama, where the army operated a program for control of venereal diseases. In July, 1944, Griffin participated in the program, studying the identification, prevention, and control of venereal diseases; later he taught the program and distributed prophylactics to fellow soldiers.[22]

In May, 1945, at the time the war ended in Europe, Griffin and his engineering aviation battalion were sent to the Pacific theater, where U.S. forces were still battling the Japanese. His outfit served on Guam, an American island that had been captured by the Japanese in December, 1941, and retaken by American forces in August, 1944. Griffin and his outfit arrived on Guam in June, 1945; this was six months after a race riot occurred in December, 1944, when friction between black sailors and white marines on the island erupted into violence, leaving two men dead. Guam, located relatively close to the Japanese home islands, was a center of aircraft operations, with American B-29 bombers taking off from there to strike Tokyo and other Japanese cities. In August, 1945, Joe Griffin and everyone on the island heard the news: American aircraft had dropped atomic bombs on Hiroshima and Nagasaki, the Japanese had surrendered, and the war was over.[23]

Griffin arrived back in the United States on December 6, 1945, and just a week later was discharged from the army at Fort Bliss, El Paso, Texas. He received various medals and ribbons for service in the American and Asiatic Pacific theaters, as well as more than five hundred dollars in travel and mustering-out payments. Returning to Beaumont, he resumed his married life with Elizabeth and soon found employment with Southern Pacific Railroad. Working in the warehouse, he handled locomotive and freight car parts and earned sixty-nine and a half cents per hour. This job was better than any he had found before the war. Beginning in 1937, after graduating from high school, and until the war, Griffin had held a series of low-paying service jobs in Beaumont that were common for young black men. He worked for Appling's Drug Store, making deliveries, carrying packages, cleaning the floors, and serving behind the luncheon counter, making sandwiches and pouring drinks. At Kirkwood's Café, Griffin worked as a bartender, selling beer, cigars, and candy and sweeping the floor. He was employed as a porter at the Heisig Hotel, making beds and cleaning rooms and hallways. For a while he lived in nearby Galveston, where he was employed at Saint Mary's Infirmary; working under the supervision of Sister Adrienne, Griffin swept and waxed the hospital floors. It was at Saint Mary's that he had met and fallen in love with Elizabeth, who worked there as an elevator operator.[24]

Delivery boy, bartender, porter, and hall boy—these were Griffin's job titles before the war. But after the war and during the postwar economic boom, Griffin found better employment: first with the railroad, later, and more importantly, with the federal government. In June, 1948, Griffin applied for a job as letter carrier with the United States Postal Department. He filled out the Application for Federal Employment, listing personal information and outlining his education and work experience. He reported his formal education: eleven years in public schools with graduation from Charlton-Pollard High School in Beaumont and six months at Prairie View Normal and Industrial College near Hempstead, Texas. At Prairie View he had followed a machinist vocational program as a Defense Student under the National Youth Administration, one of the New Deal programs orchestrated by FDR and his administration. On one occasion, Griffin had extended his education further, taking a six-month correspondence course in photography from the University of Nebraska. He liked photography and for a while practiced the art part-time.[25]

Griffin's postal department employment application was the Standard Form 57 issued by the U.S. Civil Service. The standardization of the form was important; it symbolized the ideals of equal opportunity in the civil service, ideals critical to African Americans for a long time in all parts of the nation. As early as 1883 significant numbers of black Americans began finding decent employment with the federal government, especially in Washington, D.C. By 1938 almost 10 percent of all federal employees were African Americans, and six years later their proportion amounted to nearly 12 percent. These and subsequent increases resulted in part from legislative, bureaucratic, and executive actions. In 1940 Congress passed the Ramspect Act that outlawed racial discrimination in federal hiring, and the same year the civil service commission issued new regulations forbidding discrimination because of political affiliation or religious preference. Presidents Roosevelt, Truman, and Eisenhower all took steps to increase federal employment of black Americans, with significant numbers being hired and promoted during the administrations of Truman and Eisenhower.[26]

Generally black Americans had good success with the postal department, especially in major cities around the nation where many found employment and some rose to supervisory and management positions. Even lower-level jobs, such as postal clerk and letter carrier, were desirable positions with steady employment and salaries sufficient to begin a middle-class life. Working in the postal department, as well as other federal agencies, offered another benefit: Civil service status protected the religious and political freedom of all employees, including African Americans. This protection was important during the 1950s and 1960s, when many black postal employees became leaders in civil rights campaigns in the South. With this security Joe Griffin, as well as fellow postal workers Thomas Parker and Johnnie Ware, were able to join the NAACP, attend their meetings, and participate openly in the Tyrrell Park desegregation campaign.[27]

Griffin started as a letter carrier in 1949 and in subsequent years thrived with the postal department. In 1954 he and his wife Elizabeth were living in a comfortable house on East Plum Street and rearing three sons: Vernon, age eleven; Tony, age nine; and Joseph Jr., age seven. Vernon presented a profound challenge to his parents; born November 10, 1943, he was afflicted with Down syndrome, a genetic condition that produced mental retardation and other problems. Dr. Joseph R. Fama, the white physician who delivered Elizabeth's sons, and other medical professionals urged the Griffins to place Vernon in a mental institution because of the many difficulties associated with rearing Down syndrome victims and the likelihood he would die before reaching age twenty. But Joe and Elizabeth rejected the advice—they kept Vernon and made a decent life for him.[28]

Joe and Elizabeth Griffin were devout Catholics, and they reared their sons in that religion. They lived in the North End but attended mass at Blessed Sacrament Church in the South End. Every Sunday morning, they got up early, dressed, piled into their 1950 Plymouth automobile, and drove across town, arriving in time for mass at 5:30 A.M. and beginning a day of worship, fellowship, and education. The family believed in parochial education, as both Tony and Joe Jr., completed at least eight years of formal schooling at Blessed Sacrament school. Directed by Rev. Joseph M. Schmirtz and staffed by Sister Maureen Patricia and other white members of the Order of the Blessed Sacrament, Blessed Sacrament school's mostly white leaders demonstrated a strong commitment to serve their black parishioners. Tony and Joe Jr., later transferred to Charlton-Pollard High School, from which they graduated. At Blessed Sacrament, Joe and Elizabeth were active in various groups: the Knights of Peter Claver, Ladies Auxiliary of the Knights of Peter Claver, Holy Name Society, and the Saint Joseph Society. Joe had a booming melodious voice and loved singing in the choir and elsewhere; during the war, he had sung to entertain the troops in the Pacific. Well liked at Blessed Sacrament and around town, he was known affectionately as "Sonny" or "Posey," the latter being his middle name. As already noted, he believed in the NAACP and was a leader in the local chapter. He liked to play golf, having learned the game as a youth while working as a caddy at the Beaumont Country Club. Husband, father, golfer, Catholic layman, NAACP activist, postal worker, World War II veteran—all these accomplishments and more led Joe Griffin into his role as a plaintiff in the Tyrrell Park desegregation campaign.[29]

Johnnie R. Ware

Like Joe Griffin, Johnnie Ware was a postal worker and a World War II veteran. Ware served in the army quartermaster corps between 1942 and 1945, most of that time in the Pacific theater, with two years in Hawaii and three months in Korea. Little is known about his military career, but clearly it provided him the benefits of travel. He traveled through the western United States, spent time in California, and sailed across the vast Pacific Ocean, seeing places and cultures greatly different from those of southeast Texas.

Born in Beaumont in 1919, Ware completed eleven years of formal schooling and graduated from Hebert High School. At Hebert he played football and followed an academic course, studying English and math. After high school, he attended Tillotson College in Austin, then an all-black institution affiliated with the United Methodist Church and other religious groups.[30]

At Tillotson between 1938 and 1941, Ware pursued a general education program, studying English, math, philosophy, the Bible, and Spanish, a language in which he later claimed a "fair" ability in reading and speaking. He excelled in physical education classes, earning a letter as a tennis player and probably developing his golf game. A small wiry man, Ware was a gifted athlete; he was truly ambidextrous and could play golf from either side. During 1943, when home on leave from the army, he married Ruth Banks, a graduate of Martin High, a North End school later merged with Charlton-Pollard High. After the war they lived in the North End, first on Simmons Street, where they had two children, Linda, born in 1946, and Michael, in 1948; they later lived on Pine Street, where another daughter, Toni, was born in 1954. The new Pine Street residence was convenient for Ware and his family. Nearby were Martin Elementary School, where Linda and Michael attended classes, and Pioneer Presbyterian Church, where Ware served as an elder and the family worshiped on Sundays. Organized in 1950, Pioneer was Beaumont's first black Presbyterian congregation, sponsored and partially funded in the early years by Westminster, the town's oldest white Presbyterian congregation.[31]

At the far north end of Pine Street was the Beaumont Country Club, where Ware was employed before getting a job with the postal department. He worked at the club between 1946 and 1949, serving as a waiter in the men's locker room. Earning about twenty-seven dollars a week, he provided various services to the golfers, greeting them, delivering them food and drinks, and taking care of the lockers, showers, and card rooms. Seeing many of the members regularly, often once or twice weekly, Ware became friends with a number of them: I. D. Polk, an auto dealer; Brian Sumrall, a banker; and C. F. Graham, a department store owner; others included Lamar Cecil, the lawyer who would become a federal judge, and his golfing comrades, Mose Sampson, L. W. Pitts, Gene Davis, Dave Marcus, and Dr. Julian Fertitta. Ware enjoyed knowing these men and hearing their conversations over drinks and cards. He liked golfing tales and loved the game himself; on

Mondays, when the club was closed, he joined other waiters and caddies and played the country club course.[32]

In 1950 Ware left the country club and went to work for the U.S. Postal Department. Beginning as a substitute clerk and carrier, he commenced a long postal career. During those years he came to know many people throughout the city, and he became a leader in the civil rights campaigns of the 1950s and 1960s, beginning with the 1954 effort to desegregate the Tyrrell Park golf course. Ed Moore, an African American leader, remembered Ware as "stubborn," "aggressive," and "intelligent." Hubert McCray, a white business leader, recalled Ware as "a strong advocate for black rights" but also a "friendly, patient, humorous man." "Johnnie knew everybody in town," McCray recalled, "and [he] had many funny stories about the town leaders."[33]

Thomas A. Parker, Jr.

Like Joe Griffin and Johnnie Ware, Tom Parker was a postal worker, but he was not a World War II veteran. Born in September, 1913, Parker was twenty-eight years old in 1941. He was too old to be drafted that year; men could also be exempted from service for health reasons. And Parker was different from Griffin and Ware in another way: He grew up in a *Gone with the Wind* setting. His parents, Thomas and Albertine Parker, worked as domestic servants for W. P. H. and Ida Caldwell McFaddin in their mansion at 1906 McFaddin Street. The McFaddins were among Beaumont's most elite families; they were ranchers, rice farmers, owners of more than sixty thousand acres of land, and direct beneficiaries of two oil discoveries: the "first Spindletop," in 1901, and the "second Spindletop," in 1925. Their Beaux-Arts mansion was grand—three stories high and fronted by tall columns, a living area of more than twelve thousand square feet, and grounds and gardens taking up an entire city block. The place was richly decorated in the Victorian style and filled with antiques, fine art, and decorative arts. On adjoining property was a handsome carriage house that included stables for horses, garages for automobiles, and rooms for servants. The McFaddins usually employed at least a half dozen domestic workers: butler, maids, cooks, gardener, laundry worker, and two chauffeurs, generally all African American.[34]

During the 1920s and 1930s, Tom Parker, Sr., worked steadily as Mr. McFaddin's chauffeur, while his wife Albertine was employed from time to time as a cook in the main house. Sometimes the couple and their young son, Tom Jr., lived in the carriage house, the three of them occupying one of the servants' rooms. Young Tom had the freedom of the carriage house and grounds and sometimes entered the big house, going in the back door to have meals with his parents and other servants in the main kitchen, after the McFaddins had finished dining. On one occasion, Tom Jr. served as a babysitter, looking after Mrs. McFaddin's young nephews, Dabney and Teddy Caldwell, who were visiting from Huntington, West Virginia; a photograph shows young Parker wearing a shirt and tie, posing with the little white boys on the front balcony of the big house. Later Tom Jr. did some chauffeuring for the McFaddins, driving family members around town and on one occasion taking them all the way to West Virginia. Living on the McFaddin property, watching his parents carry out their duties, and doing his own chores, young Tom Parker saw firsthand the world of white elites and their black servants, a complex world ruled by the traditions of the southern caste system, where racism and segregation were softened by paternalism and normal human relations. White families worked their black employees long hours at low wages, but at the same time often provided room and board along with medical, dental, and legal help. Although white employers generally looked with disdain upon African Americans, believing them an inferior race, some white families developed warm and lasting relationships with their black employees.[35]

Tom's mother, Albertine, believed in the benefits of religion and education. Under her influence, he attended services at Blessed Sacrament Catholic Church and went to school regularly, graduating from Charlton-Pollard High School about 1932. Tom's education was furthered by inheritance, when an uncle in San Antonio died and left him five hundred dollars; he used the funds to attend Tuskegee Institute for a while. In 1944 he started with the postal department in nearby Orange, Texas, but later obtained a transfer to the Beaumont office, where he worked on and off for more than fifteen years. He married Gladys Mouton in 1947 and fathered a daughter, Albertine or "Tina," who was born in 1951. The marriage ended in divorce in 1954, the year that Tom teamed with Fayson, Griffin, and Ware to begin their desegregation campaign in Beaumont. That year, or early in 1955, Parker and the others recruited two more Joe Doakes plaintiffs: William Narcisse and Earl White. Narcisse and White were newcomers to the project and they were different in another way: They were working-class people as compared to the others who had made it to the middle class.[36]

William Narcisse

Laura Narcisse, the former wife of William's nephew Dwight Narcisse, recalled the fifth plaintiff as "a very kind, humble man." Narcisse never married and had no children, but he cared deeply about family and friends. He "would sacrifice himself" to help others, Laura remembered; in one instance, he took on the responsibility of rearing and paying expenses for his nephew, Dwight, then a young boy. Maybe it was this sense of sacrifice that led Narcisse into the Tyrrell Park desegregation campaign. Or maybe it was his experiences in the army or lessons learned during his long career with Southern Pacific Railroad. William Narcisse, known to his family as "Bill," was born in Lake Charles, Louisiana, in 1921 but moved to Beaumont in time to graduate from Charlton-Pollard High School about 1937. During World War II he served almost three years in the army, attaining the rank of private first class in a quartermaster service company and seeing duty at Camp Claiborne in Louisiana and Camp Wolters in Texas. Discharged in 1946 from Camp Fannin at Tyler, Texas, Narcisse received money for travel and three medals: American Theater Campaign, World War II Victory, and Good Conduct.[37]

Narcisse returned to Beaumont and took up residence with his parents on Brooklyn Street in the South End. His father, Eddie Narcisse, was employed as a laborer at the nearby Magnolia Petroleum Company refinery. William got a job as a laborer, too, but with Southern Pacific Railroad, a company for which he worked during the time of the Tyrrell Park desegregation litigation. He lived quietly and modestly, on weekdays going to his railroad job and on Sundays attending services at Starlight Baptist Church. At Starlight Baptist, William Narcisse heard the preaching of Rev. W. N. McCarty, a fervent believer in the Christian faith and an ardent spokesman for the rights of African Americans. Perhaps he heard from Reverend McCarty about the Tyrrell Park campaign.[38]

Earl White

Among the six Joe Doakes plaintiffs, only Earl White was alive at the time the author began writing this history. However, because of old age and profound memory loss, he was unable to contribute any first-hand memories of the Tyrrell campaign. He passed away September 18, 2003, after spending his final years in a California veterans' hospital, where he received daily visits from his wife, Geraldine White. Earl White may have lost his memory, but some in Beaumont remembered him, remarking about the black man with the crippled left arm who learned to play golf one-handed. "I never met him," said Beaumont golfer Henry Durham, "but I used to see him on the practice range hitting the golf ball with one arm. It was something." Some might also mention the resilience of his spirit, how White remained determined and optimistic despite all the hard knocks he suffered throughout his life. Ruby White Harris, a sister, remembered him as "strong willed," while Louis White, a brother, recalled him as "very stubborn and opinionated." "He thought he was just as good as anybody," Ruby Harris said, "and especially after he came back from the Korean War and got out of the hospital. He wasn't afraid of anything."[39]

Born in 1927 into a working-class Beaumont family, Earl White was one of thirteen children. He earned a measure of education in public schools, completing elementary grades and attending Martin High School but dropping out after one year. Too young for military service during World War II, he spent his early adult years in a variety of short-term, low-paying jobs, working at a mattress company, a slaughterhouse, and one of the railroad companies. He waited tables at hotels and cafes, labored for a carpentry contractor, and caddied at the Beaumont Country Club, where he picked up used golf clubs and learned the rudiments of the game. He suffered hard times, on some occasions sleeping in boxcars or on rooftops.[40]

During June, 1950, world events intervened in Earl White's life; North Korea invaded South Korea, thus provoking the three-year Korean War in which thousands of American troops fought to defend South Korea. In September, 1950, White was drafted into the army, and after basic training he was assigned to Artillery Battery A in the 58th Armored Division. Sent to Korea, his outfit saw some of the action, with White winning a Bronze Star in one of the battles. In August, 1951, he and other troops were riding in the back of a transport truck when it hit a land mine. The blast demolished the big truck and sent it rolling over a hillside. Among the two dozen men on the truck, only White and two others survived. Knocked unconscious and badly wounded, White woke up two weeks later in a hospital in Tokyo. His injuries included a severe concussion, broken leg, compound fracture of his left shoulder, and paralysis of his left arm. The arm, disfigured and having no feeling in it, was almost useless. Returning to the United States, he was separated from the army at Fort Bliss, El Paso, Texas, on October 31, 1952, when he received a Permanent Disability Retirement.[41]

From that day forward, Earl lived on his military disability payments and what little he could earn in service jobs. In Beaumont he worked as a waiter at Hotel Beaumont and bused tables at Fuller's Café, a famous all-night eatery situated near the center of the Crockett Street brothel district. He returned from time to time to the Beaumont Country Club, picking up caddying jobs, reviving his interest in the game, and learning to hit the ball one-handed. At the country club, he came to know some of the members, probably Lamar Cecil and his comrades. They knew him as Earl, the tall, thin black caddy who worked with one arm, shouldering, carrying, and grounding the bag, pulling and replacing the clubs, all with his strong right arm. They heard no doubt the remarkable story that White had learned to play the game one-handed.[42]

Maybe it was White's phenomenal one-handed golf game that caused Fayson and the others to recruit him as one of the "Joe Doakes" plaintiffs in the golf course desegregation campaign. Like Booker Fayson, Joe Griffin, and the others, White was a bona fide golfer. He and the others loved golf. They wanted to play the municipal course at Tyrrell Park.

• •

White Golf, Black Golf

When Fayson, Griffin, and the others filed suit against the city of Beaumont, they had a two-fold purpose: They wanted to play golf at the municipal course, and they wanted to start dismantling the southern caste system in their hometown. In a strategic sense then, the golf course case was a means to an end, an opening salvo in a battle just beginning. But the golf itself was important. Golf was a part of American culture. Men and women of the upper classes, white and black, played the game at private country clubs, while middle-class citizens did the same at private, municipal, and daily-fee courses. Working-class Americans, white, black, and brown, enjoyed the game too, sometimes paying admission at public facilities, other times playing courses during off hours when they were closed to regular patrons.

Initially golf in America was a game exclusively of the white upper classes. Imported from England and Scotland, the game was permanently established in the United States during the 1880s when golf courses were developed at private clubs in Oakhurst, West Virginia; Foxburg, Pennsylvania; and Yonkers, New York. Other courses were constructed during the early 1890s at clubs in Newport, Rhode Island; Long Island, New York; and Chicago, Illinois. Golfers organized the game formally in 1894, establishing the United States Golf Association (USGA) and giving it the authority to promulgate rules for the game and to stage national championship tournaments: the Amateur, the Women's Amateur, and the Open, all of which they inaugurated in 1895.[1]

During the first half of the twentieth century, golf became increasingly popular, developing simultaneously with a rapid growth of private country clubs that began in the 1920s. Organized by white upper-class citizens in towns across America, the clubs served as venues for recreation and socialization as well as agencies of status and social exclusion. The clubs, often palatial houses on pastoral grounds, provided prestigious settings for social events and first-class facilities for tennis, swimming, and golf. Men and women members played golf avidly, the men often combining business with pleasure and entertaining customers on the course and in the clubhouse bar. Golf champions and their tournament victories generated publicity for the game and broadened its appeal to Americans of all classes and both genders. Francis Ouimet, the youthful caddy, won the U.S. Open in 1913; Walter Hagen, the dashing middle-class American, captured various titles, including the British Open, in 1920; and Bobby Jones, the stylish gentleman golfer, reigned supreme among professional and amateur players from 1923 to 1930, collecting thirteen national titles, including four U.S. Opens and three British Opens. Joyce Wethered of Great Britain, winner of numerous tournaments on both sides of the Atlantic during the 1920s, stimulated interest in the game among American women.[2]

During the early 1950s, when Booker Fayson and his friends campaigned for desegregation of the Beaumont municipal course, the game of golf in America was changing and expanding. Herbert Warren Wind, noted golf historian, called this period (1946–55) the "Age of Hogan," when Ben Hogan, Byron Nelson, Sam Snead, and other members of the Professional Golfers Association (PGA) traveled the nation, playing tournaments, winning prize money, and capturing headlines. President Dwight Eisenhower, an ardent golfer, further popularized the game, as did Bing Crosby, Bob Hope, and other Hollywood celebrities who staged charity and promotional tournaments. At the same time, the game attracted more women as they followed the accomplishments of Babe Didrikson Zaharias, Patty Berg, Louise Suggs, Betty Jameson, and other members of the Ladies Professional Golf Association (LPGA).[3]

The historian Wind described a great golf boom in the 1950s, when millions of Americans made the game an intrinsic part of their lives. Corporations built courses for their employees while cities and states developed more public links to promote recreation and attract new business and industry. Between 1946 and 1955, the estimated number of golfers rose from 2.5 million to 4 million, while the number of courses increased from 4,817 to 5,218, the latter figure including 2,807 private, 1,534 daily-fee, and 877 municipal courses. These numbers, compiled by the National Golf Foundation, show that 46 percent of the facilities (daily-fee and municipal) were open to the public and indicate a significant participation by middle- and working-class Americans. Historian Wind does not mention that African American golfers were barred as regular players from most golf facilities, nor did the National Golf Foundation compile statistics about black players.[4]

Also missing in reports of the National Golf Foundation is information about service workers—caddies, caddy masters, waiters, bartenders, cooks, greens keepers, mowers, sweepers, locker room attendants, shoe shiners, and others who labored at country clubs and other golfing facilities. If there were 4 million players in 1955, there might have been 200,000 service workers, men and women, most black but some white and brown, who supported the game of golf. They were on the course with Hogan, Snead, and Zaharias, in the clubhouse with Eisenhower, Crosby, and Hope, and on the scene with countless other Americans, carrying clubs, making drinks, and taking care of facilities. These were the "shadow people" described by Pete McDaniel in *Uneven Lies* (2000), his book about African Americans in golf. Many of the shadow people, particularly caddies, became "shadow players," learning the game while working at the courses and going round the links during off hours. Some became proficient golfers, performing long-drive feats, recording low scores, and winning bets and honors in caddy tournaments. Probably the number of these unofficial or "shadow players" amounted to at least ten thousand and could rightly be added to the 4 million estimated players.[5]

Caddies carried golf bags, marked flights of the ball, held flags, consulted about shots, and cleaned clubs. Laboring long hours at low wages, they worked in large numbers at private and public courses until the early 1960s, when they were replaced by the widespread use of pull carts and motorized golf carts. Stories of caddies who became winning golfers are legend. Ben Hogan, Byron Nelson, and Sam Snead all started as caddies and rose to the pinnacle of the professional game. Equally famous but of a later generation was Lee Trevino, the Mexican American from Dallas who learned the game as a caddy and went on to win the 1968 U.S. Open and four other major titles. *Uneven Lies* author Pete McDaniel, himself an African American, worked as a caddy at the swank, whites-only Biltmore Forest Country Club in North Carolina. At age eleven he began earning "sweat money," first as a "shag boy" picking up golf balls on the practice range and then, as he grew older and stronger, as a class-A caddy. While waiting in the caddy lot and while "looping," that is, carrying a bag around the links, he learned all about the game, the strokes, rules, and etiquette. After a member gave him some second-hand clubs, McDaniel learned to hit a golf ball and over the years became an avid and competent player.[6]

The interest of African Americans in golf extended far beyond the caddies and other people who played the "shadow game." Many black Americans, men and women of all economic classes in many regions of the nation, became golfers. They loved and wanted to play the game but were thwarted by racial attitudes and policies of white citizens who controlled the golfing world. During the days of Jim Crow segregation, white golfers treated black golfers as second-class citizens, excluding them from most private and public courses, barring them from membership in player associations, and refusing them entry to most professional and amateur tournaments. In some instances, when black golfers attempted to assert their rights, white citizens harassed them with verbal abuse, threats of violence, and even arrest. But African American golfers persevered. They created a golf world of their own, complete with country clubs, associations, tournaments, black celebrities who popularized the game, and black professionals who excelled on the links.[7]

Long ignored by most historians, the story of African Americans in golf is now covered in a number of books. In addition to Pete McDaniel's *Uneven Lies,* these include Marvin P. Dawkins and Graham Charles Kinloch's *African American Golfers during the Jim Crow*

Era (2000), John H. Kennedy's *A Course of Their Own: A History of African American Golfers* (2000), Ellen Susanna Nösner's *Clearview, America's Course: The Autobiography of William J. Powell* (2000), and Calvin H. Sinnette's *Forbidden Fairways: African Americans and the Game of Golf* (1998).

During three decades, from 1920 to 1950, African Americans organized almost four dozen golf clubs; some were complete country clubs with golf courses and others were associations that promoted the game at public courses. Shady Rest Golf and Country Club, for example, operated an eighteen-hole course at Westfield, New Jersey, while the Royal Golf Club and the Wake Robin Club, the latter a women's group, organized play on public courses in the Washington, D.C., area. Most of the clubs were situated in the East and Midwest, around Boston, New York, Philadelphia, Washington, D.C., Detroit, Chicago, and other cities. But two clubs were established in Los Angeles, and a few in southern cities such as Richmond, Atlanta, Jacksonville, Miami, and Houston. Formed mostly by upper- and middle-class African Americans, the clubs provided multiple benefits: social, business, and recreational. In these club venues, black Americans developed their golf game and staged tournaments for amateurs and professionals.[8]

Before 1952 all major tournaments except the Los Angeles Open, the Tam O'Shanter in Chicago, and the Canadian Open refused entry to African American golfers. The PGA barred black players from membership and excluded them from sanctioned tournaments; in 1943 the PGA had officially adopted a "Caucasian only" membership provision. This whites-only practice was reinforced by the fact that most PGA tournaments were staged at private country clubs where African Americans were excluded as members or guests; also, the tournaments were underwritten by local sponsors who often objected to black participation. Black golfers responded to this long-term, gross discrimination with the formation in 1926 of the United Golfers Association (UGA). During the 1940s and 1950s, the UGA sponsored numerous tournaments in various parts of the nation, including the annual National Open Golf Championship. In 1950, for example, the UGA orchestrated fifteen tournaments for professionals and amateurs (men and women) in cities such as Philadelphia, Cleveland, Indianapolis, Omaha, Detroit, Chicago, and Atlanta, with the National Open tournament being staged in Washington, D.C. That year top players included professionals Teddy Rhodes, Howard Wheeler, Bill Spiller, Charles Sifford, and Richard Terrell; amateur women Ann Gregory, Lorraine Sawyer, and Eoline Thornton; and amateur men Leonard Reed, Eural Clark, and Joe Louis, the former heavyweight boxing champion. Admired by Americans of all races, Louis became an avid amateur golfer and an ardent spokesman for black players, even underwriting the Joe Louis Open in Detroit in the late 1940s. Charles Sifford reigned supreme among black professionals during the mid-1950s, winning the UGA open championship five years running, 1952 through 1956.[9]

While excelling in UGA events, Joe Louis, Teddy Rhodes, Charles Sifford, Bill Spiller, and other players campaigned to end racial discrimination at PGA tournaments. During the 1940s and early 1950s, they employed tactics of confrontation, publicity, and litigation. In 1952 Louis finally broke the PGA color line, playing as an amateur in the San Diego Open and drawing national publicity to the plight of African American golfers. The same year the PGA partially amended its whites-only policy and permitted blacks to play in ten sanctioned tournaments, but none in the South. The first was the ten-thousand-dollar-purse Phoenix Open, in which Teddy Rhodes, Bill Spiller, and Eural Clark qualified to play. None of the three finished in the money, but along with Joe Louis in San Diego they enjoyed the satisfaction of having forced a partial change in the racial practices of the PGA. (The PGA dropped its "Caucasian-only" membership rule in 1961.) Black newspapers such as the *Chicago Defender, Pittsburgh Courier,* and Houston *Informer* gave generous coverage to the golfing exploits of Louis, Sifford, Spiller, and others, creating more African American golfers and increasing demand for access to courses and tournaments. Other black celebrity golfers such as Billy Eckstine, Jackie Robinson, and Sugar Ray Robinson generated more publicity for the game and additional support for the cause of African American golfers.[10]

Inspired in part by the golfing of African American professionals and celebrities, black recreational players worked for more access to public golf courses. Racial segregation on public golf courses was widespread, but its application was varied. In some cities, such as Baltimore, black players were limited to "colored" courses, "colored" days, or "colored" hours; in others, Atlanta, for example, they were barred completely from municipal courses. During the 1940s and 1950s, black golfers resorted to legal action, suing municipalities in more than two dozen instances to eliminate or reduce segregation practices. They sued various city governments, including Baltimore (1942 and 1948), Cleveland (1949), Kansas City (1949), Houston (1950), Miami (1950 and 1951), Nashville (1952), Atlanta (1954), Beaumont (1955), and Fort Worth (1955). In Cleveland the black plaintiffs won the unrestricted right to play a public course, but in most other cases their cause was frustrated, at least partially. Until the 1954 Supreme Court ruling in *Brown v. Board of Education,* federal courts generally ruled in favor of defendant cities, applying the "separate but equal" and other doctrines, and allowing the municipalities to maintain some form of segregation on golf courses.[11]

Texas Golf

Golf thrived in Texas during the "Age of Hogan" (1946–55); golf historian Herbert Warren Wind referred to the Lone Star State as "the New Scotland." Indeed, Texas was home to many outstanding golfers: Byron Nelson, Ben Hogan, Jimmy Demaret, Lloyd Mangrum, Jack Burke, Jr., and Dave Marr, Jr., as well as Babe Zaharias, Betty Jameson, Polly Riley, and Amelia Goldthwaite. But the game in Texas was much broader and deeper than this small group of famous white players. Thousands of men and women, most white but some black and brown, enjoyed the game during the 1950s at dozens of private, municipal, and daily-fee courses across the state. All major cities and many towns boasted at least one private country club, the most historic being the Dallas Country Club (1896), Galveston Country Club (1898), Austin Country Club (1898), Houston Country Club (1903), Beaumont Country Club (1906), El Paso Country Club (1906), San Antonio Country Club (1907), and Corpus Christi Country Club (1910). Perhaps the most notable was Colonial Country Club (1936), a Fort Worth club developed by retailer Marvin Leonard, designed by Texas golf course architect John Bredemus, and host to the prestigious Colonial Invitational tournament. Membership at these country clubs was limited to white persons, but the clubs were staffed mostly with black service workers. Many of the caddies, waiters, and other workers played the "shadow game," going around the country club links on Mondays when they were closed to members.[12]

Municipal and daily-fee courses were common in Texas during the 1950s. In addition, the state parks department offered golf at three state parks, in Bastrop, Lockhart, and Lubbock. Many cities and towns operated municipal courses as a regular part of their parks and recreation programs. San Antonio provided two public courses: Riverside Park and Brackenridge Park, the latter opened in 1916 and was the state's first municipal facility. Abilene, Amarillo, Austin, Beaumont, Bryan, El Paso, and Waco each operated at least one municipal course, while larger cities such as Dallas, Fort Worth, and Houston each had several public facilities, municipal combined with daily-fee courses. In Houston, for example, public golfers had a half dozen such courses from which to choose. Generally, black golfers were barred as regular players from Texas public courses, but many African Americans played these same courses, going around the links regularly as "shadow players."[13]

Golf in Texas during the 1950s was well organized, with various associations and tournaments that catered to the interests of amateur and professional players, both men and women. The Texas Golf Association (TGA), founded in 1906 and affiliated with the USGA, conducted men's amateur championships annually at various private clubs, such as the Austin Country Club, River Crest Country Club in Fort Worth, and River Oaks Country Club in Houston. The Texas Women's Golf Association (TWGA), organized in 1916 and also associated with the USGA, performed a similar function for amateur women, staging championship tournaments every year at country clubs around the state. In 1950 Babe Zaharias and other Texas women helped organize the Ladies Professional Golf Association (LPGA), a group that sponsored annual tournaments nationwide, including the Babe Zaharias Open in Beaumont. Texas men, including Byron Nelson, Ben Hogan, and Jimmy Demaret, routinely played PGA tournaments in the Lone Star State, including the Colonial Invitational in Fort Worth, the Dallas Open, the Houston Open, and the Texas Open in San Antonio. At the same time, the *San Antonio Light* newspaper sponsored the Texas Junior Championship, a competition for young men that attracted high school and collegiate players. Black golfers were excluded from these associations and tournaments, but many worked the tournaments as caddies, waiters, and other service employees. From these vantage points, they witnessed the unfolding of the competitions and learned much about tournament golf.[14]

Barred from play in the PGA, LPGA, and other "white" tournaments in Texas, black golfers organized their own associations and competitions. Records of these Texas groups and their tournaments are lacking and little has been written about them, but scattered articles in black newspapers shed some light on these activities. During the 1940s and 1950s, the Texas Negro Golf Association had chapters in a number of cities, including Abilene, Beaumont, Dallas, Fort Worth, and Houston. In 1941 Fort Worth hosted the First Annual Southwestern Golf Open (Negro), and five years later, San Antonio served as the site of the Texas Negro Golf Championship. Lee Elder, a Dallas resident, won the Dallas Golf Tournament in 1952; later Elder went on to become a full-fledged member of the PGA and the first African American to play in the Masters Golf Tournament. In 1955 Houston staged the Lone Star Tournament, a competition sanctioned by the UGA and drawing players from around the nation. In the Houston *Informer*, George Stephen, author of the sports column "Down the Fairway," welcomed players to town. After regretfully noting the absence of Joe Louis, Stephen bragged about the appearance of Charlie Sifford, "the champion of champions," and recognized other players for loyalty to the Houston event. He praised Allen Robertson of New York, who "comes down every year to make the tournament a success," and James Saxton of Los Angeles for the same reason.[15]

Fort Worth

While some black Texans worked to develop tournament golf, others campaigned to open public courses for recreational play. During the early and mid-1950s, black golfers in Fort Worth, Houston, and Beaumont pushed to end segregation on municipal courses. In the three cities they used similar tactics: first polite requests, then peaceful confrontations, and finally federal litigation.

In Fort Worth they achieved partial success by way of friendly negotiations. On June 26, 1954, members of the Fort Worth Negro Golf Association celebrated the desegregation of the nine-hole Harmon Field, even though they were still excluded from four other municipal courses. Meeting in the Harmon Field clubhouse, the group also recognized Jesse L. Mitchell for his leadership of the local black golf association and for "his years of fighting for golf facilities for Negroes." While admitting pleasure at the opening of one municipal course, Mitchell promised to continue the fight. "We have vowed that no force, no combination of forces, no trickery or deceit can stop the forward movement of the Texas Negro Golf Association," he said, "until we enjoy the abundance of pleasure derived from this fascinating game in an equitable manner on every municipal golf course in the state of Texas."[16]

Just two weeks later, African American golfers in Fort Worth renewed their attack on segregation at the other public courses. Appearing before a public hearing of the city recreation board, Dr. R. A. Ransom of the Negro Citizens Committee presented a formal request "that Negroes be given complete access to all of the municipal golf courses in our city." Dr. Ransom spoke cautiously but firmly: "We realize that such a decision is . . . a momentous one on your part, but as reputable, law-abiding, tax-paying citizens, we do not believe that this request is unreasonable." Alluding to ideals of "American Democracy and justice," he expressed confidence in the leadership of the recreation board and promised "exemplary" conduct on the part of "our men, women, and children." Also appearing before the board were several white citizens who opposed the desegregation plan. George Seaman, for example, argued that "white people will stop using the golf course[s] if they are opened to Negroes" and suggested privatizing the courses "in order that they might be retained for exclusive use by whites." After hearing a weekly report that 348 blacks had played the nine-hole Harmon course and that 4,413 whites had played the four eighteen-hole courses, the recreation board closed its meeting without taking any action on Ransom's request for further desegregation of the golfing facilities. Later black golfers in Fort Worth would file a federal lawsuit against the city in order to gain full access to all municipal courses.[17]

Developments in Fort Worth, where black golfers complained of their relegation to a second-rate course, were not unprecedented. In 1948 Charles Law and other African Americans sued the city of Baltimore, protesting their assignment to a nine-hole course situated in an industrial area bordered by railroad tracks. District Judge Chesnut had sympathized with the plaintiffs, discussing at some length the nature and psychology of golf: "Among outdoor sports, golf is a unique game in many of its characteristics. . . . The success of the individual player is dependent largely upon his own ability . . . [and] successful play . . . is largely affected by his own personal concentration, absence of distractions and by his personal temperament and poise. And these faculties . . . are often affected by surrounding conditions. They are helped by quiet and pleasurable surroundings . . . and hindered by noise and other distracting influences." Judge Chesnut ruled in favor of the plaintiffs, ordering Baltimore to devise a plan allowing black golfers access to the city's better courses but also preserving racial segregation.[18]

Beaumont

At the same time that Fort Worth African Americans were working to desegregate public golf, black golfers in Beaumont and Houston were carrying out similar campaigns. Beaumont boasted strong golfing traditions, and it provided white men and women with good facilities at private, public, and municipal courses. During the period from the 1930s to the 1950s, the city operated a municipal course, first at Central Park and later at Tyrrell Park. At the same time, there were two other golf clubs in town, the Beaumont Country Club and the Pine Grove Golf Club, the latter being a nine-hole, daily-fee facility that closed about 1952. The Beaumont Country Club was one of the older private clubs in Texas. Organized in 1906 and situated on the wooded banks of the Neches River, the club featured an eighteen-hole golf course, boat house, swimming pool, and clubhouse with a ballroom that overlooked the river. The membership was limited to white persons, but the staff included both whites and blacks, with African Americans holding most of the service jobs. Alex Findlay, a Scottish émigré who also designed the San Antonio Country Club and more than one hundred courses in the eastern and southern United States, laid out the golf course. The course was relatively flat and simple but also notorious for towering pine trees that crowded the fairways and complicated otherwise routine tee shots.[19]

Caddies and waiters at the Beaumont Country Club played the "shadow game," as explained in June, 1954, by the club pro, Jimmy R. Witcher. "Monday is the day on which the country club course is closed to members and caddies are allowed to play," he said. "All of the caddies, with the exception of two, and [all] locker boys are Negroes," he added. Sometimes caddies used their own clubs, but often they played with clubs belonging to members for whom they caddied regularly and from whom they obtained permission; in this way caddies had the experience of using the best and most modern golfing equipment. Witcher went on to explain how playing privileges in the "shadow game" might be extended to nonemployees and even people from out of town: On occasion "Negroes from Houston . . . played on the course but only when caddies or locker boys at the club were with them." This hospitality to nonemployees on Mondays was an informal extension of rules applicable to members on other days of the week. Nonmembers were welcome to play the course, if members accompanied them and if they paid the appropriate greens fee.[20]

Members of the Beaumont Country Club worked to promote the game of golf and on occasion arranged competitions for men and women, amateurs and professionals. On May 4, 1946, the club joined with the Beaumont Golf Association to host an exhibition match featuring the "Big Four" of American golf: Ben Hogan, Byron Nelson, Jimmy Demaret, and Sam Snead. Directed by club professional Dave Marr, Sr., the match was covered by KRIC radio and the *Beaumont Enterprise* newspaper and drew a paid attendance of almost a thousand persons. Club member Randolph Reed served as master of ceremonies, introducing the golfing stars to fans thronged around the number one tee; perhaps the crowd included Reed's brother-in-law, Lamar Cecil, and golfing friends such as L. W. Pitts, Julian Fertitta, and Mose Sampson. In the exhibition, Nelson and Snead won a 3-2 match-play victory over Hogan and Demaret, while Snead took medalist honors with a score of 70. Probably all the paid attendees were white, but numerous black caddies and other workers witnessed the events and saw the famous players. Johnnie Ware, for one, was employed then as a locker room attendant and may have served and even talked to Ben Hogan and the others.[21]

In 1953 the Beaumont Country Club again hosted a competition among America's top golfers, this time the best professional women players in the nation. April 3–5, 1953, members of the Ladies Professional Golf Association played the first ever Babe Zaharias Open, a tournament honoring Babe Didrikson Zaharias, a phenomenal athlete who grew up in Beaumont. Zaharias was one of the greatest female performers of all time, setting records and winning national fame in basketball, track and field, and golf. Sponsored by the men's 20-30 Club and offering thirty-five hundred dollars in prize money, the Beaumont tournament drew more than a dozen players, both professionals and amateurs. Professionals included Louise Suggs, Patty Berg, Jackie Pung, Betty Jameson, and Babe Zaharias, while among the amateurs were Polly Riley of Fort Worth, Lesbia Lobo of San Antonio, and fifteen-year-old Diane Garrett, a former Beaumonter who lived in Houston. All the women golfers were white, but black caddies carried the bags and black waiters mixed the drinks and served the food. Zaharias won the inaugural tournament in dramatic fashion, sinking a ten-foot birdie putt on the eighteenth green to defeat Louise Suggs by one stroke.[22]

Zaharias participated in her namesake tournament two more times, taking second place behind Suggs in 1954 and finishing out of the money in 1955 when Betty Jameson took the title. "The Babe" died of cancer in 1956. The Beaumont Country Club continued to host the Zaharias Open until 1964, when a racial controversy erupted over the entry of Althea Gibson, the African American tennis champion who had switched to golf and become a member of the LPGA. Officials of the whites-only club enforced the traditions of the southern caste system and barred Gibson from entry to the clubhouse. Nevertheless, she played the entire tournament, where she was teamed with white male club members in the "Pro-Am" round and with white female professionals in the regular rounds. The next year the LPGA moved the tournament across town to the Bayou Den Golf Club, where it was played three more years: 1965, 1966, and 1967. The controversy about

Gibson revealed the ironic contradictions of the caste system, when white members of a private club refused hospitality to a black guest at the same time that they employed, promoted, and befriended African Americans who worked in the dining halls, locker rooms, and throughout the clubhouse.[23]

African Americans in Beaumont suffered discrimination in public golf and were prevented from playing the municipal courses for many years. Public golf in Beaumont dated back to 1927–28, when the city developed a municipal facility in Cartwright Park, later known as Central Park. A nine-hole course with sand greens and a small lake, the "Muny" was equipped with a pro shop and locker room, managed by a white professional, and served by white and black caddies. As already noted, Johnnie Barlow, the future white professional, caddied there with Booker Fayson, the black golfer who would help lead the golf desegregation campaign in Beaumont. Next door to the "Muny" course was a public airfield that served planes carrying the U.S. mail. The proximity of the two facilities and an amazing coincidence combined to produce a legendary event. According to a story oft repeated by Beaumont golfers, local business leader Kyle Wheelus drove his ball off a tee at the very moment that a mail plane was taking off from the nearby airfield for a flight to Houston. The flying ball landed inside the flying plane and rested there until the craft landed ninety miles away, thus creating "the longest drive in golfing history."[24]

The Central Park municipal course served Beaumont public golfers until the 1940s, when the city opened new links at Tyrrell Park. Located south and west of town, Tyrrell Park was a five-hundred-acre tract donated to the city in 1920 by Capt. W. C. Tyrrell, an Iowa businessman who lived and prospered in Beaumont during early years of the twentieth century. In 1922 Tyrrell also gifted the city with a 1906 church building that became the Tyrrell Public Library, a facility reserved officially for white patrons until the 1960s. The city began development of the Tyrrell Park property during the late 1930s, using funds from the Works Progress Administration and laborers from the Civilian Conservation Corps and building roads, bridges, a meeting hall, campgrounds, shelters, horse stables, and a golf course. By 1943 nine holes were open for play, and four years later the entire eighteen-hole Tyrrell

Park municipal golf course was in full operation. The city closed the "Muny" at Central Park about 1950.[25]

During the mid-1950s, when Booker Fayson and his friends carried out their desegregation campaign, Tyrrell Park golf course was managed by Henry Homberg, a Beaumonter who had come up through the ranks of local golfing. Having caddied as a youth at Central Park "Muny," Homberg went to work as the city golf professional about 1941. He managed the Central Park course and helped develop the Tyrrell Park links. A friend and mentor to many golfers, especially young people, Homberg encouraged the play of high school and college students. A number of his protégés, including Butch Baird, Johnnie Barlow, Ed Campbell, Andy Herbert, Bruce Lietzke, Ron Pflieder, and Bert Weaver, built professional golfing careers as players, teachers, and managers. With respect to racial practices, Homberg adhered to the southern caste system and followed the lead of the Beaumont mayor and city council: At Tyrrell Park he hired African Americans as caddies but barred them as regular players.[26]

Houston

Because Booker Fayson and his friends were excluded from the Tyrrell Park course, they traveled on occasion to nearby Houston to play a public course in that city. There they enjoyed the benefits of a long-fought desegregation battle. The struggle had begun in 1948 when four unidentified African Americans attempted to play golf at Hermann Park and were refused; black golfers were at that time barred from all public courses in Houston. For several months afterward, the city council debated means to mollify the black golfers, discussing plans to build a golf course for black Houstonians but never bringing the project to reality.[27]

In 1950 Dr. A. W. Beal and four more black golfers—two other physicians, Dr. Hughes J. Lyman and Dr. W. J. Minor, and two businessmen, J. H. Jamison and Milton A. Pruitt—started legal action in Houston. Assuming the role of "Joe Doakes" plaintiffs, the group hired W. J. Durham, a veteran NAACP lawyer from Dallas. They also retained the services of Mandell & Wright, a well-established Houston law firm composed of four white lawyers and identified in a local newspaper as one that "represents the NAACP in Houston." Herman Wright, who was a University of Texas law school graduate, a personal injury and labor lawyer, and an ardent supporter of liberal causes, was prominent in the beginning of the Beal litigation, but his associate Ben N. Ramey did much of the work and argued the case in court. Like Wright, Ramey was a graduate of the University of Texas law school, where he earned the prestigious position of editor of the *Texas Law Review*. The combination of black plaintiffs with black *and* white lawyers demonstrated interaction between the races, unusual for the time and place, as well as complexity in the NAACP desegregation campaign.[28]

On January 24, 1950, lawyers Durham and Ramey initiated a federal lawsuit against Mayor Oscar Holcombe and the Houston city council, demanding on behalf of Dr. Beal and the other plaintiffs the right to play the three municipal golf courses: Memorial, Glenbrook, and Hermann Park. Ramey and Durham filed the *Beal v. Holcombe* suit papers in the district court of Judge T. M. Kennerly, Southern District of Texas, Houston Division. With city attorney Will Sears defending the mayor and city council, the case went to trial in Judge Kennerly's court on July 18, 1950. Lawyers for the opposing sides argued various issues and points of law, including the doctrine of "separate but equal." Derived from the famous Supreme Court decision in *Plessy v. Ferguson* (1896), the "separate but equal" principle had been used for decades in numerous cases across the nation to justify segregation of the races.[29]

The city of Houston operated nineteen public parks, with seventeen reserved for white citizens and two set aside for black citizens. The "white" parks included Memorial, Glenbrook, and Hermann, each equipped with an eighteen-hole golf course, while the two "black" parks had no golfing facilities whatsoever. Although conceding that the parks for blacks offered no golfing, city attorney Sears described their tennis, swimming, and other facilities and argued that those parks were substantially equal to the facilities at the parks for whites. Attorney Ramey countered on behalf of his clients, saying that availability of swimming pools and tennis courts did not satisfy the needs of "men who prefer to play golf and by physical condition and station in life are best suited to play golf for recreation."[30]

Judge Kennerly ruled in favor of the city on December 18, 1950, saying, "I do not think the failure to provide golf courses in parks used by Negroes is . . . a discrimination against Negroes."[31] Ten days later Ramey and Durham appealed Judge Kennerly's ruling to the Fifth Circuit Court of Appeals in New Orleans. In the appeals court the lawyers continued their arguments, debating many of the same issues covered in the district court, including the meaning and interpretation of "separate but equal." On March 22, 1952, Chief Judge Joseph C. Hutcheson, Jr., ruled in favor of Dr. Beal and his fellow golfers, saying that Judge Kennerly had "erred in fact and in law": "If an individual Negro citizen desires to play golf on a municipal course and is prevented from doing so only because he is a Negro citizen . . . the fact he is being discriminated against . . . because of his color, stands out like a sore thumb." Judge Hutcheson reversed Kennerly's ruling and sent the matter back to the district court, ordering that black golfers be allowed to play the municipal golf courses on the same basis as white golfers. But he also provided for the continuation of racial segregation, decreeing that the city be given "reasonable opportunity to promptly . . . put into effect regulations for the use of the municipal golf facilities . . . [and for] preserving segregation."[32]

While Dr. Beal and his associates won a partial victory in Judge Hutcheson's court, they did not immediately obtain the right to play golf on the municipal courses. The city delayed issuance of the necessary ordinance and then opted to appeal the Hutcheson ruling to the United States Supreme Court. City attorney Sears filed the necessary papers in June, 1952, and there the matter rested for two years, languishing behind the more important school desegregation cases that became known collectively as *Brown v. Board of Education.*[33] On May 17, 1954, the Supreme Court issued its historic ruling in the *Brown* cases, overturning *Plessy v. Ferguson,* discrediting the "separate but equal" doctrine, and outlawing segregation in public schools.

Only one week later, the Supreme Court acted on the Houston golf case; it refused to consider the city's appeal and sent the matter back to the lower courts, thus apparently allowing for the implementation of Hutcheson's plan for segregated play on Houston's golf courses. But city attorney Sears perceived matters differently. Because of new legal precedents established in *Brown* and other cases, Sears concluded that continuance of the litigation would be "meaningless." He recommended a complete desegregation of all municipal courses in Houston. Agreeing with Sears's recommendation, Mayor Roy Hofheinz and the city council issued an ordinance immediately opening all public courses to black players. Charles M. Washington, a postal employee, became the city's first black player, teeing off on the Memorial course on the afternoon June 2, 1954. Later that day, Dr. Beal, Mr. Pruitt, and other African Americans played their first round at Hermann Park.[34]

The Beaumont Campaign, 1954

While Dr. Beal and other black golfers were celebrating their complete victory in Houston and Mr. Mitchell and Dr. Ransom were enjoying a partial victory in Fort Worth, Booker Fayson and his friends were beginning their campaign in Beaumont. On Monday, June 14, 1954, they began with a two-pronged attack. One man, probably Fayson himself, drove out to Tyrrell Park, while another three, Joe Griffin, Tom Parker, and Johnnie Ware, went to city hall. According to a page-one story in the *Beaumont Enterprise*, "an adult Negro" appeared at the Tyrrell Park pro shop and "asked to be allowed to play . . . on the municipal course." Digressing, the man mentioned "he had been playing golf on Mondays at the Beaumont Country Club but could not do so . . . because the course was being readied for a tournament." When the city pro Henry Homberg declined to admit him, "the Negro left the course without pressing to be allowed to play."[35]

At the same time, Griffin, Parker, and Ware drove to city hall and entered the offices of Mrs. Willie Brockman, the city manager. They introduced themselves as members of the NAACP and asked for desegregation of two city parks: Central and Tyrrell. Mrs. Brockman declined to give them an answer but promised to refer their inquiry to city council. She also mentioned that the city had received no instructions yet from the state attorney general regarding recent decisions by the Supreme Court, a remark that shows that the recent *Brown* decision and other desegregation matters were being discussed widely and at the highest levels of state government. Everyone, Fayson's group as well as Beaumont city officials, must have seen the June 3 story on page one of the *Beaumont Enterprise:* "Houston Opens Golf Links to Negro Players."[36]

Mrs. Brockman reported promptly to Mayor Beard, who in turn issued positive-sounding statements. The request for desegregation of the two parks would be given "careful study," the mayor promised. "The city attorney will be asked to check . . . [all] legal matters which might pertain to the issue." Beard "expressed certainty the matter can be worked out . . . on a basis of the good relations which have existed here," noting that "for several years city officials have been meeting regularly with a Negro Goodwill Council (NGC) to discuss . . . matters of concern [and that] another meeting . . . is expected to be held this week." The mayor went on to enumerate various improvements in streets, sewers, and parks that the city had completed recently in African American neighborhoods.[37]

Mayor Beard moved quickly. Just one week later, on June 21, he helped create the United Racial Council (URC), a group composed of black and white citizens. Members included Dr. E. D. Sprott, Jr., the black physician who was a member of the Negro Goodwill Council and president of the local NAACP, and Charles D. Smith, a white lawyer who chaired a long-standing race relations committee of the Beaumont Chamber of Commerce. Other white members included Albert Shepherd, laundry company owner; Frank Evans, Missouri Pacific general agent; and O. B. Archer, Lamar College official. Charles Smith, a civic leader, public benefactor, and former city attorney, was elected chair of the new United Racial Council. For vice chair the group elected an African American, a man identified in the newspaper as "C. F. Price." But certainly this was Archie L. Price, high-school principal, church pastor, and close friend of Dr. Sprott. Later the URC issued a lengthy statement explaining that the group was created by a merger of the Negro Goodwill Council and the chamber's race relations committee. Obviously Smith drafted the statement, as it bears the unmistakable touch of a veteran lawyer and is replete with chamber sentiments about the history and importance of good race relations in Beaumont.[38]

At the same time, a group of black Beaumonters traveled to Dallas for the forty-fifth annual convention of the NAACP, a six-day meeting drawing seven hundred delegates and beginning June 29, 1954; the timing was propitious, just six weeks after the momentous *Brown* decision. A mostly African American organization, the

NAACP national membership included a number of prominent white Americans, such as Eleanor Roosevelt, Sen. Wayne Morse of Oregon, and labor leader James Carey. Representing the Congress of Industrial Organizations (CIO), Carey was a featured speaker in Dallas, along with Thurgood Marshall, director of the NAACP litigation campaign, and Dr. Ralph Bunche, United Nations official. R. L. Thornton, the white mayor of Dallas, appeared at the opening session and welcomed delegates to town, while President Dwight Eisenhower sent a message calling for "continued social progress" but at the same time urging, "We must have patience." Convention sessions were held at Good Street Baptist Church, and black delegates stayed in private homes, because most Dallas hotels refused to accept black guests.[39]

The exact makeup of the Beaumont delegation is not known, but the group certainly included Dr. Sprott, the energetic president of the local NAACP, and probably Pauline Brackeen, its able and efficient secretary. At the convention, Dr. Sprott and other members of his party found plenty of opportunities to attend work sessions and meet with other black Texans who were pushing for desegregation. U. Simpson Tate, the NAACP lawyer from Dallas, was there as was A. Maceo Smith of Dallas and George D. Flemmings of Fort Worth, both members of the NAACP national board. Everyone was talking about the *Brown* decision and how it could be used to desegregate public facilities.[40]

On June 30, while Dr. Sprott and the others were in Dallas, Charles Smith released a mission statement for the United Racial Council to the *Beaumont Enterprise*. After referring to "recent decisions of the United States supreme court striking down segregation in our public schools," he proceeded to assume their application to "our municipally owned and operated parks, playgrounds, swimming pools, tennis courts, and golf links." Here, leaping ahead of many Americans, Smith agreed with Houston city attorney Will Sears, believing that the *Brown* decisions would lead ultimately to the desegregation of all public facilities. Fearing public unrest about these developments, Smith urged biracial consultations, suggesting that the URC could "bring calm, sensible minds of both races around the counsel table in mature, rational discussion ... [to] contribute as much as possible ... to the peaceful, orderly adjustment to the law as laid down by the supreme court."[41]

CHAPTER 4

When Dr. Sprott and the others returned to Beaumont, use of the *Brown* decision to advance the desegregation cause was much on their minds. Sprott met with Smith and other members of the URC and there debated various strategies for desegregating public facilities in Beaumont. According to *Beaumont Enterprise* editor Robert W. Akers, who later interviewed two white URC members, the council was divided; some white members favored aggressive action while some black members urged a gradual, step-by-step approach. A white member suggested desegregating all city parks immediately, but black members rejected this proposal. Another white member recommended opening three parks: Magnolia, Central, and Tyrrell, but this idea also was rejected. Akers wrote, "The Negro members expressed the belief that three parks at one time would be too big a start and the interest of both races would be better served by beginning with a single park. They recommended Tyrrell as being remote from a concentration of white population . . . [and because] the Negroes have no golf course."[42]

The strategy of moderation adopted by black leaders in Beaumont drew praise in other quarters. Carter Wesley, the black publisher of the *Dallas Express,* urged black Texans to go slowly and be cautious in selecting targets for desegregation. He thought African Americans in San Antonio erred in trying to desegregate municipal swimming pools and urged them to fight instead for less controversial facilities such as libraries, parks, and golf courses. He reported that white "hoodlums" in Beaumont "have been ranting . . . because Negroes . . . have asked for the opening of the golf links." He counseled that black leaders in Beaumont "should refuse any public statement but quietly keep . . . talking with the people who control the parks and golf links." This was a time for "easy does it," Wesley said.[43]

The URC adopted a conservative stance, targeting only Tyrrell Park and its golf course and thereby merging its effort with the NAACP campaign begun several weeks earlier by Fayson, Griffin, Parker, and Ware. On August 6 a delegation from the URC met with city officials in the city manager's office. According the *Beaumont Enterprise,* URC representatives included Charles Smith, Albert Shepherd, Frank Evans, and O. B. Archer, all white, while Mayor Beard, council members Paul Anger and Jimmie Cokinos,

Mrs. Willie Brockman, and city attorney George Murphy were on hand for the city. After hearing a "unanimous recommendation" from the URC, the mayor and other city officials adopted their proposal for desegregating Tyrrell Park. Mayor Beard moved quickly, announcing that the park would be opened to black Beaumonters on September 20, 1954. He also directed Mrs. Brockman to make necessary arrangements, including construction of more cooking facilities and new restrooms. Beard noted that no official action by the city council was needed since the change "involves a matter of custom rather than law."[44]

Mayor Beard's announcement about the impending desegregation of Tyrrell Park provoked a sharp backlash among white golfers. In a meeting at the park clubhouse on August 9, the all-white Beaumont Golf Association (BGA) adopted a resolution calling for the city council to rescind its desegregation order and threatening to initiate a citywide petition campaign that could trigger a public referendum. After complaining that the city had made its decision "without consulting or considering the golfers of this association," the BGA put forth an argument designed to inflame public opinion among white citizens. It should be all or nothing, the BGA demanded. If the city desegregates the golf course, then it must open "the entire park system, including swimming pools, tennis courts, . . . all of the facilities at Central Park, the library, and the city auditorium." This proposal for immediate and wholesale desegregation was the very one opposed earlier by conservative black members of the URC; too much too soon would provoke too much opposition, they feared.[45]

The BGA worked hard and effectively to defeat the city's plan for desegregating Tyrrell Park. They roused public opinion and geared up for a petition campaign; they even floated the idea of initiating a "colored day" at the park, allowing black golfers exclusive use of the course on Mondays. Mayor Beard scrambled to contain the growing controversy, calling two special meetings to address the problem. For a meeting on September 16, he invited representatives of the BGA and the United Racial Council but for some reason did not include Charles Smith or any of the other white members of the URC. Perhaps Mayor Beard thought Smith had moved too far too fast on the desegregation issue. Demonstrating solidarity with the white URC members, Dr. Sprott and other black members of the group declined to attend and the meeting failed to take place. The next day Mayor Beard convoked a meeting of council members Anger and Cokinos, city manager Brockman, planning and zoning chair Otho Plummer, and nine members of the BGA. In this all-white meeting, Mayor Beard and the others discussed the unhappy political situation. As a result of the proposed desegregation of Tyrrell Park, city hall was "besieged on all sides from many and varied sources," he explained. With public opposition mounting, Mayor Beard decided to reverse his course. On September 17, just three days before the proposed opening of Tyrrell Park, he announced, "We now deem it to be in the best interest of the entire population that no change be made in the operation of our parks at this time."[46]

Booker Fayson and the other black golfers had begun their desegregation campaign in June, and now, three months later, they were defeated. They had teamed with Dr. Sprott and the local NAACP, they had enjoyed the support of Charles Smith and other white civic leaders, and for a while they had the approval of Mayor Beard and the white city council. But they were defeated. The tactics of polite requests and friendly negotiations had not worked—opposition in the white community was too great. Racial traditions of the southern caste system were too strong. New tactics were needed, and in the coming months Fayson and his group would opt for legal action. Following the example of black golfers in Houston, they would join the litigation campaign orchestrated by Thurgood Marshall and the national NAACP. To break the color line at Tyrrell Park, they would become Joe Doakes plaintiffs, hire "crusading lawyers," and sue the city of Beaumont in federal court.

Crusading Lawyers

To break the color line at Tyrrell Park, Booker Fayson and his fellow golfers hired two black lawyers, Theodore R. Johns and Elmo R. Willard III. They were young men in the summer of 1955, Johns being twenty-seven and Willard only twenty-four. Also, they were newcomers to the local legal fraternity. Johns had opened a solo practice in Beaumont during 1954 before forming a partnership in 1955 with Willard, who had just graduated from law school. Theo Johns and Elmo Willard were of the same generation, born and reared in the world of the southern caste system. Both had graduated from Howard University law school and both were imbued with the crusading spirit of the NAACP. But the two men were different. They differed in style and demeanor, as indicated by newspaper reporter Terry Wallace, who interviewed the men in later years. Wallace described Theo Johns as "a soft-spoken, down-home Marine Corps veteran of medium height with meticulous habits, conservative dress and understated style," and Elmo Willard as "a tall, rangy, talkative man with an earthy wit displayed with a booming voice, [and] a flamboyant style." The men also differed in background and experience.[1]

Theodore R. Johns

Theo Johns was born December 29, 1927, in Silsbee, a small town of twenty-five hundred persons in East Texas, a wooded region long associated with the timber industry and much influenced by the racial traditions of the American South. His parents, Mr. and Mrs. C. A. Johns, were schoolteachers. Johns attended segregated schools and graduated from Carl Blake High School in 1943. He enrolled in Prairie View A&M College near Hempstead in central Texas. Organized in 1876 as a Morrill Land Grant college, Prairie View was then the state's only public four-year college for African Americans. The enrollment then was about fifteen hundred, with virtually all students and faculty living on campus. Johns recalled paying his tuition and expenses with money earned on summer jobs and funds provided by his parents. Expenses were very modest, he said: "Eighteen dollars a month and that was for food . . . and the dormitory and your laundry, that was for everything."[2]

Johns always wanted to be a lawyer and had gone to Prairie View A&M College believing erroneously that he could study law there. But he soon learned the truth. Dr. Henry A. Bullock, sociology professor, called Johns aside and explained about pre-law programs at colleges like Prairie View A&M and law schools such as Howard University. So Johns studied sociology under Dr. Bullock and later made application to the Howard University law school. He graduated from Prairie View in 1946 but was not accepted at the Howard University law school until the fall of 1948. In the meantime, he lived for a year in Jasper, Texas, and taught school at J. H. Rowe High School, an all-black institution. Jasper, like Silsbee, was a part of "Deep East Texas," a region in which the white and black people adhered closely to the southern caste system.[3]

Johns entered Howard University law school in Washington, D.C., in the fall of 1948. Admission and class work at Howard were very competitive, Johns recalled. Veterans from World War II were coming back and joining the classes. "Some of those guys even had Ph.D.s . . . they were so much more mature . . . and everything," he said. Johns remembered a degree of diversity in his class, a group that included "about four females" and "one or two Caucasians." He also recalled a strong spirit of public service among his classmates: "Ninety percent of the students . . . were there trying to get out of law school . . . not to make money but to try to be of some . . . service to their community. . . . They had no idea that you could make money with the law."[4]

At Howard University law school between 1948 and 1951, Johns took classes from James M. Nabrit, Jr., and other professors who were actively engaged in civil rights litigation. He also heard presentations by several guest speakers, including Thurgood Marshall, who directed the nationwide litigation campaign of the NAACP. Johns remembered going to the Supreme Court and seeing Marshall in action, watching him argue the famous *Sweatt v. Painter* case that eventually desegregated the University of Texas law school. Johns graduated from law school and in June, 1951, took the examination for admission to the State Bar of Texas. He passed the bar exam on his first attempt, receiving the good news by mail on the same day in December that he received his draft notice for military service.[5]

Drafted into the U.S. Marine Corps, Johns reported to Liberty, Texas, where he met up with other draftees from southeast Texas. At Liberty the men were separated into two groups, whites standing in front and blacks to one side. The white mayor of Liberty appeared and addressed the white men, giving them a patriotic address and thanking them for service to the nation. The mayor ignored the black men, Johns recalled: "He only talked to the whites, like we weren't going anywhere, like we were just intruding or something." But when Johns entered Marine Corps boot camp in San Diego, California, he found better race relations. President Harry Truman had ordered the complete desegregation of the military forces. Johns's platoon and the whole camp were integrated, a situation that was new for him and many others. "Blacks and whites were trying to make the best of it," he recalled.[6]

After completing boot camp, Johns was able to use his legal training, working in the Marine Corps justice system and on some occasions defending sailors and marines in courts-martial trials. He represented white and black troops and generally enjoyed good relations with all. But one time he had trouble with a white drill sergeant. The man bullied him, saying "You a lawyer?! You another Calhoun!" At first Johns did not understand; he did not think of the *Amos 'n' Andy* character "Calhoun," "the lawyer who . . . wasn't a lawyer but he acted as a lawyer and he was just a joke." Soon Johns figured out the Calhoun remark and understood the insult. He confronted the man. They had words and traded pushes, an exchange that could have presented serious troubles for Johns. But his commanding officer was sympathetic to his position and dismissed the matter, saying "I don't blame you for what happened. . . . I'm not filing anything against you."[7]

Johns was discharged from the Marine Corps in December, 1953, and soon moved to Beaumont to begin practicing law. Not knowing exactly how he wanted to begin, he paid a visit to George White, Jr., the only other black lawyer in town; he had an office practice and rarely if ever appeared in the courtrooms of Jefferson County. White gave Johns a friendly welcome but declined to offer him any affiliation or office space. Instead, White suggested that he situate his practice in the Pear Orchard area and referred him to Booker Fayson, who had a new office building on Washington Boulevard. Johns met Fayson, rented office space, and sometime during 1954 hung out his shingle. He commenced his practice slowly, handling some property and criminal cases.[8]

Because he was an African American, Johns was not invited to join the Jefferson County Bar Association. But generally he enjoyed good relations with other lawyers and the judges. On one occasion, however, when he was just starting out and looked very young, one of the district judges challenged him, asking bluntly if he really was a lawyer. When Johns replied in the affirmative, the judge said, "Do you have any proof?" "I have my license," Johns replied. "Well, go and get the license," the judge ordered. So Johns hurried out of the courthouse, heading toward his office on Washington Boulevard and intending to walk the entire distance because he had no automobile at the time. Along the way, a black taxi driver recognized him and stopped. In those days African Americans had a sense of racial solidarity, Johns recalled: "Blacks knew that we were striving for a single purpose." "Well," the driver said, "it looks like you're excited, something is going on." When Johns explained his mission, the driver said, "Jump in, I'll carry you to get your license." Johns returned immediately to courthouse, showed his license to the judge, and the problem was solved. "I proved I was a lawyer," Johns remembers, "so I never had any trouble with him since that time."[9]

After opening his practice in Beaumont, Johns returned to Silsbee from time to time to visit family and friends. While there he met and fell in love with Bobbie Brown, who was teaching in the Silsbee public schools. He and Bobbie married and set up housekeeping on Lincoln Street in Beaumont's South End. They started a family, eventually having two sons, Theodore Jr., and Kent, and became members of West Tabernacle Baptist Church. At West Tabernacle, Johns came to know the pastor, Archie L. Price, a prominent black leader who also served as principal of Hebert High School. At the same time, he met Dr. Ed Sprott, Jr., O. C. Hebert, Pauline Brackeen, and other NAACP leaders and became involved in the Fayson campaign to desegregate the Tyrrell Park golf course.[10]

Elmo R. Willard III

Born September 14, 1930, in Beaumont, Elmo R. Willard III was the only child of Elmo R. Willard, Jr., and Faye Durden Willard, a couple who divorced soon after he was born. The child's father was a prominent member of the black business community. He operated Willard & Willard, Inc., Funeral Directors and owned rental properties on Forsythe Street as well as a comfortable dwelling on Houston Street. After the divorce, Faye Willard and young Elmo lived with "Grandma Durden" on Plum Street in the North End. Nearby was Adams Elementary, where Faye taught school. The Durden residence was equipped with modern conveniences, including indoor plumbing, electric lights, gas heat, telephone, radio, and in 1947, two automobiles, a 1937 Dodge and a 1942 Packard. Willard attended segregated public schools, first Adams Elementary and Pipkin Junior High in the North End and then Charlton-Pollard High School in the South End. During his high school years, Willard worked part-time, caddying at the Beaumont Country Club, waiting tables at Hotel Beaumont, and serving as an office assistant at his father's funeral home.[11]

Before graduating from Charlton-Pollard High in 1947, Willard applied for admission to Fisk University, a predominantly black university in Nashville, Tennessee. The application filled out in his hand reveals something about the sentiments of this sixteen-year-old youth. He embraced American middle-class values, but he understood he was an African American and something about what that meant in America. He reported that his favorite high school subjects were history, English, and science. He had served as president of the science club and treasurer of the junior class, and he had learned to type and drive an automobile. His favorite amusements included movies, dances, stage shows, and sports; he played football and basketball in high school. He reported regular reading of the *Beaumont Enterprise* newspaper and various magazines, including *Life, Newsweek,* and the *Saturday Evening Post,* as well as *Liberty* and *Tomorrow,* the last two being African American publications received in his home by subscription. Among books he had read during the previous two years were *On Being a Real Person,* the Bible, *Sexology, Parliamentary Rules,* and the *African American Almanac,* the last being most interesting because "it gives the notable accomplishments of the Negro."[12]

Fisk University, organized during the Reconstruction era, was one of the nation's premiere universities for African Americans; its former students included W. E. B. Du Bois, John Hope Franklin, and other black leaders. Willard was accepted for admission there, and in September, 1947, he traveled to Nashville and began his freshman year. He lived off campus in a rooming house and joined Kappa Alpha Psi, a black fraternity; he liked being one of the "Kappas," enjoying the social life and playing intramural basketball for the group. He majored in economics and business administration but was of two minds about his future. On one hand he talked about returning to Beaumont to join his father in the mortuary business; on the other, he dreamed of going to law school.[13]

At Fisk University Willard met and fell in love with Patricia Green, a young African American student from Chicago. She had graduated from Inglewood High School and completed a year at the University of Wisconsin before enrolling as an English major at Fisk in September, 1949. She remembered her girlhood days in Chicago, when relations between black and white persons were dictated by a northern version of the southern caste system. Discrimination by whites against African Americans was "more hidden [there] than in the South," she recalled. "We could go to the movies and restaurants and ride in the front of the bus, but still whites treated us as second-class citizens in terms of jobs and housing," she said.[14]

Willard married Pat Green on Valentine's Day, 1951, just a few months before he graduated from Fisk. At the same time, he applied for admission to the law school at Howard University in Washington, D.C. The head of the Fisk business administration department, Dr. A. S. Arnold, wrote a glowing letter of recommendation to George M. Johnson, dean of the Howard University law school. Dr. Arnold praised Willard as "a student of high moral character [and] keen interest with a desire and ability to learn" who had done "exceptionally well with the courses taken under my direction." Dr. Johnson authorized Willard's admission to the law school, and he began classes there in September, 1951.[15]

Willard completed the Howard law program over the standard three-year period. He and Pat resided in an off-campus apartment, where they cared for their first son, Michael, born November 17, 1951. While the young couple received scholarships and some financial help from Willard's father and other family members, they had to work to make ends meet. During fall and spring semesters, when Willard attended school full-time, he earned extra money working as a bartender and waiter at private parties; during the summer, he found a variety of jobs: janitor, truck driver, and bricklayer's helper. With the help of a friend at the university, Pat Willard found good employment as the receptionist for an all-white group of psychiatrists. Pat remembered fondly their family routine at Howard University. "Every morning, we climbed into our old Buick automobile. First we delivered Michael to the house of a babysitter, then Elmo took me to my job at the doctors' offices, and then he drove to the law school. Every evening, he made the same trip," she said, "only in reverse, going from the law school, to the doctors' offices, to the sitter's house, and finally to home." "Those were good days," she recalled.[16]

During his senior year, Willard interned for a firm of black lawyers and also worked on a criminal defense project for indigent defendants in the District of Columbia. "We intended to stay in Washington," Pat recalled. "We liked living there and I was reluctant to move to Texas. I had never lived in the South and was afraid," she said. But family obligations intervened. Willard's father died suddenly in December, 1953, and the young man felt compelled to return to Beaumont to continue his family's mortuary business. Willard graduated from law school in June, 1954, and soon thereafter moved his wife and son to Beaumont, where they set up housekeeping in an apartment on Washington Boulevard. Elmo Willard III became president and general manager of Willard & Willard, Inc., and began studying for the Texas bar exam that he would take in Austin.[17]

Willard worked hard getting ready for the bar exam, moving to Austin a week before the test to cram his preparation. After he took the exam, he returned to Beaumont and awaited results. "He was very anxious to know how he did on the exam," Pat recalled as she recounted the story of how he learned the news. Every day that passed, Willard became more nervous. He cornered their postman, telling him about the envelope that would bring the news and making him promise to call the moment it was received. Sure enough, early one morning the postman called on the telephone to say that the long-awaited envelope had arrived. Willard jumped in his car and rushed downtown to meet the man at the post office. He returned soon to the apartment and jumped out of his car, waving his arms, shouting and hollering, and announcing the good news that he had passed the test. He and Pat drove to Austin in November, 1954, to appear at the Supreme Court of Texas so that he could be sworn in as a member of the State Bar of Texas. In early 1955 he and Theo Johns formed Johns & Willard, a partnership with offices in Booker Fayson's office building on Washington Boulevard. At the same time he continued to manage Willard & Willard, the family's mortuary business on Forsythe Street.[18]

Howard University

When Theo Johns and Elmo Willard became involved in Beaumont NAACP activities, they made use of the legal training and inspiration they had received at Howard University. During the years 1948–54, when Johns and Willard studied at Howard University, the law school was a workshop for NAACP civil rights litigation, a national campaign that was spearheaded by black lawyers closely associated with the school. Thurgood Marshall was its most esteemed graduate, while James M. Nabrit, Jr., George E. C. Hayes, and others were professors there. At the university, Johns, Willard, and their fellow students followed a conventional three-year program for a bachelor of laws degree. They studied the principles and practices of Anglo-American law, taking a variety of courses, including civil procedure, contracts, criminal law, torts, evidence, domestic relations, federal jurisdiction and procedure, civil rights, and constitutional law.[19]

But Johns, Willard, and their fellow students learned more than the regular law school curriculum. They learned about the growing civil rights campaign. They heard first-person accounts from law professors who were directly involved in civil rights litigation; Professors Nabrit and Hayes taught law to their students at the same time that they worked with Thurgood Marshall and the NAACP on a number of important desegregation cases. Johns and Willard also witnessed moot court sessions, mock trials where Marshall, Nabrit, Hayes, and others argued and tested their cases before an audience of students and professors. Willard, reminiscing in later years, recalled participating in the moot court sessions and serving on a student team that critiqued legal arguments presented by Marshall and the other NAACP lawyers.[20]

NAACP

The NAACP, founded in 1909, comprised black and white members from around the nation. Its legal arm, the Legal Defense and Education Fund (Legal Defense Fund or LDF), was also biracial, receiving financial contributions from black and white donors and being staffed by both black and white attorneys. For example, Charles H. Houston, an African American, and Nathan R. Margold, who was white and Jewish, were among the lawyers who conducted NAACP legal activities during the 1920s and 1930s; later, Jack Greenberg, also white and Jewish, served as director of the Legal Defense Fund. The mission of the LDF was broad: using the rule of law to improve the lives of African Americans. Among other things, the LDF defended African Americans in the criminal justice system and used the courts to dismantle the southern caste system.[21]

Thurgood Marshall, a graduate of Lincoln University and Howard University law school, joined the LDF staff in 1936, becoming director in 1940 and serving in that capacity until 1961; later he became the first African American to serve as a Supreme Court justice. As the director of the LDF, Marshall had offices in New York City. From there he traveled the nation with Robert L. Carter and other assistants, strategizing with local attorneys and developing lawsuits aimed at ending segregation. Often they devised cases that attacked some aspect of the "separate but equal" doctrine, the judicial theory derived from *Plessy v. Ferguson* (1896) that served as the legal underpinning of the southern caste system. Marshall personally managed many of the cases, recruiting "Joe Doakes" plaintiffs, preparing legal papers, and arguing in the courts. Frequently the work was tedious and prolonged, with Marshall appearing repeatedly in district and appellate courts before fighting the final battles in the Supreme Court. He eventually argued thirty-two criminal and civil cases before the Supreme Court and won twenty-nine.[22]

In various Supreme Court victories, Marshall and other NAACP lawyers knocked down racial barriers in venues such as transportation, housing, voting, and education. A partial listing of these high court decisions demonstrates the goals of the NAACP and the scope of the LDF legal activities. In *Mitchell v. United States* (1946) and *Henderson v. United States* (1950), the Supreme Court outlawed segregation of interstate railroads; in *Shelley v. Kraemer* (1948) the court prohibited state enforcement of racial covenants in housing; and in *Smith v. Allright* (1944) the court declared unconstitutional the exclusion of black voters from primary elections in Texas. In the field of higher education, Marshall teamed with Professor Nabrit to defeat segregation practices in graduate programs at universities in Texas and Oklahoma. In *Sweatt v. Painter* (1950) the Supreme Court ordered the admission of Heman M. Sweatt, an African American, to the University of Texas law school; and in *McLaurin v. Oklahoma State Regents* (1950) the court outlawed discriminatory practices directed by the University of Oklahoma against George W. McLaurin, an African American graduate student. Professor Nabrit's work on the *Sweatt* and *McLaurin* cases was highly relevant to his students at Howard. At the same time that he and Marshall argued these cases, Nabrit taught civil rights and constitutional law to Theo Johns and other students. In these classes, Johns and his fellow students saw at close range the development of civil rights litigation.[23]

After breaking the color line in higher education, Marshall and other LDF lawyers moved to attack segregation in public schools, hammering away at the "separate but equal" theories on which the separation of the races was justified. They devised five lawsuits, four in state jurisdictions (Virginia, Delaware, South Carolina, and Kansas) and one in the District of Columbia. In these cases, black parents filed class-action lawsuits on behalf of their minor children, demanding their right to attend "white" schools; in Topeka, Kansas, for instance, Oliver Brown sued the local board of education on behalf of his seven-year-old daughter, Linda Carol Brown. Marshall and his team pushed the cases through the lower courts until they reached the Supreme Court, where the four state cases were consolidated and became known as *Brown v. Board of Education of Topeka.* The District of Columbia case, *Bolling v. Sharpe,* was identified separately but handled at the same time. Howard University professors Nabrit and Hayes worked closely with Marshall on the school cases and were largely responsible for the District of Columbia suit, carrying the case through the lower courts and arguing the matter before the Supreme Court.[24]

In the school cases, Marshall, Nabrit, Hayes, and other LDF lawyers won a resounding victory for the NAACP and the civil rights cause of African Americans. In *Brown v. Board of Education* and *Bolling v. Sharpe,* the Supreme Court overturned the "separate but equal" doctrine of *Plessy v. Ferguson* and ruled that segregated schools were unconstitutional. On May 17, 1954, Chief Justice Earl Warren announced the momentous ruling, a decision approved unanimously by the other eight justices: Hugo L. Black, Harold H. Burton, Tom C. Clark, William O. Douglas, Felix Frankfurter, Robert H. Jackson, Sherman Minton, and Stanley F. Reed. "We conclude . . . that in the field of public education the doctrine of 'separate but equal' has no place," Warren said. "Separate educational facilities are inherently unequal." But the Supreme Court had done more than outlaw racial segregation in public schools. By throwing out *Plessy v. Ferguson,* the court had also laid legal groundwork for ending segregation in libraries, parks, golf courses, swimming pools, and other public facilities.[25]

The Beaumont Campaign, 1955

In the summer of 1955, twelve months after the *Brown* decision, the Beaumont golfers resumed their efforts to desegregate the Tyrrell Park municipal course. Repeating tactics used in their 1954 campaign, they began with a two-pronged attack, petitioning city council and applying to play the course. But this time, they would add a new tactic: litigation. As noted in the prologue of this book, they opened their new campaign on June 14, 1955, with an appearance before Beaumont city council. Booker Fayson, Joe Griffin, Thomas Parker, and Johnnie Ware attended the public meeting along with Theodore Johns, their lawyer and spokesman. Speaking on behalf of his clients and the NAACP, attorney Johns asked for the desegregation of the golf course while Fayson explained the needs of the black members of the Beaumont Golfers Club. After council member Jimmie Cokinos asked questions about the previous year's campaign, the local United Racial Council, and the national NAACP, Mayor Elmo Beard issued a conclusive statement on behalf of the city administration. "In the judgment of the Council," Beard said, "a majority of the people in town are not ready to accept this desegregation."[26]

Rebuffed officially by the city council, Fayson and his group proceeded with the next step: applying to play the Tyrrell Park course. They moved cautiously, on the morning of June 20 placing telephone calls to the mayor's office and the police department, advising authorities of their plans to go to the golf course. Later that day, Fayson, Griffin, Parker, and Ware walked into the Tyrrell Park pro shop and attempted to pay their admission fees to Johnnie Barlow, the white assistant manager of the course. It was an awkward moment, Barlow recalled. He knew Fayson and Griffin personally. Years before, when they were youngsters, they had caddied together at the old Central Park municipal course. He knew they were competent golfers and was not completely indifferent to their desires. But he had specific instructions from Henry Homberg, the course manager: No black golfers were to be admitted. He refused their money and they left the premises. He remembered hearing rumors then that black golfers were getting ready to file a lawsuit, that their appearance at the pro shop was just a preliminary step. After leaving Tyrrell Park, Fayson and his group continued their attack, the same day paying official visits to Mrs. Willie Brockman, city manager, and Reese Martin, the city's parks commissioner. Speaking separately with Brockman and Martin, the men asked for free and unrestricted use of Tyrrell and Central Parks. But in both instances, the officials refused them, citing prior decisions by city council.[27]

The next day the *Beaumont Enterprise* reported the black golfers' foray to the municipal course and speculated about impending litigation. "Four Negroes" had been refused admission at Tyrrell Park golf course, the newspaper reported, and "it appeared . . . legal action may be in the offing to seek unsegregated use of the course." Sure enough, just two days later, on June 23, 1955, Theo Johns and Elmo Willard went downtown to the federal building, a massive neoclassical structure that doubled as courthouse and post office. They made their way to the second floor and entered the clerk's office, where they filed suit papers in the United States District Court, Eastern District of Texas. Mary Wakefield, the white deputy clerk, and her all-white staff must have been shocked, as this was the first time a black lawyer had filed a suit in the federal court. Wakefield accepted the legal documents, logging in the case as Civil Action No. 2920 and noting its abbreviated title: *Fayson, et al., v. Beard, Mayor of Beaumont, et al.* She referred the case automatically to Judge Lamar Cecil, who presided in the Beaumont court of the Eastern District. At the same time, in the post office downstairs, Griffin, Parker, Ware, and other black postal workers must have been rejoicing quietly, having known in advance what was going to happen.[28]

The suit papers named Fayson, Griffin, Parker, and Ware, the original four who had started the campaign in 1954, as plaintiffs. But the plaintiff's group had been expanded to include William Narcisse, railroad laborer, and Earl White, disabled Korean War veteran. Listed as defendants were the City of Beaumont and four individuals: Elmo Beard, mayor; Mrs. Willie Brockman, city manager; Reese Martin, commissioner of parks; and Henry Homberg, manager of Tyrrell Park golf course. Theo Johns and Elmo Willard signed as attorneys for the plaintiffs, while U. Simpson Tate was listed "Of Counsel." Tate, an African American lawyer who lived in Dallas, served as regional counsel for the Legal Defense Fund of the NAACP. The involvement of Tate and the rapidity with which the suit papers were produced show clearly that the Fayson litigation was a coordinated action involving Fayson and the other "Joe Doakes" golfers, lawyers Theo Johns and Elmo Willard, the local NAACP, the local Legal Redress Committee, and the Dallas office of the Legal Defense Fund. These facts also indicate how the Fayson suit was part of a wider civil rights campaign being waged by NAACP chapters throughout the Lone Star State.[29]

The Beaumont NAACP chapter, headed by Dr. Ed Sprott, Jr., was a vibrant organization with a growing membership of three hundred and an expanding civil rights agenda. The same was true for numerous other towns and cities in Texas, where about one hundred local chapters had counted almost thirty thousand members in 1949. The Beaumont chapter was a member of the Texas State Conference of Branches of the NAACP (otherwise known as the State Conference), an umbrella organization that coordinated litigation and other civil rights activities in the Lone Star State during the 1940s and 1950s. Juanita Craft, William J. Durham, Maceo Smith, Carter Wesley, and Lulu B. White were among the leaders of the State Conference that had offices in Dallas. White, whose career was chronicled in a biography by Merline Pitre, served simultaneously as director of the state branches and executive director of the Houston branch of the NAACP. Other groups based in Dallas were the Legal Redress Committee, a statewide association of volunteer lawyers, and the Legal Defense Fund of the NAACP. The Legal Defense Fund regional office was staffed with two full-time employees: Donald Jones, regional secretary, and U. Simpson Tate, special counsel.[30]

U. Simpson Tate reported directly to Thurgood Marshall in the national headquarters of the Legal Defense Fund in New York City. Tate enjoyed a long-standing association with Marshall, having attended Lincoln University with him and much later following in his footsteps at Howard University law school. After graduating from the law school in 1946, Tate practiced for a while in the District of Columbia and then moved to the Lone Star State in 1948. As regional counsel for the Legal Defense Fund, Tate worked closely with the State Conference, an organization credited by historian Michael Gillette with great influence in the Texas civil rights struggle. Between 1937 and 1957, "the Texas State Conference . . . was the principal vehicle for civil rights activism," Gillette wrote, "planning and initiating lawsuits [and coordinating] them with the local branches and the national headquarters in New York. It largely financed the expensive court actions, obtained plaintiffs, and assured that cases conformed to the NAACP's policies and strategies." They attacked employment discrimination by corporations and labor unions, for example, complaining between 1952 and 1954 about racial discrimination by Sheffield Steel Company and the United States Steelworkers Union in Houston. They sponsored desegregation suits against public schools, colleges, public transportation systems, hospitals, libraries, and parks. As described here, they also participated in the litigation aimed at the desegregation of public golf courses in Houston, Fort Worth, and Beaumont.[31]

In the Beaumont litigation, U. Simpson Tate joined forces with local lawyers Theo Johns and Elmo Willard, working with them in the preparation of documents and arguments for the *Fayson* case. The papers they filed in Judge Lamar Cecil's court represented a class-action lawsuit, demanding relief and benefits for Fayson and his fellow golfers, as well as "all other Negro persons similarly situated in the city of Beaumont, Texas." In simplest terms, the plaintiffs and their lawyers asked Judge Cecil and the federal court for two things: (1) They wanted the city to end its segregation practices at Central and Tyrrell Parks, and (2) they wanted all African Americans to be granted free and unrestricted use of those facilities. Here Fayson and his group continued their conservative strategy, limiting their targets to Central and Tyrrell Parks and not seeking the immediate desegregation of swimming pools, libraries, and other municipal facilities.[32]

Mayor Beard and other city officials received a civil summons from a federal marshal on June 28 and soon hired lawyer John D. Rienstra to represent them and the city. Rienstra was a senior partner of King, Sharfstein & Rienstra, an insurance defense firm that frequently served as outside counsel for the city. A forty-seven-year-old veteran lawyer, Rienstra enjoyed a friendly relationship with George Murphy, the city staff attorney, and was well experienced in the federal courts, having served earlier as U.S. assistant attorney for the Eastern District of Texas. Rienstra was comfortable working in Judge Lamar Cecil's courtroom. He knew the judge personally and professionally; both had graduated from the University of Texas law school.[33]

In their original complaint, Johns, Willard, and Tate set forth a variety of legal arguments, declaring among other things that the city's exclusion of Fayson and other black golfers was unconstitutional, denying them their liberty and property without due process of law and also denying them equal protection of the law

CHAPTER 5

as secured under the Fourteenth Amendment of the U.S. Constitution. The plaintiffs recounted events of 1954, when Fayson and his group had first attempted to desegregate Tyrrell Park and when city officials had allegedly issued an administrative order excluding the black golfers because of their race and color. They also recounted events of 1955, when Fayson and the others applied to play the Tyrrell course and were refused. Arguing that the city's administrative order of 1954 and its exclusionary practices were unlawful, the plaintiffs asked Judge Cecil for a declaratory judgment and a federal injunction, ruling that such practices were unconstitutional and ordering their termination. They made no mention of the *Brown* decision or other recent legal developments; they would do that later.[34]

On July 19 John Rienstra and George Murphy filed the Defendants' Original Answer on behalf of the city, Mayor Beard, and the other city officials. Here Rienstra and Murphy conceded various facts about events of 1954 and 1955 but denied that the city had ever issued an exclusionary administrative order in 1954. They concluded their answer with a contingency provision. If Judge Cecil found that Fayson and his fellow golfers were entitled to play the Tyrrell Park course, Rienstra and Murphy asked that the city be given "a reasonable opportunity to prepare . . . reasonable rules and regulations for use of said facilities upon a segregated basis, as authorized by Article 1015b, Vernon's Civil Statutes of Texas." Here they referred to a 1927 statute that authorized Texas cities to promulgate ordinances requiring and enforcing segregation of the races in housing and other venues.[35]

Judge Cecil moved quickly, on August 1 promising a verdict in mid-September. He applied himself assiduously to his cases and expected the lawyers in his court to do the same. On August 19 and 24, the opposing lawyers followed customary litigation procedures. They filed documents of admission and stipulation, setting forth facts about events during 1954–55 and itemizing facilities at Central and Tyrrell Parks. Generally both parties agreed about these matters, although the city denied issuance of the alleged 1954 administrative order. On the other hand, Rienstra and Murphy readily conceded that the city had excluded Fayson and the other black golfers from Tyrrell Park solely because of their race and color.[36]

At the same time that Theo Johns helped Willard and Tate push the Fayson golf course case, he worked with Dr. Sprott and other local NAACP leaders to attack segregation elsewhere in Beaumont. On August 23 Johns joined a delegation that appeared at a regents' meeting at Lamar State College of Technology asking for the admission of black students from Beaumont and Port Arthur. In addition to Johns and Dr. Sprott, the delegation included Pauline Brackeen, Bessie Mae Fontenot, O. C. Hebert, Marion Lewis, and D. A. Davis, a white minister from Port Arthur who acted as the delegation's speaker. As reported on the front page of the *Beaumont Enterprise,* college officials denied admission to black students for the time being but promised to give the matter further consideration.[37]

Dr. Sprott and the NAACP widened their attack, the next day sending a delegation to a board meeting of the Beaumont Independent School District and asking for the desegregation of public schools. In this instance, the group was composed exclusively of African Americans and included Pauline Brackeen, Terry Charlton, A. C. Robinson, Marion Lewis, and Dr. Sprott. Marion Lewis, an insurance agent, acted as speaker and presented a carefully worded petition referring to the *Brown* decision and urging the school board to reorganize the schools "on a non-discriminatory basis." Mrs. R. Jack Orrick, board president, announced that the trustees would defer all desegregation decisions pending "a complete study and understanding of the problems involved."[38]

At the same time that Beaumont blacks pushed for desegregation, African Americans elsewhere in Texas carried out similar campaigns, working with the LDF of the NAACP and attacking segregation in schools, colleges, hospitals, and other public facilities. As shown by samplings from the front page of the *Beaumont Enterprise* during July and August, 1955, black Texans conducted wide-ranging desegregation campaigns that attracted substantial publicity and provoked mixed reactions among white citizens. In Houston, Thurgood Marshall met with U. Simpson Tate and other NAACP leaders in a closed-door strategy session, after which Tate issued a public statement asking for prompt desegregation of all state-supported schools. Black citizens petitioned for school desegregation in various towns, including Lubbock, Waco, Big Spring, and Kilgore. In Kilgore, opponents of desegregation organized a Citizens' Council, vowing to maintain segregation and promising to cooperate with similar councils in Mississippi, Georgia, and other southern states. A federal judge in El Paso ordered the admission of black students to Texas Western College (now the University of Texas at El Paso), while Gov. Allan Shivers, after hotly denouncing the *Brown* decision, appointed a statewide biracial committee to study the school desegregation issue.[39]

On August 24 the lawyers in the Fayson case filed their most important documents with Judge Cecil. Attorneys for Fayson delivered their Memorandum of Points and Authorities, while attorneys for the city produced their Memorandum Brief in Behalf of Defendants. In these detailed statements, the opposing lawyers outlined the facts of the case and cited the latest and most relevant legal precedents that they believed would win victory for their respective clients. The federal judiciary was a hierarchy of courts—district, appellate, and finally the Supreme Court. The courts operated on a system of precedents, meaning that once a legal question had been decided in a certain way by a superior court, it must be decided in the same way by inferior courts, until it was changed by a superior court. Precedents evolved constantly and lawyers had to be ever alert, searching the courts nationwide for the latest developments. The lawyers had the critical responsibility of advising the judge about the newest precedents established in superior courts.[40]

Rienstra and Murphy, representing Mayor Beard and the city, submitted to Judge Cecil a memorandum with legal arguments that were relatively simple and straightforward. Citing the Houston golf course case of *Beal v. Holcombe,* they conceded right away that Fayson and his group were entitled to play the Tyrrell Park course. But as permitted in the Houston case, and also in *Holmes v. City of Atlanta,* another golf course case, they suggested that the city of Beaumont was entitled to establish a segregation system for the Tyrrell Park facilities. (Apparently the fact that the city of Houston on its own initiative had already completely desegregated its public golf courses was not relevant in terms of legal precedents.) Anticipating arguments prepared by attorneys for Fayson and his group, they avowed that the desegregation precedents established in the recent *Brown* decision were limited to the field of education and did not apply to recreation facilities. In the view of Rienstra and Murphy, the "separate but equal" doctrine of *Plessy v. Ferguson* was "still constitutional and applicable" elsewhere.[41]

Johns and Willard worked with Tate in the preparation of a lengthy memorandum setting forth their arguments for consideration by Judge Cecil. They made the same assumption as Rienstra and Murphy, that Fayson, Griffin, and other black golfers were entitled to play the Tyrrell Park course. But they argued that the imposition of any segregation system by the city would be unlawful. In support of their position, Johns, Willard, and Tate cited well-known cases, including *Sweatt v. Painter, McLaurin v. Oklahoma State Regents*, and *Brown v. Board of Education.* They pointed to other cases, such as *Lonesome v. Maxwell,* in which blacks won the outright desegregation of public beaches and bathhouses in Baltimore, and *Holmes v. City of Atlanta,* in which African American golfers gained access to public courses but on a segregated basis. Tate later recalled working with Johns and Willard and together fine-tuning their arguments to handle the apparent and untimely contradiction between the *Lonesome* and *Holmes* cases. The Fayson "suit was drawn to fall within the case of *Lonesome v. Maxwell* decided in the Fourth Circuit," Tate reported. But during the course of the Fayson litigation, "the case of *Holmes v. City of Atlanta* was decided by the Fifth Circuit which seemed to take the opposite position to the *Lonesome* case. We undertook to show . . . that the cases were not decided on the same pleadings and that there is a clean and clear distinction between the two cases."[42]

In addition to submitting their arguments on behalf of the Fayson group, Johns and Willard filed another document, a motion to allow oral argument. Judge Cecil granted their motion immediately and scheduled the oral argument for the next week. Everyone would assemble in his courtroom on September 1. Fayson, Griffin, and other black golfers would be pitted against Mayor Beard and other white officials of Beaumont. The black lawyers Johns, Willard, and Tate would do battle with the white lawyers Rienstra and Murphy. The opposing parties would make their arguments before Judge Cecil, a white judge, and be ruled by his decision. Lamar Cecil had federal judicial power, but he was new to the job, on the bench for less than one year, and had no experience with civil rights cases. In the *Brown* case the Supreme Court had ruled that segregation was unconstitutional in public schools. But what about municipal golf courses and other public recreational facilities? Would Judge Cecil apply the new legal principles of *Brown* to the golf course at Tyrrell Park? Everything would depend on Judge Cecil.[43] So, who was Lamar Cecil?

• •

Lawyer Lamar Cecil

During the summer of 1955, Lamar Cecil suffered serious health problems, including hypertension and others, but otherwise he had many reasons to feel good about himself. He had a lovely and affluent wife, three handsome children, a comfortable home, ample income, private club memberships, and plenty of friends for golf, cards, and socializing. He could point with satisfaction to his position and credentials: He was a prominent lawyer, Republican Party leader, and most important, a federal judge, a newly won position in which he enjoyed high prestige and wielded great power. Indeed, he had accomplished much in his fifty-two years.

Lamar John Ryan Cecil was born in Houston, Texas, November 2, 1902, the son of Anna May and Lamar H. Cecil. His father held various management positions with Southern Pacific Railroad, jobs that caused the family to relocate on several occasions when Lamar was growing up. At various times they lived in New Orleans, Lafayette, and De Ridder, Louisiana, as well as Austin, Texas, before settling in Houston. While residing in Lafayette, May gave birth to the couple's second and last child, a daughter named Edith. When the family lived in De Ridder, young Lamar became very active in the Roman Catholic Church. His mother, an avid Catholic, reared him in the church, even though his father was a life-long but nonpracticing Methodist. From De Ridder, the teenaged Lamar traveled to Grand Coteau, Louisiana, where he became a boarding student at Saint Charles College, a Jesuit school that offered high school and college classes for young men. Under the instruction of Jesuit fathers for one year, Lamar earned good grades, making A's in Christian doctrine, elocution, English, and history, B's in Latin and penmanship, and a C in algebra; it seems he always had trouble with math courses. Later, when the family resided in Austin, Lamar attended a Catholic church regularly and on occasion was an altar server.[1]

While living in Austin, young Lamar fell victim to the devastating flu epidemic that swept the nation in 1918–19. His younger sister Edith, only five years old at the time, remembered knowing that her brother was terribly ill, hearing worried talk between her parents, and seeing the family doctor come and go every day at their house on Rio Grande Street. She recalls peeking through Lamar's bedroom door, seeing him in his bed, coughing loudly and bleeding from his nose and mouth. Lamar recovered from the flu, but Edith speculated that internal injuries caused by that disease might have contributed to heart and lung problems that worsened his health and eventually took his life.[2]

Despite his illness, Lamar completed his high school education in Austin in 1918, earning college entrance credits in English, history, algebra, civics, and Latin. The next year he embarked on a plan to become a Catholic priest, probably with the enthusiastic encouragement of his mother May. He traveled to Washington, D.C., and enrolled in Catholic University of America, where he majored in philosophy and took classes in English, French, Greek, and history. At the same time he joined the Paulists, a missionary brotherhood dedicated to preaching and disseminating Catholic doctrine. With Paulist brothers and other seminarians, Lamar resided at nearby Saint Paul's College, where he engaged in rigorous spiritual training. The daily schedule included two half-hour periods of meditation, daily mass, spiritual reading, community prayer, and evening devotional services. The seventeen-year-old Lamar participated in religious services, on occasions taking roles as acolyte, thurifer (censer carrier), and lecturer. One evening in May, 1920, he delivered a lecture about the Virgin Mary and her role as the "Seat of Wisdom," a fundamental tenet of Catholic doctrine. Once or twice a week he attended conferences to hear discussions of spiritual topics, and every month he participated in a day of retreat.[3]

Lamar performed well in his classes at Catholic University, making mostly A's and B's, though he barely passed his math course. And apparently he conformed himself to the discipline and training of the Paulist program. But after one year, he changed his mind and his plans. Withdrawing from the university and the seminary, he returned to the bosom of his family, then living in Houston. His sister Edith remembered that when he came home he had given up all ideas of becoming a priest. Even more, he stopped attending mass and dropped completely out of the church. She never heard him explain this change in his life, but the results were profound. He abandoned priestly ideals of celibacy, piety, and self-sacrifice and embarked on a conventional bourgeois life that would emphasize money, materialism, and hedonistic pleasures.[4]

In Houston, Lamar resided with his family in a dwelling on Marshall Street in an all-white neighborhood not too far from the campus of Rice Institute. The Cecil family owned a comfortable two-story house, suitable for Lamar's father, who prospered with the Southern Pacific Railroad and enjoyed valuable business and civic connections. As assistant to the Southern Pacific general manager, the elder Cecil associated with top officials, including Henry Tallichet, a prominent lawyer and bank director who served as general attorney for the railroad company; later Tallichet's friendship would be important when young Lamar began his legal career. Like many in the Marshall Street neighborhood, the Cecil family employed African Americans as domestic servants, women and men, some residing from time to time in the garage apartment. Edith Cecil Flynn recalled a black man whose first name was Leon; he was the "houseman," a domestic worker who served as butler, chauffeur, and gardener. In this way, Edith and her brother Lamar became accustomed to the practices of the southern caste system.[5]

In 1920 Lamar enrolled at Rice Institute, a private university endowed by Houston merchant William Marsh Rice. With Oxford-style buildings and an Ivy League faculty, Rice provided tuition-free education for male and female students, though

African Americans were excluded. Lamar entered the university as a sophomore and thus probably escaped the hazing suffered by freshmen (nicknamed "Slimes"), such as the Slime nightshirt parade when the newcomers were reduced to pajamas and nightgowns and paraded along Main Street. On the other hand, he probably socialized with fellow students and may have taken drinks of alcohol, a practice strictly forbidden by university rules during the Prohibition era. On one occasion students at an on-campus party scandalized the university, when, according to the student newspaper the *Thresher,* "some wild man threw a cognac bottle into the middle of the dancing floor." Excessive drinking by students on Rice and other college campuses was common during the Roaring Twenties, or Jazz Age, when many young Americans abandoned the Victorian inhibitions of older generations and experimented with freer and more exuberant forms of dancing, drinking, and sexual practices.[6]

A member of the class of 1923, Lamar pursued a bachelor of arts degree program. Over three years he took arts and sciences courses, including math, French, English, chemistry, philosophy, biology, and history. In English he read Shakespearean and Victorian literature; in biology, he studied bacteriology, immunology, and prevention of human disease; and in history, he read accounts of English history, from medieval times to the Norman conquest. He passed all the courses but excelled in none, compiling a C average and graduating in June, 1923. That year the *Campanile* yearbook featured ninety-six seniors, including thirty-nine women. Pictured in cap and gown, Lamar was credited with a B.A. degree but nothing else, no athletics or club affiliations, no extracurricular activities.[7]

In the fall of 1923 Lamar set out to become an attorney and enrolled in the law school at the University of Texas in Austin. Perhaps he took these steps with the encouragement of his father and the assistance of Henry Tallichet, the family friend and Southern Pacific lawyer. The Texas law school program, directed by Dean Ira P. Hildebrand, comprised twenty-four courses over three years. All the students were white and mostly men, but there were a few women. During his first semester, Lamar did well enough, passing contracts and two other courses. But in the second semester, he failed miserably. He flunked three courses and was kicked out of the university. His sister Edith, then ten years old, remembered hearing the bad news and the worried discussions between her parents. She did not know the reasons for Lamar's troubles but speculated they stemmed from fraternity life. He was a member of Kappa Sigma, one of several fraternities that probably engaged in late-night parties and excessive drinking. Whether Lamar learned to drink alcoholic beverages at Rice Institute or the University of Texas is not known, but he did learn. Later in his adult years, he drank whiskey routinely and in copious amounts.[8]

Expelled from the University of Texas law school, Lamar returned to Houston to live with his family on Marshall Street. His father arranged a job for him with Southern Pacific Railroad. The company put the failed student to work on a labor gang, maintaining roadbeds and railroad tracks. The work was hard and the weather was hot. It was a learning experience for the young man, according to a family story recalled by Edith. One day, when Lamar and his fellow workers were slaving away on railroad tracks, they were ordered to step aside to make way for an oncoming train. Lamar stood in the broiling sun, looking up, watching a string of passenger cars going by. There, on the rear of a private executive car, he saw his father standing comfortably on the shaded deck and conversing with other well-dressed officials. So the story goes, the elder Cecil said nothing but merely tipped his hat to the wayward son. The event was pivotal. The young man had learned his lesson; he wanted out of the labor gang. Vowing to mend his ways, Lamar returned to Austin, where he gained readmission to the University of Texas law school.[9]

During a summer session of 1925, Lamar passed two law courses, and from that time forward, he performed satisfactorily. He made grades of B or C in most of his classes and completed his course work in 1927. He graduated that year along with sixty-one other students, a group that included Leona M. Barrier and three other women, but no African Americans or Mexican Americans. Joe E. Estes, future U.S. district judge in the Northern District of Texas, was a member of the class, as were Percy Foreman, later a renowned criminal lawyer, and Ralph W. Yarborough, who graduated with highest honors and later gained fame as a liberal Democrat and United States senator.[10]

Lamar Cecil started his legal career in Beaumont, where he went to work for Duff & Duff, a law firm that handled cases for Southern Pacific. Probably he found this employment through the influence of his father and Mr. Tallichet. In Beaumont he lived in a garage apartment on Calder Avenue, worked in the Duff offices in the San Jacinto Building, and assumed the life of a young bachelor. He readily gained acceptance in local society and was invited to parties hosted by leading families. While attending a party at the Cooke Wilson home, he met Mary Reed, a pretty twenty-year-old girl who had just returned home from Randolph-Macon, an exclusive women's college in Virginia. Mary was the daughter of T. S. Reed, Jr., and granddaughter of T. S. Reed, Sr., men of substantial wealth and high standing. Mary's sister Ruby also attended Randolph-Macon, and both the girls enjoyed the traditional "Grand Tour" of Europe. Her brother Randolph likewise benefited from private education, having attended Virginia Military Institute. Clearly the Reeds qualified as one of Beaumont's elite families when measured in terms of business and social distinctions.[11]

Lamar courted Mary and won her hand. They married September 15, 1930, in ceremonies reported in local newspapers as "outstanding in social prominence" and noted for "exquisite music" and "elegance of appointments." Rev. J. B. Holmes from Fort Worth conducted "Episcopal-style" services at First Christian Church while the Mozart Violin Choir provided classical music. Mary was reported to be "a lovely blonde," her beauty "accentuated by her bridal array": "an exquisite gown of ivory satin fashioned along simple, elegant lines," "a diamond drop suspended from a platinum chain," and "a veil of tulle" covering her face. Her sister Ruby served as maid of honor while her brother Randolph appeared as one of Lamar's six groomsmen. The couple knelt and said their vows, then withdrew to the strains of Mendelssohn's "Wedding March." Afterward, the wedding crowd of four hundred attended "a brilliant reception" at the Reed home on Victoria Street where "the entire home was thrown open" and guests paraded on "the great three-sided porch." The newspapers made no mention of domestic servants, but probably the Reed reception was staffed with African American men and women attired in black and white, the butlers, cooks, and maids who served the food and poured the drinks.[12]

Lamar's sister, Edith Cecil, had served as a bridesmaid in the wedding, and his parents, Lamar and May Cecil, were welcomed as honored guests at the reception. The elder Cecils must have marveled at the sight of their son, a handsome young lawyer being accepted officially as a member of one of Beaumont's leading families. To get to this place, Lamar had followed a circuitous and sometimes tortured course: first Jesuit scholar and Paulist seminarian, then fraternity man and failed student, then railroad laborer, and finally law graduate and promising young attorney. They probably did not think of it, but their son had solidified a high position on the socioeconomic ladder. By virtue of his profession and marriage, young Lamar now proved his membership in the upper class. Now he was a bona fide member of the Beaumont elite.

After a wedding trip to Asheville, North Carolina, Lamar and Mary set up housekeeping in an older dwelling on Hazel Street. But in 1932 they moved into a new two-story English-style house at 2495 Broadway Street. Mary's father, T. S. Reed, Jr., bought the property from the builder and made it available to his daughter and son-in-law at a bargain price. The couple lived there for more than twenty-five years, rearing three children: Lamar, a son born in 1932; Grayson, a daughter born in 1934; and Reed, a son born in 1939. Mary cared for the house and children with the assistance of black domestic workers, an arrangement that was common in the households of many upper-class and elite families in Beaumont. The Cecils' daughter, Grayson, remembered maids and cooks whose first names were Hallie, Esther, and Louis. Another African American worker was Morris Morehead, who served the family many years as gardener and butler, sometimes wearing a white jacket to welcome guests and serve meals. Within the context of the southern caste system, Morehead's relations with Mary and Lamar Cecil were mutually warm and respectful. Grayson Cecil recalled that her father and Morehead shared a genial relationship, frequently joking together about Morehead's payday and other matters.[13]

Over the years, as Mary and Lamar reared their children, he matured and prospered as an attorney. First he won a partnership in the Duff firm, then he practiced by himself, and later he formed a partnership with Quentin Keith that evolved into the firm Cecil,

Keith & Mehaffy. Cecil's association with Quentin Keith, a Port Arthur native and University of Texas law school graduate, and James W. Mehaffy, an Arkansan and graduate of the University of Michigan law school, proved beneficial to all three men. Their partnership thrived during the 1940s and 1950s, when they had many valuable clients and employed a number of associates, including John P. Blair, Frank C. Cox, Woodson E. Dryden, Hugh Freeland, James D. McNicholas, and Harold Peterson. Cecil, Keith & Mehaffy was a "defense" firm—they defended railroads, oil refineries, insurance companies, and other corporations against claims brought by employees and other plaintiffs. Cecil himself controlled several of their most lucrative accounts, including Southern Pacific Railroad and Employers Casualty Insurance Company, companies that had substantial operations in southeast Texas and generated numerous law cases that needed to be handled in local courts. Cecil's close relationship with Southern Pacific was long-standing and derived of course from his father, as well as from Mr. Tallichet and Mr. Duff, while his influence with Employers Casualty stemmed from his father-in-law, T. S. Reed, Jr., who served on the insurance company's board of directors. In this way, Cecil profited handsomely from family and personal relationships.[14]

Lamar Cecil loved the law. He knew the law. He understood how to make it work. He knew statutory law, common law, state law, and federal law. He understood judges, juries, and courtroom procedures. During his twenty-five-year legal career he earned prominence in various professional associations, serving a term as president of the Jefferson County Bar Association and on occasion delivering papers at national meetings of the American Bar Association. He handled many law cases personally, appearing in state and federal courts and gaining a reputation as an outstanding trial lawyer. James D. McNicholas, a former associate, remembered seeing Cecil argue cases before juries: "Lamar was very intelligent, talented, and persuasive. He charmed the jurors."[15]

But if Cecil excelled in the courtrooms, his attention to work in the office was probably less than 100 percent. The one-time Paulist seminarian now spent countless hours in the company of friends at private clubs, golfing, playing cards, and drinking. He enjoyed life at the Beaumont Country Club, at the Beaumont

Club, and at Town Club. He was a competent golfer, good card player, and master teller of aphorisms, jokes, and stories. He shared the club life with close friends, among them Gene Davis, banker and publisher; Ed Edson, investor; Julian Fertitta, physician; John Hart, physician; Bruce Jackson, investor; Dave Marcus, lawyer; Llewellyn Pitts, architect; and Mose Sampson, steel distributor. All his club friends probably qualified as members of the Beaumont elite in terms of their business and social positions. Other friends were his brothers-in-law Fletcher Graham, member of the prestigious Graham family and husband of Ruby Reed, and Randolph Reed, who was married to Margaret Phelan, a member of one of Beaumont's wealthiest and most elite families. Lamar Cecil and Randolph Reed were the closet of companions; they shared family matters as well as an interest in Republican politics, a sardonic view of life, and an inclination to hedonistic pleasures.[16]

Lamar and Mary Cecil, Randolph and Margaret Reed, their friends and their friends' wives were greatly influenced by the Roaring Twenties or Jazz Age. It was an era studied by historians such as William E. Leuchtenburg and Michael E. Parrish, fictionalized by novelists such as F. Scott Fitzgerald, Ernest Hemingway, and Sinclair Lewis, and epitomized by H. L. Mencken, the cynical magazine writer who satirized many aspects of American culture. Cecil, his friends, and their wives were born during the first decade of the twentieth century; they went to high school and college and came of age during the 1920s. In general historical terms, it was a time when many Americans suffered a profound disillusionment brought on by the horrific and seemingly pointless slaughter of World War I, when they lost their fear of a wrathful God, abandoned Victorian standards of decorum, and gave up the optimism of the earlier Progressive generations. It was a "lost generation," suggested writer Gertrude Stein, one that grew up "to find all Gods dead, all wars fought, all faiths in man shaken," said novelist Fitzgerald.[17]

Cecil and others of his generation experienced a revolution in morals during the Roaring Twenties, an era described by Fitzgerald as "History's Most Expensive Orgy." Many women became "flappers" or "New Women" and claimed the same freedoms as men. They drank whiskey and smoked cigarettes in public; they entered speakeasies and danced the Charleston; they read Freud, talked about sex, and told off-color stories in mixed company. In the movies they saw Mae West and other stars who celebrated the thrills of unbridled sexual activities. They "petted," "necked," and apparently became more promiscuous than women of earlier generations, bestowing sexual favors on boyfriends likewise eager to enjoy the new freedoms of the Jazz Age.[18]

At the same time, many men and women of Cecil's generation became regular and copious drinkers of alcohol, a phenomenon detailed and discussed by historian Norman H. Clark. Spurred on by advertising and movies, many Americans came to believe that drinking was "integral to the fashionable life—the world of the wealthy, the proud, the elite." The images and illusions associated with drinking were powerful, according to Clark:

Drinking man was the man of physical action and triumph, [and] distinguished in his masculinity. . . . His indulgences were deep, yet honest . . . his impulsiveness was mature and humane and firmly true. . . . By the fact and style of his drinking, he could attract not only sexual partners but loyal friends. . . . Drinking woman was her own person, liberated yet compassionate, firm-minded, yet ready to yield to the proper stimulation. . . . Thus Drinking American was warm, friendly, convivial, physically attractive, distinctively up-per-middle or upper-class in taste, demeanor, and comport-ment.[19]

Movie stars Clark Gable, Tyrone Power, and especially Hum-phrey Bogart played film roles that romanticized the drinking of alcohol. "They drank convivially," wrote historian Clark, "in pleasant cocktail lounges or at elegant cocktail parties. . . . Or they drank alone, reflectively calm and quiet, using alcohol in carefully measured applications. . . . For the Bogart character, especially, life was serious and the kicks hard. A man suffered and surely he deserved his honest indulgences. He need not apologize. He drank like a man who had earned it; he smoked like a man who had found in the smoke some critical expression of his manhood." Bogart was the perfect model of "a drinking and smoking person," a figure exemplified by many Americans, including Lamar Cecil, most of his club friends, and many of their wives. They were "drinking and smoking" persons—they drank whiskey and smoked cigarettes on a regular basis. Cecil himself, when he was younger and before he put on weight, bore a striking resemblance to Bogart, having a dark complexion, hooded eyes, and full, sensual lips.[20]

Cecil indulged himself deeply in the club life, playing golf at the Beaumont Country Club at least once a week and playing cards several times weekly at the country club, Beaumont Club, and Town Club. Ed Edson, Bruce Jackson, and Randolph Reed were among the regulars in his frequent card games. He was an excellent player and frequently won games of pitch and gin rummy. Gene Davis, Julian Fertitta, John Hart, Dave Marcus, Llewellyn Pitts, and Mose Sampson were with him weekly on the golf course; there he demonstrated real competence and often recorded scores in the mid-eighties. Like his fellow golfers, he employed black caddies regularly and over the years came to know a number of them, including perhaps Joe Griffin, Earl White, and Elmo Willard, all of whom caddied at the club and would appear later in his courtroom. After a round of eighteen holes, Cecil and his golfing friends retired to the men's locker room for drinks, cards, and showers. Here, during the late 1940s, he came to know Johnnie Ware, the African American waiter who managed the locker room. Cecil and Ware developed a long-term relationship, one that extended outside the country club. Over the years, Cecil and Randolph Reed hired Ware to serve them as driver, cook, and bartender at private poker parties and other such events. Cecil, the future white judge, and Ware, the future black plaintiff, shared warm and friendly relations, as permitted by customs of employment, distinctions of class, and traditions of the southern caste system.[21]

While Cecil and his friends enjoyed the pleasures of club life, they cultivated the art of locker-room conversation. They kidded one another unmercifully, making fun of golfing mistakes, card game defeats, physical insufficiencies, social gaffes, and domestic embarrassments. Among themselves they used nicknames, often insulting and obscene. They told jokes and stories, some ironic, cynical, or sardonic, others blasphemous and outrageous. In attitude they often mimicked H. L. Mencken, the acid-tongued writer who ridiculed religion, marriage, and other ideals of American life. Mencken issued various blasts: about Religion, "Say what you will about the Ten Commandments, you must always come back to the pleasant fact that there are only ten of them"; about Puritanism, "The haunting fear that someone, somewhere, may be happy": and about Conscience, "The inner voice which warns that someone maybe looking." He lampooned as middle-class the values of love and fidelity, saying, "Love is the delusion that one woman differs from another." In the same vein was a locker-room joke told and retold by Cecil and his club friends: "The two most overrated things in the world are home cooking and home f———." The sentiment was pure Mencken and probably borrowed by Cecil and his friends from the unexpurgated writings of the master.[22]

Cecil reflected also the sentiments of Sinclair Lewis, the American writer who satirized Rotary, the chamber of commerce, and other booster organizations. Sometimes Cecil dismissed these groups as "childish," but other times, when his good friends were involved, he probably softened his opinions and restrained his comments. He often expressed disdain for the Neches River Festival, an annual event in which debutante celebrations were combined with chamber-of-commerce promotions of the town. But when his daughter Grayson came of age in 1950, he dutifully joined the Knights of the Neches, bought a Knight's yachting cap, and escorted his wife Mary to festival events. Other debutantes that year included Carolyn Hart, daughter of his good friend John Hart, as well as Johanna Phelan, Ida McFaddin, and Suzanne Stedman, all members of elite Beaumont families. No young African American women or their families participated in the festival, but numerous black men and women worked festival parties as butlers, cooks, and waiters. Cecil's support of the Neches River Festival was not wholehearted or long-lasting, however, as he soon gave his Knight's yachting cap to his butler, Morris Morehead. The black man sported the cap while mowing Cecil's front lawn, a scene that caused great insult to more serious Knights and produced much amusement for Cecil.[23]

If Cecil and his club friends made verbal fun of marriage, and if some may have violated their marriage vows, most of them stayed married to their first wives and carried out their obligations as husbands and fathers. Cecil himself assisted his wife Mary with family and social affairs, sharing concern for their children, escorting her to parties, receptions, and dances, and on occasion going with her and the children to Sunday services at Saint Mark's Episcopal Church. Mary Cecil was an ardent member of Saint Mark's and the first woman elected to its vestry. She required her three children to be baptized and confirmed in the Episcopal faith, and over the years she longed for the conversion of her husband, the apostate Roman Catholic. She got her wish one Sunday in 1952 when she and Cecil attended services at Saint Mark's. Much to her surprise and delight, Cecil got up from his seat, walked to the altar railing, and was received by a visiting bishop as an official member of the Protestant Episcopal Church of the United States. Thus, after a hiatus of more than thirty years, the one-time Paulist seminarian came back to the fold of organized religion. Whether he returned to the church for spiritual or other reasons, or a combination of such factors, of course cannot be known. But it is interesting to speculate about whether his Catholic training and his spiritual feelings, if any, had any influence upon his actions as federal judge, especially with respect to desegregation cases that some said involved profound moral questions.[24]

Almost every evening Cecil came home from the office, or the country club, or the card room, in time for dinner with Mary and the children. Dinner was a formal affair, with Cecil at the head of the table carving the meat and Morris Morehead in white coat delivering the plates to Mary, Lamar Jr., Grayson, and Reed. The ritual and decorum of the evening dinner symbolized the high standards that Cecil and his wife imposed on their children. The parents demanded excellence in behavior, manners, and school-work. For high-school education, Lamar and Mary sent their children to prestigious private schools, with Lamar Jr., and Reed attending Episcopal High School in Alexandria, Virginia, and Grayson going to Mount Vernon College in Washington, D.C.[25]

Grayson remembered many evenings at home when she and her brothers were hushed. "Be quiet," her mother would say, "your father is not feeling well." Her father would sit in his living room chair, resting and reading quietly. Lamar Cecil was a sick man and sick for a long time. For many years he suffered from arteriosclerosis and hypertension, some said malignant hyperten-sion, conditions that caused fatigue, headaches, and shortness of breath, and threatened heart attack, stroke, even sudden death. In addition he experienced episodes of ulcerative colitis, an ailment that produced discomfort and intestinal distress. Doctors in Beaumont diagnosed the ailments and rendered treatments but could not offer a lasting solution for the hypertension, except perhaps words of caution about drinking, smoking, and other matters of lifestyle.[26]

Anxious to find a cure for the hypertension, Cecil traveled to the famous Mayo Clinic in Rochester, Minnesota, sometime during the early 1940s. Doctors there proposed a bilateral sympathectomy, a radical surgical procedure in which doctors opened both sides of the patient's back and severed certain sympathetic nerves that influenced functions of the vascular system. Sympathectomy was "the state-of-the-art treatment for advanced high blood pressure" during the 1940s, according to one writer. But "the major problem with this complex and extreme procedure was that it didn't work for most patients—at least not over the long term." Such was the case for Cecil; he underwent the surgery but in the long run his hypertension was not cured. In the short run, however, he recovered from the surgery and resumed his busy life, going to the office, trying cases, and enjoying himself at the clubs. In the showers of the men's locker room of the country club, he was famous for the two awful C-shaped scars that marked his lower back. "That's where they took out my kidneys," he always quipped.[27]

· ·

Republican Lamar Cecil

After his surgery, Lamar Cecil resumed his busy life, attending to his family, working in his law firm, and enjoying himself at the clubs. But somehow he found time and energy to pursue a new interest—Republican Party politics. Texas then was controlled entirely by the Democratic Party, at all governmental levels, while the Republican Party had few members and was largely impotent in terms of electing public officials. Cecil joined a small cadre of Texas men and women who embraced the theory of a two-party state, believing the Lone Star State would benefit by the development of a viable Republican Party. They espoused Republican ideology; they filed for public office, raised campaign funds, and rallied voters.

Why Cecil became a Republican is not known. Maybe he harbored a secret ambition for a federal appointment, but this notion seems unlikely since prospects for its realization were so slim and so far in the future. Or perhaps his motivations were economic and ideological; as a member of the Beaumont elite and a corporate lawyer, he might be inclined toward the party long associated with business and property interests. His sister Edith remembered that their parents were life-long Democrats, loyal supporters of President Franklin D. Roosevelt. Leading the nation during the Depression and World War II, Roosevelt was adored by millions of Americans and elected four times to the presidency. But many conservative Americans, including numerous Texans, opposed Roosevelt, believing he was too beholden to organized labor and judging his New Deal programs as too liberal, even socialistic or communistic. Edith recalled that her brother Lamar, the professional lawyer, was offended by Roosevelt's "court-packing" scheme, a proposal to increase the number of Supreme Court justices and thereby create a new majority favorable to the policies of his administration.[1]

Campaign 1944

Whatever his motivations, Cecil plunged headlong into Republican Party politics in the summer of 1944, early in the modern era of Texas Republicans and eight years before the pivotal Eisenhower campaign of 1952. He filed as a Republican candidate for Congress in the 2nd Congressional District, a seat being vacated by East Texas Democrat Martin Dies, Jr., the controversial head of the House Un-American Activities Committee. To fill Dies's place and oppose Cecil, the Democrats nominated Jesse M. Combs, an East Texas lawyer who served on the Ninth Court of Civil Appeals in Beaumont. Combs and Cecil knew one another, and according to Edith Cecil Flynn, Combs went to see Cecil for a pre-election parley. In Cecil's office on the ninth floor of the Goodhue Building, Combs asked Cecil bluntly if he actually thought he could win the race. "Hell no," Cecil retorted, "if I thought I'd win, I'd jump out of that window."[2]

Cecil may have joked about his chances in the race, but filing for office was an important step in a long-term plan for building the Republican Party in southeast Texas. In all likelihood, he made the race with the encouragement of L. J. "Brub" Benckenstein, an affluent corporate lawyer who served many years as Republican Party chairman for Jefferson County. Cecil and Benckenstein knew one another, both being attorneys, having offices for a while in the same building and holding memberships in the Beaumont Club and Town Club. Benckenstein was eight years older than Cecil and, in the party, much senior to him in authority and length of service. Prominent in GOP affairs since the late 1920s, Benckenstein served in a number of important state and national party positions, including county chairman, state delegate to the national executive committee, chairman of state conventions, and keynote speaker at state conventions. In the 1944 race, Bencken-stein probably advised Cecil and perhaps helped him raise money for the campaign. Probably they became friends. But later they would become bitter rivals.[3]

In the 1944 election, carried out during the height of World War II, Roosevelt ran for an unprecedented fourth term. Some Democrats in the Lone Star State opposed Roosevelt and came out against the incumbent president and his new vice presidential nominee, Harry Truman; they organized the Texas Regulars, a rump organization that presaged later groups, such as Democrats for Eisenhower. Texas Republicans, meanwhile, backed the GOP ticket of Thomas E. Dewey for president and John Bricker for vice president. They also supported a slate of state candidates headed by gubernatorial candidate B. J. Peasley of Tyler and including Lamar Cecil in the southeast Texas congressional race.[4]

Cecil and Benckenstein worked together in the 1944 campaign. They attended a GOP rally in Beaumont during which Col. Alvin M. Owsley, a lifelong Democrat and former head of the American Legion, spoke in favor of the Dewey/Bricker ticket and urged Texas voters to support other Republican candidates. About two weeks before the election, Benckenstein issued optimistic predictions, reporting a dramatic shift in voter sentiments in favor of Dewey and the Republicans. "Telephone messages of support . . . have been pouring into the Republican headquarters," he said. "Small businessmen are calling in to pledge their support for the Repub-lican Party. . . . They feel the Republican Party is the only defense against the Hillmanish regime the Democrats are trying to foster on the public again for another four years." Here Benckenstein referred to Sidney Hillman, the CIO labor leader who had great influence in the Roosevelt administration. While Benckenstein appealed for support from small business owners and refinery workers, he said nothing about African Americans, apparently ignoring prospective black voters. Benckenstein pushed the campaign hard, announcing a two-week schedule of daily radio broadcasts, some on national and statewide networks, others on a local station. In Beaumont he orchestrated a series of election-eering broadcasts by pro-Republican business and labor leaders, including Ben Lashley, a Port Arthur union man; Richard Bloss, an executive with International Derrick & Equipment Company;

CHAPTER 7

and George Booth, owner of Booth Sheet Metal Works. Lamar Cecil took the last spot on the local radio schedule, on election eve broadcasting a plea for voter support of Republican candidates.[5]

Not long before the election, Democrats from southeast Texas rallied in Port Arthur. At a meeting of five hundred, Jesse M. Combs, Cecil's opponent for Congress, introduced Tom Tyson, the state senator who urged support for President Roosevelt and the Democrats. Adopting a war theme and urging voters not to change horses in the middle of the stream, Tyson blasted the Republicans, saying they have "no respect for the American fighting men who are making it possible for them to campaign in a land of free men." He defended Roosevelt's relationship with Sidney Hillman, reminding the audience that the labor leader "represents those who have produced the munitions of war." Tyson made no overt bid for the votes of African Americans, but he did allude to racial issues. "The Republicans have attempted to create disunity among the Democrats on racial disunity," he said. "I am not so concerned about Negroes as I am about political white trash."[6]

On election day, Roosevelt and Truman won the national race handily and led the Democrats to sweeping victories in Texas. In the Lone Star State Roosevelt polled 821,605 votes while Dewey received only 191,425. In state races, the Democrats swamped the Republicans. Coke Stevenson, the Democratic nominee for governor, defeated the Republican Peasley by a margin of about 10 to 1. In the southeast Texas congressional race, Democrat Jesse M. Combs demolished Republican Lamar Cecil, winning 94 percent of the vote against 6 percent for Cecil. In all Cecil attracted only 3,442 votes out of almost 58,000. In Jefferson County, his results were miserable; he even lost Averill School, his home box, 909 to 225, and Hebert High, a large African American precinct, 204 to 3. Mary Cecil remembered that her husband's humiliating defeat drew rueful comments from his card-playing friends. Reviewing box-by-box election returns, Ed Edson poked fun at Cecil. "Hey Lamar," Edson chortled, "I see you won three votes in Port Neches and one in Sabine Pass. Let's go down to Sabine Pass and thank that guy for his support."[7]

Thoroughly beaten, Cecil apparently retired from Republican politics for an extended time. But not so for "Brub" Benckenstein; he forged ahead, playing important roles in the elections of 1946,

1948, and 1950, all of which resulted in overwhelming defeats for Republican candidates. He presided at state conventions and served on the credentials committee at national conventions. In these capacities, Benckenstein worked closely with other Republican leaders, including R. B. Creager, who chaired the Texas Republican Party; Alvin H. Lane, a Dallas attorney; Marrs McLean, a San Antonio oilman; and Joe Ingraham, a Houston lawyer. He also came to know Henry Zweifel, Fort Worth lawyer, and H. J. "Jack" Porter, a Houston oilman, the two men who fought for control of the Texas party after Creager died in 1950. The struggle between Zweifel, a longtime party functionary, and Porter, a relative newcomer, symbolized a strategic battle that was played out in the 1952 elections. Zweifel epitomized the Old Guard Republicans in Texas, a small group that for years measured success not in election victories but in patronage—they worked for judgeships, new federal buildings, and other emoluments handed out by Republican administrations. Porter, on the other hand, represented a new breed of Texas Republicans, men and women who believed in the two-party system, worked to build the party at the grass roots, and expected to elect party members to public office at all governmental levels. Sometimes Porter and other newcomers referred disparagingly to the Zweifel faction as "the never-say-win Old Guard."[8]

Campaign 1952

Party leaders Zweifel and Porter were divided further by loyalties to prospective presidential nominees for the 1952 elections. Zweifel favored Robert A. Taft, the conservative senator from Ohio and longtime Republican leader who had sought the presidential nomination in 1948, while Porter supported Dwight D. Eisenhower, the World War II military hero and newcomer to party politics. Porter believed that the freshness and popularity of "Ike" Eisenhower, a Texas native, would attract the votes of many Democrats and thus pave the way for development of the Republican Party in the Lone Star State. The competition between the Zweifel/Taft faction and the Porter/Eisenhower faction became contentious, dividing Texas Republicans into warring camps and setting off battles at every party level—precinct, county, and state.[9]

In Beaumont and Jefferson County, Benckenstein commanded the Zweifel faction, working to maintain Old Guard control of the local party apparatus and giving strong support to the nomination of Taft. But he was challenged by Lamar Cecil, who came out of political retirement in 1951. That year Jack Porter and other Texas Republicans for Eisenhower began putting together a statewide, county-by-county organization. Their goal was to win control of the state convention and send an Eisenhower delegation to the national convention. In December Hobart K. McDowell, a party worker from San Angelo, wrote to Porter about a prospective chairman for Jefferson County. He and Malcolm McCorquodale, a Houston lawyer, had just returned from Beaumont, where they went to meet and evaluate Lamar Cecil. McDowell gave an enthusiastic report, enumerating Cecil's many attributes: "He is a member of one of Beaumont['s] leading law firms . . . a good friend of Malcolm's [McCorquodale] . . . a close friend of Governor Allan Shivers . . . [and] is married into one of Beaumont's very wealthy families." Additionally, McDowell reported, "We were told by all that he was a very fine and upright man." McDowell surmised, "He really looks like a winner to me," adding the salient fact that Cecil said "he would gladly take out after Benckenstein."[10]

Cecil took the job and, true to his word, set out to challenge Benckenstein. He assembled a team of Eisenhower Republicans to battle the Old Guard for control of the precinct and county conventions. Among his recruits was his brother-in-law, Randolph Reed, who became an avid Republican. Reed worked hard for the party and even filed as a Republican candidate for Congress in the upcoming election, seeking the same seat that Cecil had lost in 1944. Why Cecil and Reed devoted so much time and energy, and perhaps money, to Republican Party politics is not known. Perhaps their reasons were ideological; both members of the Beaumont elite, they opposed the Fair Deal policies of the Truman administration. Perhaps Cecil yearned for political power; maybe he planned to run again for public office or seek nomination for a federal judgeship. Whatever their reasons, they probably entered the political fray with a sense of fun and amusement. The two men shared an ironic, even sardonic view of life. They laughed at everyone, including themselves.[11]

Beaumont

At the precinct conventions on May 3, Cecil and Reed took the first steps in Jack Porter's plan to win control of the Texas GOP for Eisenhower. The Porter strategy reflected the realities of the nominating process: Precinct voters would elect delegates to the county conventions, which would elect delegates to the state convention, which would elect delegates to the national convention, which in the end would select the presidential nominee. In the precincts of Jefferson County, the Cecil group challenged the forces of Benckenstein and Taft, recruiting large numbers of pro-Eisenhower delegates. Some were authentic Republicans, but many others were longtime Democrats who decided to support Eisenhower. In some precincts, large numbers of Eisenhower supporters overwhelmed the Old Guard members for Taft, causing them to bolt precinct meetings and hold rump sessions.[12]

A classic battle occurred in Cecil's home precinct, Averill School, where Eisenhower supporters made up the large majority of an unprecedented turnout of more than 125 persons. The Eisenhower forces took control of the meeting and elected Cecil to chair, events that caused the Taft people to bolt the meeting and organize a rump session elsewhere in the school building; there the bolters chose lawyer Sterling D. Bennett as precinct chair and elected a slate of Taft delegates for the upcoming county convention. A similar thing occurred in Benckenstein's home precinct, where delegates met as usual in the living room of his residence on Victoria Street. Much to Benckenstein's chagrin, he, his wife, and other Taft loyalists were outvoted by Eisenhower supporters and forced to retreat to his two-car garage, where they elected Taft delegates to the county convention.[13]

In other Jefferson County precincts results were mixed, with some groups favoring Taft and others making no commitment for a presidential nominee. But Cecil, Reed, and their Eisenhower cohorts had won important victories and laid the groundwork for the upcoming county convention. Elsewhere in the state, especially in urban areas, Porter and the Eisenhower group achieved similar results. In many precinct conventions in Houston, Dallas, Fort Worth, Austin, and El Paso, Eisenhower forces outnumbered the Old Guard Republicans, causing many more instances of "bolt-and-rump." Sometimes it was the Eisenhower group that bolted. In Beaumont and elsewhere, Old Guard Republicans complained bitterly, saying that many Eisenhower supporters were not legitimate Republicans and should not be allowed to control the all-important nominating process. Porter and the Eisenhower group countered, arguing that enlisting the support of Democrats was essential if the Texas GOP was to become a viable party. The Old Guard and the Eisenhower people argued this point again and again, in the precincts, the county, the state, and finally the national convention.[14]

Zweifel and the Old Guard tried to solve the legitimacy question and maintain control of the party by introducing the requirement that convention delegates sign a loyalty oath: "I am a Republican and I intend to participate in the party's activities in 1952." They hoped the oath would discourage the influx of Democrats, the so-called "presidential Republicans." But their plan backfired. Porter and the Eisenhower group soon determined that the oath was harmless, that it would not limit the electoral choices of Democratic voters but would facilitate their entry into Republican processes. At Porter's recommendation, many Eisenhower supporters, Republicans and Democrats alike, signed the oath and thus provided valuable ammunition for future arguments about the legitimacy of convention delegates.[15]

Cecil, Reed, and the Eisenhower forces went into action again on May 6, when they battled Benckenstein and the Taft Old Guard for control of the GOP county convention. Crowding into a courtroom of the Jefferson County Courthouse, the two groups contested with one another, disputing precinct results and selection of the nineteen delegates needed for the upcoming state convention. Arguments became heated over the issue of certain delegates who were disqualified by the executive committee headed by Benckenstein. Cecil protested strongly, charging that Benckenstein had eliminated only delegates favorable to Eisenhower. Cecil's "faction rent the warm . . . courtroom air with protests," reported a local newspaper, and "arguing [that] was lengthy, punctuated by high-pitched remarks from several women among the Eisenhower followers."[16]

The two factions tried to compromise, appointing a mediation committee of six persons, including Benckenstein, his secretary Mary Montgomery, Cecil, and Reed. But when the compromise committee failed to agree, Benckenstein suggested an even split of delegates for the state convention: nine and one-half for Taft and an equal number for Eisenhower. Cecil and Reed might have agreed to the compromise, but Ike supporters rejected the idea spontaneously, booing down the proposed coalition. Thus rebuffed, Benckenstein and his group walked out of the meeting and reassembled in another courtroom. "It was the Taft group which left," Cecil reported gleefully to the newspaper. "We held the convention in the appointed place," he said.[17]

Cecil, Reed, and their group proceeded to elect Eisenhower delegates for the state convention: nineteen regulars and nineteen alternates, a group that included Cecil and Reed as well as Reed's sister, Ruby Graham. Randolph Reed was elected chair of the Eisenhower delegation. At the same time, Benckenstein and the Taft supporters selected its own group of regulars and alternates, a delegation that included Benckenstein, his wife Elaine Benckenstein, his secretary Mary Montgomery, his son Fred Locke Benckenstein, his sister-in-law Thekla Benckenstein, and George Duncan, a young attorney who worked in his law office. Apparently no African Americans or labor union members were included in either group.[18]

At the same time that Cecil contested with Benckenstein over control of the Jefferson County Republicans, his partner James W. Mehaffy plunged into Democratic politics. He ran for the position of county chair, a job held by labor union official George Cowart. Why Mehaffy took this action is not known. Perhaps he worked covertly with his partner Cecil, covering "both sides of the street" and trying to increase the influence of their law firm. Perhaps he was a bona fide Democrat and wanted to diversify the leadership of the local party, an organization controlled by Cowart and members of local labor unions. Whatever his motivation, his plan did not work, at least in the short run, as he was disqualified in the race because of filing technicalities. But later in the year, Mehaffy did gain prominence in "Democrats for Eisenhower," an influential statewide group led by Gov. Allan Shivers.[19]

Mineral Wells

The Taft and Eisenhower factions of Jefferson County collided again at the state convention in Mineral Wells. Convening May

26–27 in the Baker Hotel, the meeting registered more than a thousand delegates. The main business was the election of delegates to the GOP national convention, and the overriding question was whether the Texas delegation would favor Taft or Eisenhower. From the beginning the Taft Old Guard controlled the convention apparatus, including the State Executive Committee that decided critical disputes between rival delegations from the various counties. For Jefferson County, the executive committee awarded all nineteen seats to the Benckenstein/Taft faction, while they rejected all members of the Eisenhower group led by Cecil and Reed. The executive committee took similar action with regard to other large urban delegations, such as Houston, Dallas, and Fort Worth, throwing out Eisenhower supporters and seating Taft loyalists. Porter and the Eisenhower people protested vociferously, claiming their delegates, many of whom had taken the loyalty oath, had been elected properly and were entitled to the convention seats. Ratcheting up their arguments, the Porter group accused the Old Guard of "stealing" the delegates, a charge that soon would become a valuable argument for the Eisenhower forces. The Zweifel/Taft faction countered, denying that the Eisenhower delegates were "real Republicans" and claiming that the Old Guard was saving the party from "mob rule."[20]

When the convention opened its formal session on May 27, its membership was weighted heavily in favor of the Old Guard, with Taft delegates numbering approximately eight hundred and Eisenhower supporters amounting to only about two hundred. The Beaumonter Benckenstein presided as convention chair, overruling objections and orchestrating convention votes that confirmed decisions of the executive committee. Under the GOP rules, the Taft delegates were permitted to vote whether to seat themselves or their Eisenhower opponents; naturally, they voted to seat themselves. Meanwhile Eisenhower delegates expelled from the convention gathered for a rump meeting that already was being organized.[21]

Several things triggered the Eisenhower bolt. In one case, apparently a committee hearing, Lamar Cecil argued with convention officials over the issue of the loyalty oath. Having been a bona fide Republican since at least 1944, the indignant Cecil refused to sign the oath and loudly urged others to refuse also. According to an account given later by Benckenstein's secretary, Mary Montgomery, Cecil "caused so much disturbance" that the chair ruled him out of order, ordered him to leave, and told him to "take his faction with him." Whereupon, Montgomery reported, "Cecil and a large number of persons left." Later Alvin Lane, Dallas party leader, spoke to the assembled convention and protested the mistreatment of Eisenhower supporters. "Our appeal has been thrown out," he said. "There is no reason for any Eisenhower people to remain here any longer." Then Lane and large numbers of Eisenhower delegates left the convention hall.[22]

After bolting the "Taft" convention, Porter and the Eisenhower Republicans reconvened in a community center across the street from the Baker Hotel. In a classic rump operation, they conducted a formal convention complete with speeches, resolutions, and election of delegates to the national convention. Porter orchestrated the program with the help of Herbert Brownell, Jr., a Wall Street lawyer and Eisenhower campaign official who had traveled to Texas for the state convention. Porter and others made speeches to the convention, lauding the candidacy of Eisenhower and blasting the highhanded tactics of the Zweifel Old Guard. One referred to the "forty thieves" on the executive committee that had disqualified so many Eisenhower delegates. Houston lawyer Joe Ingraham came over from the Taft convention and spoke spontaneously to the Eisenhower supporters, reaffirming his loyalty to Taft but at the same time condemning the mistreatment of the Eisenhower delegates. Soon Ingraham would switch sides and join the Eisenhower camp.[23]

The Taft and Eisenhower conventions each elected thirty-eight delegates plus alternates for the upcoming national convention in Chicago. The Taft group included Henry Zweifel; Mrs. Carl J. Stearns, a member of the national committee; Orville Bullington, who chaired the state executive committee; Marrs McLean, a member of the national finance committee; and L. J. Benckenstein, party leader of Jefferson County. Jack Porter headed the Eisenhower delegation, a group that included Alvin H. Lane, a former Republican candidate for governor; Joe Ingraham, chair of the Harris County executive committee; H. L. Hunt, Dallas millionaire and party contributor; Malcolm McCorquodale, a party official from Houston; and Lamar Cecil from Beaumont. The Eisenhower delegation included Mrs. Jack Bliss of Midland and four other women, while the Taft group counted three women, including Mrs. Stearns. No African Americans, Mexican Americans, or labor union members were selected for either group.[24]

The Eisenhower state convention passed resolutions endorsing their candidate for president and blasting the Truman administration. They called for housecleaning in all departments and condemned "bureaucratic forms of government, particularly the FEPC." Many white Americans, especially southerners, condemned the Fair Employment Practices Committee, a Democratic program intended to outlaw racial discrimination in defense industries during World War II. Addressing another issue of great political potential, Eisenhower Republicans demanded the return of the tidelands, oil-rich lands in the Gulf of Mexico that President Truman had appropriated for federal ownership by way of an executive order. The Taft state convention drafted similar resolutions, recommending their candidate and vowing to "clean up the mess in Washington." They also called for the return of the tidelands, but awkwardly so, because Taft favored federal ownership of the disputed territories.[25]

The tidelands question would become an important issue in the Texas contest between Taft and Eisenhower, who endorsed state ownership of the properties. But in the weeks leading up to the national convention, the tidelands question was overshadowed by controversies arising from events in Mineral Wells, where Zweifel, Benckenstein, and the Old Guard had expelled so many Eisenhower delegates. The Old Guard defended its actions, vowing to protect the party against a mob invasion of Democrats posing as Republicans. Meanwhile, Jack Porter and other Eisenhower supporters blasted the Taft faction, charging repeatedly that they had stolen control of the nominating process at Mineral Wells. They accused the Taft Old Guard of "stealing," "dishonest rigging," "deceit," "an unforgivable injustice," and a "high-handed lockout" of delegates at Mineral Wells. Reported widely in national newspapers and magazines, the factional dispute in Texas gave the Eisenhower group valuable arguments for upcoming contests in the national convention. The candidate Eisenhower referred to the

Taft people in Texas as "rustlers," while his campaign manager, Henry Cabot Lodge, Jr., described events at Mineral Wells as "an infamous national scandal."[26]

Chicago

In late June the Taft and Eisenhower groups traveled to Chicago for the Republican National Convention, each wanting to be seated as the official delegation from Texas and each vowing to support their candidate. Zweifel, Benckenstein, Orville Bullington, and others led the Taft group, while Porter headed the Eisenhower team, which included Alvin Lane, Malcolm McCorquodale, Joe Ingraham, and Lamar Cecil. Cecil and his wife Mary departed from Beaumont, probably going by railroad through New Orleans to Chicago, while Porter, his wife Ilona, and others took the train from Houston. Both groups arrived by July 1, when the national executive committee began hearings about disputed state delegations. A number of the disputes were similar to the one in Texas, where rival factions favored either Taft or Eisenhower, the two leading candidates. Other presidential prospects that year included former Minnesota governor Harold Stassen, California governor Earl Warren, and Gen. Douglas MacArthur, the controversial military commander in the Far East who had just been dismissed by President Truman.[27]

The convention registered 1,206 delegates, a group that included 128 women. With 604 votes needed to win the nomination, the question of disputed delegations loomed large. Especially critical were 68 seats from three southern states: Georgia, 17; Louisiana, 13; and Texas, 38. In Georgia two factions, one favoring Taft and the other Eisenhower, battled for disputed seats. The Louisiana and Texas cases were much alike, Old Guard Republicans challenged by Eisenhower Republicans, but the Texas question was more important on account of the large number of delegates and the intense public controversy arising from the Mineral Wells convention.[28]

The disputes over the Georgia, Louisiana, and Texas delegations were heard first in the national executive committee and later in the credentials committee, both groups being controlled by Taft majorities. As the hearings proceeded, committee members received a variety of messages aimed at settling the delegation disputes. Former president Herbert Hoover urged mediation, a Republican governor's group recommended a "Fair Play" rule, and Senator Taft himself proposed a compromise for the Texas delegation, giving twenty-two seats to himself and sixteen to Eisenhower.[29]

In the highly controversial Texas case, the committees heard extended arguments from both sides. Taft majorities on both committees voted in favor of the Taft compromise, but Jack Porter and other Eisenhower leaders demanded certification of their entire Mineral Wells delegation. Monte Appel, a Washington attorney, and others presented the case for the Zweifel/Taft delegates, while Alvin Lane, Malcolm McCorquodale, and Lamar Cecil represented the Porter/Eisenhower supporters. Cecil, the veteran trial lawyer, headed the team, outlining presentations and making closing arguments.[30]

Credentials committee hearings opened July 10 under the bright lights of television coverage, the first time that such events were broadcast live to the nation. Already the Eisenhower delegates from Louisiana had won their seats, so the committee proceeded to hear the cases from Georgia and Texas. In the Texas contest, the Zweifel/Taft group made their arguments first, followed by the Eisenhower team: Lane, McCorquodale, and Cecil. Urging the justice of their cause, the Cecil team recounted details of the Mineral Wells convention, where the Zweifel faction had expelled hundreds of Eisenhower delegates. Not one of the Eisenhower delegates had been excluded because of irregularities, they argued, or because they had not been elected legitimately by county conventions. In fact, they pointed out, the Eisenhower delegates had been elected by majorities ranging from 2 to 1 to 10 to 1. They defended their publicity campaign inviting participation by longtime Democrats, pointing to the wisdom of such action and reminding everyone that the Zweifel faction had done the same thing. They rejected completely the accusation that the Eisenhower delegation was composed of "Johnny-come-lately" Republicans, citing the well-known credentials of Porter, Lane, and Cecil, among others.[31]

Edith Cecil Flynn remembered sitting in her library in New Hampshire, watching her brother speak on national television. "He looked marvelous," she said. Wearing a dark suit, white shirt, and striped tie, the polished trial lawyer leaned slightly forward, spoke persuasively, and gestured to the crowd. Closing his argument, Cecil returned to the legitimacy question, reminding committee members that the Zweifel forces had not presented "one word of evidence to prove their contention of bad faith" on the part of Porter and the Eisenhower delegates.[32]

But the credentials committee rebuffed Cecil and his Eisenhower team, voting to sustain the action of the national committee and splitting the delegation, twenty-two for Taft and sixteen for Eisenhower. Managers for Eisenhower, in consultation with Porter and the other Texans, refused the compromise and demanded the issue be decided by the whole convention. Before the convention considered the Texas issue, however, they took up the Georgia question; the national and credentials committees had awarded all of Georgia's seventeen delegates to Taft. In a classic floor fight and a dramatic roll call vote of 607 to 531, the convention overturned the committee actions and gave all the Georgia seats to Eisenhower delegates. This action was a turning point; the convention had voted for the first time to favor Eisenhower in the matter of disputed delegates.[33]

The convention proceeded quickly to the Texas question. Eisenhower managers demanded a roll call vote, but to the surprise of many, Taft managers waived the proceeding and apparently conceded the issue of the disputed Texas delegates. The convention acted then by voice vote, awarding all the Texas seats to the Porter delegation that had been elected in the rump convention in Mineral Wells. The Texas vote was "the final coup," a death blow for Taft, according to Eisenhower biographer Herbert S. Parmet. It touched off a riotous celebration among the Eisenhower supporters, especially Jack Porter and his fellow Texans. "A thunderous shout went up as the victory was won and the band boomed out with 'The Eyes of Texas,'" reported the *Beaumont Enterprise*. Mary Cecil rushed over from a seat in the gallery to congratulate her husband, who later issued a brief statement to the press. "Justice has been done," Cecil said, "and the will of the people of Texas upheld."[34]

The seating of the Eisenhower delegations from Georgia and Texas was pivotal, leading ultimately to the nomination of their candidate. Eisenhower was selected as the presidential nominee, and Richard M. Nixon of California was later nominated for vice president. The decision on Texas also overturned the state's Republican organization, unseating Henry Zweifel and his Old Guard associates and giving power to Porter and his Eisenhower team. Jack Porter and Mrs. John R. Black of Dallas were appointed to represent Texas on the Republican National Committee, while Lamar Cecil was named to replace L. J. Benckenstein as a congressional district representative to the convention. "Lamar Cecil Is Given Benckenstein Seat" was the headline in a Beaumont newspaper. Events at the convention had amounted to a double insult for "Brub" Benckenstein, who saw his candidate go down to defeat and then lost his party position to Cecil, his Beaumont rival.[35]

Mary Cecil recalled the triumphant celebrations in the Chicago convention hall and hotels. She remembered being with her husband in a crowd and meeting Eisenhower. Someone introduced Cecil to Eisenhower, saying "Here, General, meet Lamar Cecil, the man who won Texas for you." Of course this remark was much too generous and in reality amounted to a falsehood. If any one man had won Texas for Eisenhower, it was Jack Porter: He planned the campaign, recruited key people, and carried the fight to victory. But Lamar Cecil did play a key role in winning Texas, an event of great importance. O. Douglas Weeks, author of *Texas Presidential Politics in 1952*, concluded that the Texas victory was crucial for Eisenhower, that he won the national nomination because he and his managers had exploited the issues and controversies arising in the Lone Star State.[36]

While convention delegates selected their presidential and vice presidential nominees, the Republicans also hammered out a platform, twenty-five campaign issues drafted to appeal to a broad spectrum of public opinion. In the areas of foreign policy and national defense, Republicans blasted the Truman administration for its handling of the Korean War, vowed support for collective security abroad, and promised to speed up the development of the armed forces; they also favored a homeland for Jews and recommended a policy of "true reciprocity" in foreign trade. On the domestic side, Republicans addressed many issues, such as government corruption, communism, small business, agriculture, labor, taxation, health, education, veterans, and social security. In the area of women's rights, they endorsed an equal rights constitutional amendment and legislation ensuring equal pay.[37]

The platform also included a civil rights plank, a program that Republicans hoped would help them capture the middle ground and win the favor of liberals while not offending conservatives, especially white southern Democrats whom they hoped would vote as "presidential Republicans." They denounced Democratic administrations for bigotry, duplicity, and insincerity and declared that the main responsibility for civil rights should be carried by the states. At the federal level, Republicans promised action against lynching, poll taxes, and segregation in the District of Columbia. On the sensitive issue of fair employment practices, they compromised between liberal and conservative positions, recommending federal legislation but promising to defer to states already addressing these issues. Whether Lamar Cecil was involved in the civil rights discussions or even paid attention to such matters is not known. But soon, within just three years, he would be dealing with civil rights questions in an important way.[38]

The entire platform, including the civil rights plank, was adopted by a voice vote of the convention on a motion from the platform chair, Sen. Eugene Millikin of Colorado, and with a second from Harold Burton, an African American delegate from Harlem. Burton was the only African American identified as a delegate in *Presidential Nominating Politics in 1952*, a scholarly work by Paul T. David of the Brookings Institution and other political scientists who studied the Democratic and Republican nominating conventions that year. David and his coauthors did mention other African American delegates in related regional studies, but in the first volume of their work, which focused on the national scene, they provided no quantification or summary of participation by African Americans, Mexican Americans, or other minority groups in the Republican National Convention.[39]

After the convention, Texas Republicans returned to the Lone Star State and began work for the national elections in November. The Zweifel faction joined the Porter faction in "a harmony meeting," pledging to campaign together for the election of Eisenhower and Nixon. They began building a statewide organization, setting up groups in every county and precinct. In Beaumont Lamar Cecil teamed with his brother-in-law Randolph Reed and other local Republicans to organize the campaign throughout the southeast Texas area. Reed, running for the region's congressional seat, framed his own candidacy as part of the national Republican ticket, hoping to ride Eisenhower's coattails to victory in a region that by tradition voted heavily for Democratic candidates.[40]

While Porter and his group pushed the Republican program in Texas, the Eisenhower candidacy received a tremendous boost from Gov. Allan Shivers, the popular Democratic leader. He jumped ship during the election, publicly opposing the national Democratic ticket of Adlai Stevenson and John J. Sparkman and spearheading a "Democrats for Eisenhower" campaign. This move was a critical development throughout Texas, including southeast Texas. Shivers had lived in Port Arthur and had many social and political friends in the region, including Lamar Cecil and his two law partners, Quentin Keith, a Port Arthur native and former Shivers law partner, and James Mehaffy, who joined Shivers's "Democrats for Eisenhower" organization. For Governor Shivers and other Democrats, the tidelands question was a handy issue, a solid Texas reason for turning away from Stevenson and giving support to Eisenhower.[41]

Eisenhower, Nixon, and other Republicans campaigned in Texas, making speeches and raising money. O. Douglas Weeks, aforementioned author of *Texas Presidential Politics in 1952* and then chairman of the University of Texas government department, reported that political "sums collected and expended in Texas throughout 1952 were without precedent in the history of the state." While not having access to precise campaign finance records, Weeks estimated that "one million dollars were spent to carry the state for Eisenhower and were donated mainly by Democrats for Eisenhower." Among these were Oveta Culp Hobby and Jesse Jones of Houston and Sid Richardson of Fort Worth. Whether Lamar Cecil or Randolph Reed made substantial financial donations to the Eisenhower campaign is not known. They were affluent persons but not wealthy on the scale of Hobby, Jones, or Richardson. Cecil contributed much by way of time, expertise, and travel funds, and he may have donated cash as well. Reed likewise may have sent money to the Eisenhower organization, but he probably spent more personal funds for his own congressional race.[42]

In the southeast Texas congressional contest, Reed ran against Jack Brooks, a former Texas legislator who had defeated twelve opponents in Democratic primary and runoff races. Brooks campaigned as a "Loyalist" or "blue-collar Democrat" appealing to working-class voters and staying clear of the "Shivercrats" who supported Eisenhower. Reed took another tack, openly professing his conversion from the Democratic to the Republican faith and urging others to do likewise. In large newspaper advertisements, he explained that he was "born and raised a Democrat" but "cast his lot with the Republican Party" because the Democratic Party "deserted its time-honored principles, insulted the south, and stole the Texas tidelands." Pledging his solidarity with General Eisenhower on the Korean War issue, Reed promised to "do everything in my power to bring our boys home from Korea at the earliest possible moment and to keep them out of future useless wars." Reed placed heavy emphasis on his affiliation with the Republican national ticket. "It's time for a change," he said. "Let's make the change complete. Elect Eisenhower, Nixon, and Reed."[43]

On election eve Governor Shivers came to Beaumont and appeared at an Eisenhower rally at the city auditorium. Planned strictly as a Democrats for Eisenhower affair, the rally featured well-known members of the Beaumont business establishment, including lawyer A. D. Moore, lawyer Beeman Strong, advertising executive Jack Dahmer, insurance agent David Hearn, and newspaper editors R. W. Akers and T. T. Hunt. Randolph Reed, Lamar Cecil, and other Eisenhower Republicans were given no part in the program and received no recognition, even though James Mehaffy, Cecil's law partner, served as local chair of the Democrats for Eisenhower group and enjoyed the distinction of introducing Governor Shivers. Apparently Mehaffy and the "Shivercrats" decided that bringing in Republicans would be divisive and counterproductive.[44]

Even without Republicans, the Eisenhower rally drew a large and diverse audience. The crowd of seventeen hundred included at least twenty-five Democratic Loyalists, probably union members, who opposed Eisenhower and supported the party ticket of Stevenson and Sparkman. Before the meeting, Loyalists picketed the auditorium entrance, and when Governor Shivers began to speak they jeered and booed him. When spectators friendly to the governor tried to quiet the rowdy protesters, tempers flared and fistfights erupted. Police arrested four of the hecklers while the others yielded to the crowd that gave loud cheers and applause to Shivers as he continued his message of support for Eisenhower.[45]

Eisenhower Victory

The large and energetic crowd at the Beaumont rally proved indicative of a tremendous voter turnout in Texas on election day. Almost 2.1 million Texans cast ballots that day, as compared with 1.1 million in 1948. The Eisenhower/Nixon ticket captured 53 percent of the Texas votes, giving 24 electoral votes to Eisenhower and contributing to his sweeping victory in the race for the presidency. Across the nation he took 53.4 percent of the popular vote and won 442 electoral votes while Stevenson received only 89. In Texas, Eisenhower racked up big victories in most large urban centers, including Dallas, Austin, Houston, San Antonio, and Fort Worth. But Stevenson won majorities in others, such as Waco, Wichita Falls, Corpus Christi, Galveston, and Beaumont–Port Arthur, the last three being strongholds of labor unions and Loyalist Democratic organizations. Stevenson also captured majorities in rural counties of East Texas where large numbers of African Americans cast their ballots for the Democratic ticket.[46]

Eisenhower's victory in the presidential race did little to weaken Democratic power in Texas politics in other areas of government or, in the near term, to build a viable Republican Party. At the congressional level, for example, Texas had twenty-one district seats, all won as usual by Democrats. In the 1952 election, only one Republican, Randolph Reed, even ran for Congress, and he was soundly defeated. In the race for the 2nd Congressional District, Democrat Jack Brooks captured 83,267 votes as compared to 22,108 for the Republican Reed. In Jefferson County, where Stevenson led Eisenhower by 29,352 to 25,373, Brooks beat Reed 35,928 to 17,946. Reed won his home precinct, Averill School, 920 to 537, but lost by wide margins in "blue-collar" and African American precincts. At Hebert High, for example, black voters rejected Reed 960 to 29. Thoroughly defeated, Reed had the grim satisfaction of having bested his brother-in-law Lamar Cecil in the infamous Sabine Pass precinct, where he won 45 votes as compared to the measly 1 vote captured by Cecil in 1944. Probably they kidded one another and together suffered verbal abuse from their card- and golf-playing friends. But Reed and Cecil, especially Cecil, had accomplished much. They had helped Eisenhower win the Republican nomination, a step that led the former general directly to the presidency.[47]

Now Lamar Cecil had new and powerful friends, men and women who ruled the Republican Party in Texas and were closely associated with Eisenhower. Immediately after the election, Cecil wrote to Eisenhower himself, sending "sincere congratulations on your splendid victory" and congratulating the American people "because a man of your character and ability has been elected President." Cecil proceeded to discuss the role of Texas: "We . . . are quite proud that our State . . . returned a majority in your favor. I can assure you it has been a long and hard fight in which I had the pleasure of participating in some small degree. The major part of the credit in my judgment should go to Jack Porter who has been an indefatigable worker in your behalf . . . and who has never spared himself in the fight." Perhaps Cecil sent a blind copy of his letter to Jack Porter, as Porter's assistance would be important in the future.[48]

Two weeks later, Cecil received a brief and perfunctory letter bearing Eisenhower's signature, thanking him for his "generous sentiments" and his support of "our Crusade." The exchange of correspondence between Cecil and Eisenhower mattered little in itself, but Cecil's letter demonstrated his understanding of Republican politics and his confidence in dealing with people of great power and prestige. Now Cecil moved in high circles, now he longed for more power and prestige for himself, now perhaps he yearned for a federal judgeship.[49]

Judge Lamar Cecil

After the 1952 Eisenhower victory, Lamar Cecil continued working in the law business, but he also capitalized on his newfound power in the Republican Party. He played the patronage game, exploiting and cultivating new friendships to get benefits for himself and fellow Republicans. In June, 1953, just six months after the Eisenhower inauguration, he wrote a patronage letter to William P. Rogers, the new deputy attorney general. Cecil recommended Glenn D. Gillette, a Washington, D.C., radio-engineering consultant, to fill a vacancy on the Federal Communications Commission. Apparently he had not met Gillette but sent the letter at the suggestion of other Texas Republicans. Cecil did know Rogers personally, as well as Attorney General Herbert Brownell, Jr., having worked with them on the Eisenhower team at the Chicago convention. He opened his letter to Rogers with "Dear Bill" and closed with vague promises to visit Washington, D.C.: "I am going to try my best to get up your way before too long, and I am looking forward to a visit with you." Rogers forwarded Cecil's letter to Sherman Adams, Eisenhower's top advisor, an action that indicated Cecil's access to the inner circles at the White House.[1]

Soon Lamar Cecil played a patronage card for himself. During the fall of 1953, when Congress considered legislation to create new federal judgeships for Texas, Cecil became a prospective nominee for one of the judgeships. He traveled to Washington,

D.C., where he made an appearance before the Senate Judiciary Subcommittee headed by Sen. William Langer, a Republican from North Dakota. Congress deferred action, but early the next year it created more than twenty additional federal district judgeships around the nation, including two for Texas—one for the Southern District and one for the Eastern District. The *Beaumont Enterprise* covered the story, speculating that President Eisenhower would nominate Joe Ingraham of Houston for the new Southern District post, while Lamar Cecil was the likely candidate for the Eastern District position. If Eisenhower named Ingraham and Cecil, they would be the first Republican nominees in Texas since 1931, when President Herbert Hoover nominated Robert J. McMillan for the Western District of Texas. The newspaper writer suggested that Texas Republican leader Jack Porter would recommend Cecil, "the Beaumont attorney who championed the case of the Texas Eisenhower delegation at the Republican convention in 1952." When questioned by the *Enterprise* reporter, Cecil indicated he would accept the judgeship.[2]

The Eastern District of Texas, where Cecil aspired to judgeship, was one of four districts in the state of Texas. The state was part of the Fifth Circuit, a larger judicial region that then included Texas, Louisiana, Mississippi, Alabama, Georgia, and Florida. Cases appealed from district courts were referred to the U.S. Court of Appeals for the Fifth Circuit in New Orleans, and from there to the Supreme Court of the United States. The Eastern District of Texas comprised forty-one East Texas counties and six division courts: Beaumont, Jefferson, Paris, Sherman, Texarkana, and Tyler, the last being district headquarters and home to the chief judge, Joseph W. Sheehy. If Cecil obtained the judgeship, he would be based in Beaumont and travel the district to supplement the work of Sheehy, a Democrat appointed in 1951 by President Truman. With a population of 1.3 million that included about 300,000 African Americans, the Eastern District shared a long history with the Deep South; most of its citizens adhered closely to the traditions of the southern caste system.[3]

Jack Porter, the Texas Republican leader, helped initiate a formal campaign for Lamar Cecil's appointment, sending a letter on February 17, 1954, to Attorney General Herbert Brownell, Jr., and suggesting Cecil as a prospective judicial nominee. In the

Eisenhower administration, Attorney General Brownell and his deputy William P. Rogers had official responsibility for judicial nominations, receiving, processing, and recommending them for the president's approval. Cecil's own nomination file, now in the possession of his daughter Grayson Cecil, demonstrated how he, his partners, friends, and fellow lawyers worked to advance his cause. Bar associations from Jefferson, Orange, and other counties in the Eastern District sent letters of recommendation, as did various Beaumont lawyers: Gilbert T. Adams, Joiner Cartwright, J. B. Morris, Will E. Orgain, Beeman Strong, and W. G. Walley, Jr., as well as Houston lawyers Dillon Anderson, Rex Baker, and Jack Binion. Many sent recommendation letters to Texas congressional leaders, including Sen. Lyndon B. Johnson, Sen. Price Daniel, and Rep. Jack Brooks, all Democrats, all of whom knew Cecil on a first-name basis, and all of whom sent him friendly letters of encouragement. The file contained no letters from NAACP officials or from persons that the author could identify as African Americans.[4]

Near the end of March, 1954, Cecil made another trip to Washington, D.C., on this occasion having lunch with Robert Cutler and Gen. Wilton B. Persons, both personal friends of and close advisors to the president. Cutler served Eisenhower as special assistant for national security affairs, while Persons was the president's congressional liaison. Cecil later recalled that he was "the guest of Bobby Cutler" at this luncheon, an event that clearly indicated his valuable ties to the Eisenhower administration.[5]

Soon after returning to Beaumont, Cecil played another patronage card, this time trying to deliver a favor for friends in the Beaumont chapter of the Texas A&M College former students' association. On April 19 he wrote to General Persons, telling him about an upcoming meeting of the Beaumont A&M Club that would honor football coach Paul "Bear" Bryant, who had just been hired by the school. "A great majority of the former students of A&M . . . were active supporters of President Eisenhower in his campaign for the presidency," Cecil explained, "and as you undoubtedly know, Texas A&M College contributed more officers to the Armed Forces during the last war than did any other college in the United States." Cecil asked for a letter signed by Eisenhower commending A&M alumni for their interest in athletics and their service to the country, promising that such a letter would be "widely publicized throughout the State and . . . be very helpful to us Republicans in Texas who are working towards building a two-party State."[6]

General Persons declined Cecil's request for the Texas A&M commendation letter, explaining that President Eisenhower could not comply for fear of offending countless others who were making similar requests. Persons reported that both he and Bobby Cutler regretted the decision, especially "knowing of the President's great admiration for Texas A&M College." Cecil did not get the commendation letter, but he received something more important to himself: a general offer of access from General Persons. "I . . . hope that on your next trip to Washington I will have the opportunity of seeing you again," Persons wrote. "In the meantime, I hope you will let me know when there is some other thing we can do or provide to be helpful to you." Of course there was "some other thing" where Cecil needed Persons's help: his nomination for the judgeship in the Eastern District of Texas.[7]

During the summer of 1954, the Eisenhower administration moved to fill the district judgeships in Texas, on August 6 giving the official commission to Joe Ingraham for the Southern District and a week later processing the nomination of Lamar Cecil for the Eastern District. Deputy Attorney General Rogers and Attorney General Brownell each sent formal letters to President Eisenhower recommending Cecil for the new judgeship. The two letters, taken together, provide a brief outline of personal, political, and security information customarily gathered to complete a nomination. In addition to biographical data, the letters confirmed that Cecil was a Republican and was recommended by party officials, including Jack Porter, Texas representative on the National Republican Committee, and Chauncey Robbins, assistant to the chair of the National Republican Committee. Rogers reported that the Federal Bureau of Investigation had investigated and cleared Cecil, while Brownell added a personal endorsement: "Mr. Cecil bears a good reputation as to character and integrity, has judicial temperament, and is qualified, I believe, to be a United States District Judge."[8]

Rogers mentioned that both Texas senators, Lyndon B. Johnson and Price Daniel, were members of the Democratic Party, an observation alluding to the importance of senators in the judicial nominating process. According to the Constitution, federal judges were to be appointed by the president with the "advice and consent" of the Senate, meaning that nominees had to be approved by the Senate Judiciary Committee. Also, in accordance with long-standing customs, judicial appointments were subject to "senatorial courtesy," a tradition that gave home-state senators Johnson and Daniel a virtual veto on Lamar Cecil and other Texas nominees. In Cecil's case, consideration by Johnson and Daniel, as well as any action by the Senate Judiciary Committee, was deferred until after a congressional recess that began August 20, 1954.[9]

On the day before Congress began its recess, the Eisenhower administration announced the nomination of Lamar Cecil for the new Eastern District judgeship. The *Beaumont Enterprise* reported the news, recounting a telephone interview with Cecil, who was in Chicago for a meeting of the American Bar Association. "I am delighted I have been nominated. I have been honored far beyond my desserts," Cecil said. "I shall endeavor to the limit of my ability to perform the duties of the office with diligence, impartiality, and courtesy to the bar and the litigants appearing before me." The newspaper noted that U.S. district judges were appointed for lifetime terms and drew annual salaries of fifteen thousand dollars. For Cecil, the judge's salary probably represented a substantial reduction in income, when compared to his earnings as a senior partner in the law firm of Cecil, Keith & Mehaffy.[10]

With Congress in recess, President Eisenhower took steps to place Cecil on the bench. He gave Cecil a "recess appointment," signing the official commission August 31, thus allowing him to commence service immediately and thereby deferring confirmation by the Senate. Why the Eisenhower administration gave Cecil a recess appointment is not known. Perhaps Brownell and the others wanted Cecil to begin service quickly to take care of a backlog of judicial work. Or maybe they wanted to avoid some awkward political matter in the Senate, knowing that it was generally easier to get confirmation for a sitting judge than a mere candidate. In any event, Cecil began service in September, and two months later the Senate considered his name for confirmation. In November, 1954, Sen. William Langer and members of his Senate Judiciary Subcommittee heard testimony for and against a number of judicial nominees, including Lamar Cecil. Jack Porter, Republican National

Committee member from Texas, appeared before the committee and recommended Cecil "very highly and most favorably" and expressed his "full wholehearted endorsement."[11]

J. G. Sourwine, counsel for the subcommittee, reported that both Texas senators, Johnson and Daniel, had sent "blue slips" approving Cecil's nomination. In addition, Sourwine noted that Cecil was recommended by federal judiciary committees of the State Bar of Texas and the American Bar Association, the latter being critical in the nomination process during the Eisenhower administration. According to Sheldon Goldman, author of *Picking Federal Judges* (1997), Eisenhower was a stickler for the selection process, delegating authority but at the same insisting that judicial nominees meet all criteria and be cleared by all appropriate parties, especially the American Bar Association. Goldman also observed that Eisenhower wanted only middle-of-the-road candidates and tried to avoid those who espoused extremist views in government and politics. On matters of race, Deputy Attorney General William Rogers reported that he and his staff avoided judicial candidates who made racist statements or held memberships in radical segregationist organizations. Whether racial questions were considered in Cecil's nomination is not known, but such issues would become important during his term of service.[12]

In his report to the committee, Sourwine noted that Cecil's file included many letters favorable to the nominee but also "a single letter which might be considered in the nature of a protest." The protest letter was sent by Sterling D. Bennett, a Beaumont lawyer, cohort of L. J. Benckenstein, and Taft supporter whom Cecil had defeated for chairmanship of the Averill School precinct in 1952. As to the exact nature of the protest, Sourwine was guarded, saying only that Bennett was not critical of Cecil's legal qualifications or his legal conduct. Perhaps Bennett tried to embarrass Cecil, maybe alluding to his personal habits and repeating stories about his card playing, golfing, and drinking. Sourwine advised that Bennett had been invited by telegram to appear personally before the committee to explain his protest, but he had not appeared. Senator Langer, who chaired the committee, mentioned that he had investigated the Bennett protest "thoroughly" but provided no details. After more discussion, Langer and the other senators voted unanimously to confirm the appointment of Cecil.[13]

CHAPTER 8

Cecil was one of 178 federal judges appointed by Eisenhower during his eight-year presidency. The group included Earl Warren and 5 others for the Supreme Court, 45 for appellate courts, and 128 for district courts. In none of these instances did the president appoint a woman or an African American, though he did just that to fill two posts on the U.S. Customs Court, appointing Mary Donlon in 1955 and Scovel Richardson in 1957. In Texas, Eisenhower named three district judges, Ingraham and Cecil as already mentioned, and Joe E. Estes, a Democrat from Dallas. The appointment of the Democrat Estes highlighted a sore subject for Jack Porter, who complained repeatedly about the lack of patronage bestowed upon Texas Republicans. It seemed that Eisenhower gave the biggest rewards to Democrats for Eisenhower, such as Oveta Culp Hobby, who became secretary of the new Department of Health, Education, and Welfare.[14]

But Cecil received his judgeship and was very pleased. On the morning of September 9, 1954, he went to the federal courthouse in Beaumont for the official swearing-in ceremonies. "More than 400 persons jammed the federal building courtroom . . . to see Lamar Cecil . . . installed as a new U.S. district judge in a brief but impressive ceremony," reported the *Beaumont Enterprise*. "Mr. Cecil . . . the first Beaumonter ever to serve as a federal judge," the article continued, "turned his back on a rich private law practice to accept a lifetime public office of prestige and importance." Earl Black, president of the Jefferson County Bar Association, and prominent local attorney Beeman Strong made speeches praising Cecil, after which Judge Joe Sheehy of Tyler administered the oath of office. Witnesses included all three judges from the Southern District—James Allred, Allan B. Hannay, and Joe Ingraham—as well as other governmental officials, such as Texas Supreme Court Justice Clyde Smith, U.S. District Attorney William M. Steger, and U.S. Marshal Peyton McKnight. Jack Porter was there, as was Pat Tynan, who chaired the Republican Party of Jefferson County. Cecil's mother, May Cecil, attended the ceremonies, as did his wife Mary, his daughter Grayson, and his younger son Reed. The older son, Lamar Jr., was away serving in the army. Cecil took the oath of office, swearing to "administer justice . . . and do equal right to the poor and to the rich, and . . . faithfully discharge and perform . . . all the duties as United States District Judge under the Constitution and the laws of the United States, and . . . support and defend the Constitution . . . against all enemies, foreign and domestic. . . . So help me God." At the conclusion of the ceremony, the new judge spoke eloquently, idealistically, and perhaps prophetically, to those assembled. "If a will to work and a sense of humility and a deep abiding love of the law will help me," Cecil said, "I can assure you my undiminished efforts for the rest of my life will be to make a good judge in the truest sense of the word."[15]

In reporting the ceremonies for Cecil's swearing in as district judge, the newspaper made no mention of African Americans who might have attended, nor did it record any reaction among local black leaders. But Johnnie Ware and the other black golfers must have seen the news. Of course Ware knew Cecil personally, having served him several years in the locker room at the Beaumont Country Club. In addition Ware as well as Joe Griffin and Thomas Parker were postal employees; they worked in the same building where Judge Cecil had his offices and courtroom. By an interesting coincidence, Cecil took the bench at the same time that Ware and the other black golfers awaited hopefully the fruition of their first campaign to desegregate Tyrrell Park golf course. As noted earlier, the city administration had ordered the course opened to black players effective September 20. But on September 17, just eight days after Cecil was sworn in, the city rescinded its order and announced that segregation practices at the municipal golf course would not be changed for the time being.[16]

Also coincident with Cecil's assumption of the judgeship were events arising out of the Supreme Court's momentous decision in *Brown v. Board of Education.* Announced May 17, 1954, just four months before Cecil's inauguration, the *Brown* decision precipitated many campaigns by African Americans and others nationwide to desegregate schools and other public facilities. Samples of these campaigns were seen in front-page stories of the *Beaumont Enterprise* in September of 1954, the month that Judge Cecil was installed on the bench. Headlines included "Segregation End in Washington Schools Upheld," "Mississippi to Bar Negroes in Medical School," and "Solons' Views on Segregation Hearing Sought," the last story dealing with questions about whether the State of Texas would participate in Supreme Court hearings concerning the desegregation of public schools. Apparently the *Brown* decision and other desegregation issues were not mentioned publicly at Judge Cecil's inauguration, but probably he saw the questions looming.[17]

The day after taking the bench, Judge Lamar Cecil began hearing cases and at the same time dispatched a letter of appreciation to his benefactor. "Dear Mr. President," he wrote, "I entered upon duty yesterday as United States District Judge . . . pursuant to the recess commission which you have issued to me. I am unable to express adequately my deep gratitude for the honor which you have bestowed upon me." He went on to promise honorable service and good behavior, perhaps alluding to questions about his personal conduct. "I . . . promise you faithfully that no act of mine, judicial or personal, will ever reflect discredit upon this high office. My unremitting efforts will be directed toward being a good Judge in the truest sense of the word." A week later Cecil received a letter from Thomas E. Stephens, secretary to the president, thanking him for his letter on behalf of Eisenhower, sending best wishes, and expressing "every confidence that you will discharge the duties of your office in a satisfactory matter."[18]

Terminating his partnership with Quentin Keith and James Mehaffy, Cecil moved his personal files and other belongings out of their offices in the Bowie Building and into his judicial quarters on the second floor of the federal building. His new offices were large and comfortable, equipped with anteroom, bathroom, and a private passageway to the bench in his courtroom. The courtroom itself was majestic, with cork floors laid out in a checkerboard pattern and walls covered with alternating panels of black walnut and ebony marble. Two green marble columns with Ionic capitals flanked the judge's bench. To staff his office and court, Judge Cecil hired Hazel E. Pluecker as secretary and Andrew P. Cokinos as bailiff. The brother of city council member Jimmie Cokinos, Andy Cokinos served as sergeant-at-arms in the courtroom and held the title "crier." He opened every court session, announcing the arrival of the judge and crying "Oyez, oyez, God save the United States and this Honorable Court."[19]

Judge Cecil presided regularly in two division courts, Beaumont and Jefferson, and handled a variety of civil and criminal cases. Jefferson was a small antebellum town in rural Marion County of northeast Texas, while Beaumont was the largest city in the

Eastern District. By far the Beaumont court had the longest docket of cases and took most of Cecil's time. During his three-and-a-half years of service, Cecil's workload in Beaumont varied from month to month; in some instances he handled twenty civil and ten criminal cases, but in other months he had fewer than ten of both kinds. In the civil cases he knew many of the litigants, such as Employers Insurance, Kirby Lumber, and Gulf Oil, as he had worked for or with them as a defense lawyer. In criminal cases he conducted trials and when necessary sentenced guilty defendants to prison, often recommending prisoners be afforded job training. He presided over numerous naturalization ceremonies, on January 27, 1955, for example, granting citizenship to one Abder-Rauof Salem Sayied Ahamed and at the man's request changing his name to Alan Salem Ahmed. Generally Judge Cecil adhered to court traditions and enforced strict standards of behavior and decorum. But on one occasion the judge suffered a hilarious loss of dignity. According to a story told by Grayson Cecil, on one occasion the crier Andrew Cokinos fumbled the introduction of Judge Cecil, crying "Oyez, oyez, God save the United States *from* this Honorable Court."[20]

Fayson v. Beard

During the summer of 1955 Judge Cecil worked a relatively short docket in the Beaumont court. In the month of August, for example, he had fewer than ten civil and criminal cases. But he had responsibility for *Fayson v. Beard,* the class-action civil rights case in which black Beaumonters demanded desegregation of the Tyrrell Park municipal golf course. The black NAACP lawyers Theo Johns, Elmo Willard, and U. Simpson Tate had filed the original suit on June 23, 1955, while John Rienstra and George Murphy, white lawyers representing the white city government, had submitted their formal answer July 19. During subsequent weeks, both sides filed written arguments and other documents, after which Judge Cecil scheduled a trial with oral arguments for September 1.[21]

That Thursday morning, September 1, Booker Fayson and the other black golfers, along with black lawyers Theo Johns, Elmo Willard, and U. Simpson Tate, drove to the federal building in downtown Beaumont. After parking their automobiles, they walked up to the front of the massive neoclassical courthouse, passing beneath a large American flag suspended high in the air and alongside tall Corinthian columns that fronted the building. Maybe they noted the building's rich architectural ornamentations, federal shields, laurel wreaths, stars, eagles, scales of justice, sheaved stalks of grain, and longhorn steers. As Fayson and the others went through the front doors, they passed close to carved images of the Great Seal of the United States, on one side the American eagle and the words *E pluribus unum* ("From one, many") and on the other a truncated pyramid bearing the date 1776, the all-seeing eye of Divine Providence, and the words *Annuit coeptis* ("He has smiled upon us"). The American flag, the Great Seal, and the federal courthouse itself represented the rule of law and other high ideals of the United States, ideals that Booker Fayson, his golfing friends, and their lawyers wanted to realize for themselves. Inside the courtroom of Judge Lamar Cecil, Fayson and the others wanted to work the rule of law to collect on the promises of the Declaration of Independence and the provisions of the Constitution.[22]

In the Beaumont courtroom Cokinos opened the session with the traditional "Oyez, oyez," calling everyone in the chamber to rise to greet Judge Cecil, who mounted the bench wearing his black robes. After preliminary remarks, Cecil proceeded with the formal hearing, listening to arguments presented by the opposing attorneys, with U. Simpson Tate speaking on behalf of the plaintiffs and John Rienstra presenting the case for the city. Summarizing arguments he had devised together with Theo Johns and Elmo Willard, Tate explained to Judge Cecil that Fayson and other black Beaumonters wanted to play the Tyrrell Park golf course and more; they wanted free and unrestricted access to all facilities at Tyrrell and Central Parks on the same basis as white citizens. Rienstra offered a compromise, conceding that Judge Cecil would probably find that Fayson and other African Americans were entitled to use the two parks, but asking that the city be allowed to make reasonable rules and regulations for preserving racial segregation. The doctrine of "separate but equal" still applied in fields other than education, Rienstra argued. The city wanted to devise a plan for black golfers to play the Tyrrell course on Mondays or some other "colored day."[23]

The lawyers Tate, Johns, and Willard called two witnesses, Booker Fayson and William Narcisse, to testify on behalf of themselves and the four other plaintiffs, Joe Griffin, Thomas Parker, Johnnie Ware, and Earl White. Fayson, the insurance agent, testified first, recounting that he and the other black golfers had asked Mayor Elmo Beard and the city council on June 14 for permission to use the golf course and other facilities at Tyrrell and Central Parks but that city officials had refused, Mayor Beard having announced that "Beaumont isn't ready for it." Narcisse, the Southern Pacific laborer, explained that both he and Fayson went to Tyrrell Park golf course on June 20 and tried to pay their greens fees, but the golf shop attendant, Johnnie Barlow, refused to accept their money or to let them play the course. Narcisse also testified that he complained later to Reese Martin, the parks commissioner, but Martin had denied responsibility, saying that city council made the rules and he could not change them. After hearing the witnesses, Judge Cecil closed the hearing with an announcement that he would issue a ruling the following week.[24]

As promised, Judge Cecil issued his Memorandum Decision on September 7, 1955. In this nine-page document, Cecil summarized the facts of the case, evaluated arguments submitted by the opposing lawyers, and rendered his decision. "It is undisputed," Cecil wrote, that African Americans "have been . . . refused the right to use Central and Tyrrell parks . . . solely because of their race and color, pursuant to . . . custom and usage of the city of Beaumont." Johns, Willard, and Tate argued that the city's policy of excluding African Americans was unconstitutional, Cecil noted, that it denied black citizens their privileges and immunities, their liberty and property without due process of law, and their equal protection under the Fourteenth Amendment and other federal laws. For Fayson and all black citizens, Johns and the other black lawyers claimed "the Constitutional right to the free and unrestricted use and enjoyment of the parks."[25]

City officials admitted "with commendable candor" the right of black citizens to use the two city parks, Judge Cecil noted. However, the white lawyers asked the judge to give the city permission to fashion "reasonable regulations" that would allow such use "only upon a segregated basis." To support their "separate but equal" argument, Rienstra and Murphy cited the famous

Supreme Court decision in *Plessy v. Ferguson* (1896), a Louisiana transportation case, and two golf course appellate decisions in the Fifth Circuit, *Beal v. Holcombe* (1951) and *Holmes v. City of Atlanta* (1955). On these points Judge Cecil disagreed with Rienstra and Murphy, dismissing their contentions one by one. In the Houston golf course case, *Beal v. Holcombe,* the appellate decision had been rendered before the famous Supreme Court ruling in *Brown v. Board of Education* and thus did not reflect the principles brought to bear in that case. In *Holmes v. City of Atlanta,* black golfers had won everything they asked: permission to play the public golf courses on a segregated basis. But black citizens in Beaumont wanted more, Cecil noted; they demanded "free and unrestricted use" of the two public parks, with no segregation whatsoever.[26]

Judge Cecil proceeded to discuss the new Supreme Court decision in *Brown v. Board of Education* (1954) and its abandonment of the long-standing "separate but equal" doctrine of *Plessy v. Ferguson* (1896). In the *Brown* education case, the high court of Chief Justice Earl Warren ruled that all public school students were entitled to equal treatment, not only in tangible facilities but also with respect to intangible or psychological factors. Racial segregation of students amounted to "unconstitutional discrimination," Judge Cecil noted, "because of the impact upon segregated students of intangible or psychological factors."[27]

Judge Cecil then asked a rhetorical question: What about golf courses and other public recreation facilities? "What . . . is the current status of *Plessy v. Ferguson?*" To answer the question, he cited recent decisions of higher courts: *Muir v. Louisville Theatrical Park Association* and *Rice v. Arnold,* two pro-segregation rulings the Supreme Court sent back to lower courts for reconsideration, and *Lonesome v. Maxwell,* in which an appellate court had recently outlawed segregation on public beaches in Baltimore. In Cecil's view, these actions "are strong indications that *Plessy v. Ferguson* will not and should not be held to be controlling in the public recreational field." If discrimination in intangible or psychological factors was unconstitutional in public education, Cecil reasoned, the same principle must also apply in public recreation. Some might argue, he observed, that intangibles were less important in public recreation than in public education, but he dismissed that reasoning, pointing to inherent and unacceptable contradictions

—that "a little discrimination is to be condoned, but a great deal be condemned."[28]

In the conclusion of the Memorandum Decision, Judge Cecil gave complete victory to Fayson and the other black golfers. "I think the plaintiffs are entitled to the relief sought in this case," he wrote. Accordingly, he ordered the preparation of a decree declaring that Fayson and his friends as well as "other Negroes similarly situated have the right under the Constitution of the United States to the free and unrestricted use and enjoyment of Central and Tyrrell Parks in the City of Beaumont." Ruling that any city policy or practice contrary to this decision was "unconstitutional and void," Cecil ordered preparation of an injunction, a written order forbidding the city from ever again discriminating against Fayson and his fellow African Americans "because of their race and color" in connection with their use of Central and Tyrrell Parks.[29]

Headlines in the *Beaumont Enterprise* broadcast the news: "RULING GIVES NEGROES USE OF PARKS. City's Facilities Must Be Open Cecil Declares." The front-page story reviewed Cecil's written decision in its entirety, naming all the parties to the suit, recapping the various legal arguments, and quoting the judge's ruling. In addition, the newspaper observed that "Judge Cecil's decision is believed to be the first in the U.S. Fifth Circuit striking down segregation in the field of public recreation." In all likelihood, the newspaper reporter was correct: This was the first decision in the South ordering an end to segregation on golf courses, public parks, and other recreational facilities. If not, if there had been others, lawyers Johns, Willard, and Tate would have cited them for the benefit of their clients, and Judge Cecil would have mentioned them; that was the way the system worked. Later Cecil's ruling in the Tyrrell Park case would be cited in at least a half dozen other park and recreational decisions, in Montgomery (1960), Birmingham (1961), Tampa (1962), Memphis (1963), Baton Rouge (1964), and Jackson (1971).[30]

Reactions from Booker Fayson and the other black golfers, along with Theo Johns and the other black lawyers, were not recorded, but they must have been very pleased. They had cracked the color line for the first time in Beaumont and won the right to play the Tyrrell course on the same basis as white golfers. A few days later, the *Enterprise* reported mixed reactions in the white community, with some citizens accepting the desegregation order and others wanting to appeal Judge Cecil's decision to the Fifth Circuit Court of Appeals in New Orleans. The newspaper did not report a threat of violence against the black golfer Johnnie Ware, but his daughter, Linda Ware Kyle, remembered one night during the golf course controversy when someone burned a cross in their front yard on Pine Street. This incident of near violence demonstrated the risks of becoming a Joe Doakes plaintiff, when Ware and the others went in harm's way.[31]

For almost a week, Mayor Beard and city council members debated the appeal question, discussing the matter with their attorneys and hearing comments from citizens. L. K. Wasson, representing the all-white Beaumont Golf Association, favored the appeals process, as did Mrs. A. W. Lightfoot, a white community activist, who said she believed "the Negro citizen is entitled to certain privileges . . . the same as . . . the white people" but argued "that no court has the power under the constitution to enforce integration of one race upon another." But after consultations with the city's lawyers, Rienstra and Murphy, Mayor Beard and the city council decided not to appeal Judge Cecil's ruling. The council mollified the Beaumont Golf Association and other white golfing groups, authorizing golf course manager Henry Homberg to reserve the Tyrrell Park course from time to time for association tournaments. At the same time, Mayor Beard assumed a statesmanlike position, saying "the council has . . . reached the best decision for all the people . . . of Beaumont" and soliciting "the co-operation of the entire citizenship in the use of the Tyrrell Park golf course."[32]

On September 13, Judge Cecil signed the final order, a document prepared as customary by lawyers for the victorious party. Drafted by Johns, Willard, and Tate, the three-page order summarized Judge Cecil's findings, decreed compliance by city officials, and refused the city's request for promulgation of segregation regulations. In brief and powerful terms, the paper decreed that Mayor Elmo Beard; Mrs. Willie Brockman, the city manager; parks commissioner Reese Martin; and golf course manager Henry Homberg and their successors were "permanently enjoined and restrained . . . henceforth and forever from executing or enforcing any administrative order or policy" that might deny Fayson and other black Beaumonters "the free and unrestricted use of . . . Central and Tyrrell parks." In addition the order declared that Judge Cecil retained jurisdiction for the case in his court, so that any of the parties involved could refer to him any questions pertaining to implementation of the desegregation order.[33]

Two days later black golfers broke the color line at Tyrrell Park. According *Beaumont Enterprise* writer Bob Price, "Local golfing history was made at Tyrrell Park . . . as A. T. Miller and Junius Dautrive became the first two Negroes to use the Municipal links. The pair checked in around 3:30 P.M. and played nine holes." Miller and Dautrive were Port Arthur residents, Miller the principal of Lincoln High School and Dautrive a teacher in one of the local schools. That A. T. Miller should play the "first round" came as no surprise to people who knew him. With college degrees from Prairie View and the University of Wisconsin, Miller was an ambitious and articulate man who broke the color line in the graduate school at North Texas State College in Denton. Johnnie Barlow, then the golf shop attendant at Tyrrell Park, remembered details of those days when black golfers first appeared. On the occasion of the "first round," when A. T. Miller drove up to the golf course parking lot and got out of his car, a white man confronted him and threatened him with a pistol. According to Barlow, Miller ignored the man, brushing past him and proceeding into the golf shop where he paid his greens fee and commenced his golf game.[34]

A few days later, Barlow witnessed another racial incident, this time when Earl White, the disabled war veteran who played golf one-handed, entered the Tyrrell Park golf shop. Two white men confronted White, shoving and pushing him against a wall. The black community responded quickly to the mistreatment of White with a show of force. The next weekend a large number of black golfers—some said a hundred, others said many more—appeared at the Tyrrell Park golf shop, paid their fees, and played the course. The identities of the black golfers were not recorded, but Barlow remembered hearing they came from Beaumont, Port Arthur, and Houston. Probably they included Booker Fayson, Joe Griffin, Thomas Parker, William Narcisse, Johnnie Ware, and Earl White, the six golfers who won the desegregation of the Tyrrell

Park course. Almost certainly Fayson, Ware, and White were there, as they were inclined to be bold and even confrontational. According to Barlow, the show of force was decisive. Afterward black golfers played the Tyrrell course freely, except on occasions when the facility was reserved by the Beaumont Golf Association or some other group.[35]

White resistance to the Tyrrell Park desegregation did not die immediately. At least two groups wanted to circumvent Judge Cecil's desegregation order by privatizing the municipal park. Nola White, R. C. Adams, L. K. Wasson, and others proposed the creation of the "Tyrrell Park Country Club," a private club that would lease the municipal golf course from the city and restrict its use to presumably all-white club members. Harry Kowalski suggested a similar plan, complaining that black golfers were taking over the park and saying that he and other white people did not "want their families mingling with the colored people." Mayor Beard and the council rejected the privatization plan after consulting with attorney George Murphy. In turning down the privatization scheme, council member Jimmie Cokinos observed that the Tyrrell Park desegregation was no longer a city question because it had "already been decided in the courts."[36]

Beaumont Enterprise editor Robert W. Akers urged moderation on the part of all citizens in dealing with the park desegregation. "Adjustments will have to be made in a calm manner," he wrote, "and it is hoped that the change-over from decades of custom and tradition will be accomplished in a gradual manner." He believed local African Americans would "cooperate in this moderate approach" and reminded all his readers that Booker Fayson and his black friends had targeted only two parks, Central and Tyrrell. "Let it be noted," he said, that Fayson's petition "might have covered ALL the parks and ALL recreation facilities. If it had, it seems logical to believe that too might have been granted. So the Negro citizens themselves have so far contributed a spirit of gradualism."[37]

Akers's prose was a bit awkward, but his thoughts were sound. The Fayson group had gained a small victory, but probably they could have won much more. If the opposing parties in the Fayson suit saw Akers's column, each would have had different reactions. Mayor Beard and other white city officials could feel thankful they did not have to handle the desegregation of swimming pools, libraries, restrooms, and other municipal facilities, at least for the time being. On the other hand, Fayson and other black Beaumonters may have felt they had "left money on the table," that if they had widened their campaign, they could have won the desegregation of all city facilities. But Booker Fayson, Joe Griffin, William Narcisse, Thomas Parker, Johnnie Ware, and Earl White did win the right to play golf at Tyrrell Park, something they had wanted for a long time. Lawyers Theo Johns and Elmo Willard, along with Dr. Ed Sprott, Pauline Brackeen, and other local NAACP officials, must have been pleased. With the help of U. Simpson Tate and the national NAACP, the Beaumonters had learned to work the federal justice system for the benefit of all African Americans. In addition they had found Lamar Cecil, a white judge able and willing to wield judicial power on their behalf.[38]

The Akers column appeared September 16, but probably Judge Cecil did not see it, as he was getting ready to leave town the next day for an extended vacation. Cecil had never been to Europe, and his wife Mary persuaded him that now the time and circumstances were right. They would take their daughter, Grayson, and younger son, Reed, to Germany to visit their older son, Lamar Jr., who was serving in the U.S. Army. In addition, they would make a seven-week "Grand Tour," crossing the ocean by luxury liner; visiting London, Paris, Rome, and Madrid; and seeing the sights. Grayson Cecil remembered that her father was reluctant to make the trip but bowed to the wishes of his wife, who had made all the arrangements.[39]

On September 17, just four days after signing the Tyrrell Park desegregation order, Judge Cecil and his family boarded a train in Beaumont and settled themselves for the long ride to New York. Perhaps, as the train pulled away from the station and headed east, Cecil thought about his desegregation order in the Fayson case and the changes it produced. Did he think about Booker Fayson, Johnnie Ware, and other black golfers and how they rejoiced? Did he consider L. K. Wasson and other white golfers and how desegregation would disturb their pleasures at Tyrrell Park? Desegregation at the municipal golf course made no difference to Cecil personally, as he and his friends would play their

CHAPTER 8

golf at the all-white Beaumont Country Club. Did he consider the wider implications of his actions? Did he recognize how the caste system pervaded the lives of all southeast Texans? Did he anticipate that his desegregation of the golf course was only the first of many steps that would be taken to break the caste system? Did he speculate about future civil rights cases, perhaps sensing that the black lawyers Johns, Willard, and Tate would bring more cases to his court? Probably, as the train passed over city streets and crossed the wide river, Judge Cecil sat back, lit a cigarette, and ordered a drink.

Epilogue

Six months after winning the desegregation of Central and Tyrrell Parks, lawyers Theo Johns and Elmo Willard returned to the court of Judge Lamar Cecil and renewed their attack on the southern caste system. This time they went after a bigger prize—the desegregation of Lamar State College of Technology in Beaumont, Texas. Lamar then was an all-white institution offering both academic and vocational programs. Founded in 1923 as a junior college, Lamar became a four-year state college with a separate board of regents in 1949. Enabling legislation conformed the college to the rules and customs of the caste system, designating Lamar as "a co-educational institution of higher learning for the white youth of this State."[1]

During the late 1940s and early 1950s, African Americans in Beaumont worked to improve education opportunities and attempted to desegregate Lamar College, an effort that resulted in the opening of a black branch of the college on the Charlton-Pollard High School campus. But the branch was short-lived, and the needs and desires of the black community were not satisfied. In 1952 James Briscoe, a graduate of Charlton-Pollard High, tried to enroll at Lamar but was refused. During July and August of 1955, local NAACP leaders renewed the Lamar desegregation campaign, an effort detailed and discussed by Amilcar Shabazz in *Advancing Democracy: African Americans and the Struggle for Access and Equity in Higher Education in Texas* (2004). In the new campaign, NAACP leaders initiated a three-step program: petitioning for change, attempting to enroll, and filing suit. As noted earlier,

D. A. Davis, a white minister from Port Arthur, as well as Dr. Sprott, Theo Johns, and other local black leaders appeared at a board of regents' meeting on August 23, 1955, and asked for admission of seven black students. College president F. L. McDonald, speaking on behalf of the regents, denied their request, citing the whites-only provision of the enabling legislation and the overcrowded conditions on the campus. Known then as "Lamar Tech," the college enrolled about five thousand students. Publicly rebuffed by college officials, the NAACP group at the same time accomplished another important task. Several of the prospective black students, including Versie Jackson and James Anthony Cormier, attempted to register for the fall semester; they filled out applications, provided high school transcripts, and offered tuition fees. College registrar Celeste Kitchen rejected their applications, sending them letters and citing the same reasons outlined by Dr. McDonald. The exclusion of Jackson and Cormier because of color alone laid the essential groundwork for a federal lawsuit, a lawsuit in which black Beaumonters would attempt to use federal judicial power to attack the state laws and customs of the caste system and to break the color line at Lamar Tech.[2]

Like the golf course case, the litigation campaign to desegregate Lamar Tech was a team effort involving black plaintiffs, black lawyers, and black leaders in the local and state offices of the NAACP. Versie Jackson and James Anthony Cormier, the two students who tried to register, became classic Joe Doakes plaintiffs as described by Thurgood Marshall. They believed in their cause, they put their names on the line, and they went in harm's way. Versie Jackson was a twenty-six-year-old woman who had graduated from a Beaumont high school in 1948 and had already completed about thirty hours of college work at Texas Southern University in Houston. Anthony Cormier, a recent graduate of Blessed Sacrament High School, wanted to attend Lamar to study electrical engineering. He was the son of Wesley and Viola Cormier, both active members of the local NAACP chapter. The selection of young Cormier as a plaintiff shows the close involvement of the NAACP, a group led by Dr. Ed Sprott, Jr., Pauline Brackeen, O. C. Hebert, Marion Lewis, Maudry Plummer, Rev. G. W. Daniels, Rev. William N. McCarty, and others. The team included the same lawyers who had handled the golf course case: Theo Johns and Elmo Willard from Beaumont and U. Simpson Tate, the NAACP lawyer from Dallas. Tate played a prominent role in this case too, demonstrating the continuing influence of the Legal Defense Fund of the Texas NAACP.[3]

The black attorneys drafted a lawsuit against Lamar Tech, naming Versie Jackson and Anthony Cormier as plaintiffs and, as defendants, F. L. McDonald, Celeste Kitchen, and all members of the board of regents, a group that included Houston oilman John W. Mecom. Johns and the other lawyers composed the suit as a class action, demanding admission for Jackson and Cormier and for all other qualified African Americans. Contending that exclusion of African American students because of race was a violation of the Constitution and other laws, the NAACP lawyers asked the federal court to order the college to end its exclusionary practices and to admit black students. Booker T. Fayson, lead plaintiff in the golf course case, witnessed the papers as notary public, while Johns, Willard, and Tate signed as "Attorneys for Plaintiffs." Also listed as plaintiff's attorneys were Robert Carter and Thurgood Marshall, top NAACP lawyers with offices in New York City. Johns recalled that when he added Marshall's name to the papers, he was thinking that it would be "good to have his name on the petition." As it turned out, listing Marshall's name may have been counterproductive. The famous lawyer did not come to Beaumont for the case, but his name did serve as a lightning rod for white segregationists who argued that most black Texans were happy with the status quo; they blamed "foreigners" and "outside agitators" for filing lawsuits and causing trouble.[4]

On March 14, 1956, Johns and Willard filed the suit papers for *Jackson v. McDonald,* in the U.S. District Court in Beaumont. Of course, this was the court of Lamar Cecil, the judge who had ruled in their favor in the golf course case. Perhaps the black lawyers were confident of the outcome, believing they would get a favorable hearing from Judge Cecil. But there was a problem of timing. The Beaumont court was in recess until May 6. Judge Cecil was in Washington, D.C., on temporary assignment, serving as special judge in the U.S. District Court for the District of Columbia. Edith Flynn, Cecil's sister, resided then with her husband and family in nearby Chevy Chase, Maryland. She remembered that her brother Lamar and his wife Mary resided in a hotel convenient to the federal courthouse in Washington, D.C. She hosted the Beaumont couple at several dinner parties, one in which another guest, a physician from the Bethesda naval hospital, consulted with Judge Cecil about his hypertension and warned him of the dangers of the disease. The hypertension was taking its toll, Edith recalled, causing Cecil to suffer episodes of fatigue and shortness of breath.[5]

John Ben Shepperd, attorney general of Texas, and his office handled the legal defense for Lamar Tech in the *Jackson v. McDonald* litigation. Shepperd, a leader in the conservative wing of Texas Democratic Party, had been elected attorney general in 1952 and reelected in 1954. On April 5, 1956, he and Horace Wimberly, deputy attorney general, filed an answer in the *Jackson* suit, asserting six defenses and making an assortment of arguments. In one instance they denied the jurisdiction of the U.S. District Court and in another they outlined and recommended diversity in Texas institutions. They explained that already Texas offered three types of colleges—"purely white," "purely Negro," and "racially mixed"—that now students were free to make their individual choices. Lamar was a white institution, they said. It was planned and developed as a college for white students, under laws promulgated before the *Brown* decision, and was already overcrowded with white students. "To require a sudden reversal of all these plans," they suggested, "presents serious problems affecting the welfare of all students." Shepperd conceded that the court might rule in favor of desegregation, but he warned against precipitous action. As "a means of minimizing local trouble and turmoil," he recommended a gradual program, suggesting that blacks might be admitted as sophomores, juniors, and seniors in the academic year 1957–58 and freshmen in 1958–59.[6]

Several times in the defense pleadings, Shepperd attacked the black plaintiffs, black lawyers, and the NAACP, accusing them of arousing "turmoil and discontent . . . between the races." He ridiculed plaintiffs Versie Jackson and Anthony Cormier, describing them as "two puppets dangled before this court by the operators of a national racial organization." Referring no doubt to Thurgood Marshall and other NAACP leaders, Shepperd expressed disdain for the "inordinate desires of those officers in certain Negro organizations to chalk up a record of 'victories.'" These verbal attacks upon the NAACP proved to be indicative of Shepperd's policies and the practices of his office.[7]

The arguments offered by Shepperd provoked a hot response from the black lawyers. On May 4, two days before Judge Cecil was to reconvene his court, Johns, Willard, and Tate filed a "Plaintiff's Motion to Strike Redundant and Scandalous Materials." Here, step by step, they refuted all or parts of Shepperd's six defenses and asked the court to strike out objectionable portions. In one instance they found Shepperd's arguments to be "totally irrelevant, immaterial, impertinent, and redundant" and in another "scandalous, argumentative, and ridiculous." As to the assertion that Versie Jackson and Anthony Cormier were "two puppets dangling before this Court by the operators of a national racial organization," Tate and the other black lawyers judged Shepperd's remarks to be "argumentative, redundant, and irrelevant and . . . [having] no probative value."[8]

For the lawyers Johns, Willard, and Tate; for the plaintiffs Jackson and Cormier; and for Judge Cecil, the legal aspects of the Lamar Tech question were easier than the Tyrrell Park golf course case. Already two other four-year state colleges had been desegregated by federal court order. On July 25, 1955, a U.S. District Court judge, Robert E. Thomason, ordered the admission of black students to Texas Western College in El Paso, and Judge Joseph Sheehy of the U.S. District Court in East Texas took similar action on December 19, 1955, ordering the desegregation of North Texas State College in Denton. But the public and political aspects of the Lamar case proved much more difficult than the golf course litigation. During the summer and fall of 1956, when they worked the college case, Judge Cecil, the plaintiffs, and the lawyers had to face rising opposition from white Texans who favored segregation and opposed making changes in the southern caste system. Gov. Allan Shivers publicly denounced actions of the Supreme Court, Attorney General John Ben Shepperd attacked the NAACP, and numerous white groups organized citizens' councils with the expressed purpose of preserving the caste system in the Lone Star State. On July 28, voters in the statewide Democratic Party primary expressed strong support for continuation of segregation and the caste system. By margins of 4 to 1, Texas Democrats approved three nonbinding referendums that favored continuation of public school segregation, prohibition of marriage between whites and blacks, and implementation of "interposition," a legal strategy designed to shield Texas from desegregation rulings of the Supreme Court.[9]

Despite the growing controversies about desegregation, Judge Cecil proceeded resolutely in the Lamar Tech litigation. On July 30 he conducted a trial in his Beaumont courtroom, hearing arguments from opposing attorneys, listening to testimony from witnesses, and issuing a verbal ruling. U. Simpson Tate called Versie Jackson to the stand, eliciting testimony that proved she was a qualified applicant and that she had been rejected from admission to the college because of her race. Deputy Attorney General Horace Wimberly handled the defense for Lamar Tech, bringing Dr. F. L. McDonald, the college president, to testify. Dr. McDonald confirmed that he had rejected Mrs. Jackson because of her race, explaining he had taken this action because of the "whites-only" provision of the law founding the college and because of instructions from the board of regents. At the conclusion of the proceedings, Judge Cecil announced a sweeping victory for the black litigants. "Negroes are eligible to be enrolled at Lamar Tech providing they meet the college requirements," Cecil said. "They are to receive no special favors, but are to be treated like all other United States citizens."[10]

Judge Cecil issued an injunction against Lamar State College of Technology, ordering school officials to stop discriminating against black students. In addition he expressed his intentions clearly and publicly to follow the rule of law. "The Supreme Court has ruled that discrimination in the field of education, at any level, is unconstitutional," he said. "The separate but equal [principle] is no longer in effect, whether we like it or not. We must follow the Supreme Court of the United States. I will follow the Supreme Court as long as I sit here."[11]

On August 30, about three weeks before the college was to begin fall registration, Judge Cecil released his "Findings of Fact and Conclusions of Law" and signed his "Order." In these two documents he outlawed discrimination against black students and ordered that Versie Jackson, Anthony Cormier, and others be admitted to the college beginning with the upcoming fall term. The attorney general filed a motion with Judge Cecil, asking him to suspend his desegregation order pending the results of an appeal the state had filed already with the Fifth Circuit Court in New Orleans. But Judge Cecil denied the state's motion to suspend his order and thus allowed the black students to begin registering on the normal date, September 19.[12]

Registration by Jackson, Cormier, and other black students touched off a thirty-day period of turmoil on the campus and in the town. Segregationist partisans burned crosses on college grounds, picketed at campus entrances, published pro-segregation petitions, harassed black students, made threatening telephone calls to the black lawyers, and committed acts of violence against the town mayor. During these volatile times, segregationists in Beaumont received encouragement from the actions and speeches of the state's highest officials, Governor Shivers and Attorney General Shepperd.[13]

On September 21 Shepperd opened an attack on the NAACP in Texas, sending his representatives and armed state troopers to seize files and membership records in NAACP offices in Dallas, Houston, Orange, Beaumont, and other Texas towns. The next day the attorney general obtained a temporary injunction from Otis T. Dunagan, a state district judge in Tyler, ordering the NAACP to stop doing business in Texas. The state charged the NAACP with "seeking to register students in various schools . . . by a method contrary to the laws of this state, and that such efforts tend to incite racial prejudice, picketing, riots, and other unlawful acts." Specifically, the state accused the NAACP, "a foreign corporation" with offices in New York, of failure to pay a franchise tax, illegal political activity, and barratry, the improper incitement of lawsuits. Among the NAACP officials named in the complaint was U. Simpson Tate, the Dallas lawyer who just three weeks earlier had helped win the desegregation of Lamar Tech in the court of Judge Lamar Cecil.[14]

Judge Cecil must have read the news about the attorney general's campaign against Tate and the NAACP, but his reactions are not known. Perhaps he saw Shepperd's actions as an attack upon himself and his actions in the Lamar Tech litigation. Clearly the Lamar case had many of the elements criticized by Shepperd: It was an NAACP effort to register black students in a school previously reserved by state law for white students. Furthermore, the connection of this case with the New York offices of the NAACP was undeniable, because the name of Thurgood Marshall had been listed in the suit papers as a counsel for the plaintiffs. But probably Judge Cecil was unimpressed by the attorney general and his actions. As Cecil had said in the Lamar case, the matter was clear: The Supreme Court had ruled that discrimination in schools was unconstitutional.[15]

Judge Cecil spoke out publicly on September 21 when he delivered a Constitution Week speech at a meeting of the local American Legion. He gave the Legionnaires a civics lesson, explaining, "A citizen should never think that the Constitution is static or immobile. It changes and grows." Changing interpretations of the Fourteenth Amendment were the cause of "all the current discussion about racial segregation," he observed. "From 1896 to 1954, a prior decision in the case of *Plessy v. Ferguson* held that . . . separate but equal facilities [were] sufficient to give a citizen equal protection of the law under the 14th Amendment." But since the *Brown* decision in 1954, he said, "the maintenance of separate but equal facilities has been declared insufficient." He urged respect for the judicial system, pointing out that as a private citizen he had a right to disagree with the Supreme Court, but that as a judge he must obey its rulings.[16]

Just three days after Judge Cecil spoke, and as registration proceeded at Lamar Tech, the controversy about desegregation was fueled by events in Beaumont. At a convention of the East Texas Peace Officers Association, a crowd of more than four hundred delegates heard speeches by Gov. Allan Shivers and Attorney General John Ben Shepperd lambasting the Supreme Court and the NAACP. Speaking to a large crowd in the Rose Room of Hotel Beaumont, Governor Shivers described the Supreme Court as "misguided" and vowed to defend states' rights in matters of public education. "We are going to see our colored brothers have an education, the best facilities, and see that colored teachers keep their jobs," Shivers said. In all likelihood there were no "colored brothers" in the Rose Room audience, except for Hughes Murdock and his fellow black waiters, who set up the chairs and poured the coffee.[17]

Attorney General Shepperd spoke to a morning session of the peace officers group, lashing out at Thurgood Marshall and the NAACP programs in Texas. "Whites and Negroes have lived peacefully in Texas for years," he said. "They will continue to do so if left alone." He promised his office "will not let the Ku Klux Klan rise again and it won't let any other organization stir up our people." Echoing the states' rights speeches of the governor and attorney general, the peace officers association passed a resolution urging the state legislature to enact new laws guaranteeing segregation in schools. Referring to the pro-segregation referendums approved in the recent Democratic primary, the resolution called on state legislators to pass "legislation implementing the public mandate."[18]

It was a remarkable coincidence in timing and convergence of opposing forces: the appearance of Governor Shivers and Attorney General Shepperd in the town where Judge Cecil had just ordered the desegregation of the local state college and on the same day that black students began attending classes. Shivers and Shepperd were Democrats, elected officials, executive and judicial officers of the state; they represented the political will of a white majority as indicated in their own election to office and by the recent referendum voting; they reflected forces that favored the status quo and the preservation of the caste system. On the other hand, Cecil was a Republican, an appointed official, and a judicial officer of the federal government; he represented the new Supreme Court law that served the interests of a black minority; he reflected forces that favored change and the dismantlement of the caste system. The federal judicial law was more powerful than the executive, legislative, and judicial law of the state. Judge Cecil wielded the greater power and wielded it decisively, but whether his Lamar Tech desegregation order would be implemented was a question that remained in doubt, at least for about ten days.[19]

With classes beginning September 24, the Lamar campus became a testing ground for the opposing forces—black students wanting change promised by federal law and white protestors defending the status quo of state law. It was a direct confrontation, a battle of sorts, with Versie Jackson, Anthony Cormier, and about twenty-five other black students trying to attend classes and white picketers attempting to stop them. Mrs. Gertrude Carruth of Beaumont and two women from Vidor, Mrs. B. L. Parker and

Mrs. H. T. Mercer, were among the leaders of the picketers, a group whose numbers ranged from several dozen to three hundred. For about ten days the white segregationists tried to block campus entrances, presented petitions, carried signs, and shouted threats, all the while observed by law enforcement officers and covered by newspaper reporters and photographers. The *Beaumont Enterprise* published front-page stories with headlines reporting "Picketers Escort Negro Students from Lamar," "Picketers Again Halt Negroes at Lamar Tech," and "Negro Student Says Picket Attacked Him on Lamar Campus."[20]

The lawyer Theo Johns stepped out front as a leader in the final battles for access to Lamar Tech. He enrolled himself as a student in the business school, went to the campus, and crossed the picket lines. On October 2, Johns accompanied a young student, Clarence Sams, to the college to attend classes. As they attempted to drive onto the campus, white picketers blocked the path of their car and threatened them with violence. They beat and rocked the car, almost turning it over. One shouted to Johns, "Get out of here and stay out if you want to stay alive." When Johns called out for help from bystanders, one a local police officer and another an Episcopal rector, a white picketer shouted, "You're going to need a priest if you don't get out of here and stay out."[21]

Johns and his law partner Elmo Willard tried another tactic: They paid an official visit to Mayor Jimmie P. Cokinos, the man who had served as a city council member during the golf course litigation. Escorting two young black students, the two lawyers went to the mayor's office and pleaded for protection from the picketers. After meeting with the mayor, Johns spoke to reporters, saying, "Administrators at the college and the students themselves have been very nice. The Negro students have been well received by both. We do not want any publicity. We merely want assurance that Negro students will be allowed to enter and leave the campus unmolested." Mayor Cokinos responded positively to the pleas of the black lawyers: "I assured them the law would be enforced at the college, and city police will be posted there to prevent any outbreak of violence."[22]

Many white students at Lamar were offended by the actions of the white picketers and wanted them removed from the campus. Bob Megarity, a student leader, presented a petition to Dr.

McDonald, the college president, expressing confidence in his leadership and urging him to stop the picketing. "We believe the matter of segregation has been decided in the courts and is not long a matter of personal opinion," the petitioners wrote. "We feel a strong sense of justice and fair play, and cannot sympathize with any group which denies to any student privileges granted by the Supreme Court."[23]

Robert Akers, editor of the *Beaumont Enterprise,* echoed the call for law and order on the Lamar campus. In an October 4 editorial, he asked, "Who is running our city?" Was it "the duly elected officials and the police department?" or was it "a fringe of society [that] has resorted to the ancient recourse of men attempting to have their way by violence?" Mayor Cokinos moved decisively the next day. Responding in part to a direct request from college president McDonald, the mayor ordered police chief Jim Mulligan and his forces to clear the picketers from the campus area. "I want city police to take complete charge out there and remove the pickets. We will not tolerate mob rule in our city," Cokinos said. In carrying out their orders, the police arrested three picketers: Durel Franks, Leisel Shelander, and Mrs. A. W. Lightfoot, a former mayoral candidate and outspoken community activist. Mrs. Gertrude Carruth, a fellow picketer, protested the arrest of Mrs. Lightfoot and defended their cause. "Dr. McDonald is unduly alarmed," she said, "and not enough concerned over . . . the integration problem." She judged picketers as "fine citizens bent upon halting . . . an evil thing that would ultimately change and disfigure our entire American social order if allowed to run unhindered."[24]

Dr. McDonald favored strong action by local police forces and warned of mob rule: "We are not debating the issue of integration now. I personally regret the Supreme Court's decision on that matter. What we have to decide at once, however, is whether a state college in the city of Beaumont has the protection of the lawfully designated police force or is it to be dictated by a mob." After visiting the campus and conferring with Dr. McDonald, Mayor Cokinos agreed that the situation had "explosive possibilities." It was an explosive situation indeed, especially for Mayor Cokinos. One night unknown persons threw a Molotov cocktail at his house on Hazel Street, and later someone bombed his church, using a dynamite charge that damaged the front doors and windows of Saint Michael's Greek Orthodox Church. Judge Cecil himself suffered at least one threat of violence, when the FBI reported that someone might attack his residence on Broadway Street.[25]

Actions by Dr. McDonald, Mayor Cokinos, and Beaumont police solved the picket line problems at Lamar Tech and allowed white and black students to attend classes without being molested. But those who protested desegregation expressed their views elsewhere. Two of the picketers, Mrs. Gertrude Carruth of Beaumont and Mrs. H. T. Mercer, published statements in the local newspaper. Mrs. Carruth protested "this integration movement as UTTERLY EVIL AND TOTALLY FOREIGN to every American concept of Christian society," while Mrs. Mercer condemned desegregation as "proceedings that would eventually destroy the white race of people." Other local segregationists organized a Beaumont chapter of the White Citizens Council for the expressed purpose campaigning against integration in public schools. In a meeting on October 16 at the Sportatorium boxing arena, a crowd of six hundred heard Dr. H. E. Masters of Kilgore lambaste the idea of school desegregation and rail against the prospect of intermarriage between the races. Covering events that night at the Sportatorium, the *Beaumont Enterprise* reported a "macabre" decoration: Mayor Cokinos hung in effigy, a black figure strung up with a white rope and bearing a sign with the name "Cokinos."[26]

At the same time, Mayor Cokinos received warm praise for his strong actions and those of the Beaumont Police Department. Robert Akers, editor of the *Beaumont Enterprise;* Earl Tipton, president of the student council; and J. E. "Johnny" Flowers, labor leader and president of the Beaumont Building and Trades Council, all thanked him publicly for restoring law and order on the campus. Certainly the mayor and police department deserved commendation, as their vigorous enforcement of the law ended the picket problems at Lamar Tech and, more importantly, may have averted a repetition of the 1943 race riot.[27]

The Lamar Tech case was finalized later when the U.S. Fifth Circuit Court of Appeals dismissed the state's appeal and affirmed the desegregation order handed down by Judge Cecil. In the meantime, more black students enrolled at the college and desegregation there was ensured. After their 1956 victory in the college case, however, leaders in the local NAACP suspended their litigation program. In Beaumont and elsewhere in Texas, the NAACP curbed many of its activities in the face of mounting opposition from white governmental officials. Using barratry and other charges, the attorney general obtained a permanent injunction against the NAACP and effectively shut down most of its legal activities. In addition the state legislature in 1957 passed several pro-segregation bills, one that targeted unnamed civil rights organizations and threatened publication of membership lists. Later, during the early 1960s, NAACP leaders and other African Americans in Texas would resume a broad civil rights program. In Beaumont Pauline Brackeen, Collis Cannon, Rev. G. W. Daniels, Theodore Johns, Rev. William N. McCarty, Edward Moore, Cleveland Nisby, Maudry Plummer, Dr. Ed Sprott, Jr., Elmo Willard, and others would instigate and coordinate a number of activities, conducting sit-ins at lunch counters, negotiating for opening of public facilities, filing suit for desegregation of public schools, and finally celebrating many new freedoms ensured by the passage of the 1964 Civil Rights Act.[28]

The conclusion of the Lamar Tech case marked the end of a three-way judicial relationship among Lamar Cecil, "the receptive federal judge"; Theo Johns and Elmo Willard, "the crusading lawyers"; and Booker Fayson, Versie Jackson, and other "Joe Doakes" plaintiffs. But the three parties alluded to by Thurgood Marshall had produced significant changes. Using the new law of the Supreme Court, they had started breaking down the southern caste system in Beaumont and southeast Texas. Now black students matriculated freely at Lamar Tech, and now black citizens enjoyed the unrestricted use of the tennis courts at Central Park and the golf course at Tyrrell Park.

Among the six black golfers in the Fayson suit, four—Booker Fayson, Joe Griffin, Johnnie Ware, and Earl White—collected handsomely on their litigation victory and enjoyed playing the Tyrrell course many times. Such was not the case for the other two, as Thomas A. Parker died in 1959 and William Narcisse apparently gave up the game. Later Earl White married Geraldine Malbrough and moved with her to California, where they settled in Richmond and had three children. White perfected his one-handed golf game, eventually reducing his handicap to 13 and becoming known as "the one-armed bandit," a nickname alluding to his golfing and betting skills. In later years he spoke with pride about having played golf with Charlie Sifford and Jim Dent, both prominent black professionals, and having lost a twenty-dollar golfing wager to baseball legend Willie Mays.[29]

Henry Durham, an outstanding black golfer in the Beaumont area, benefited early from the desegregation of the local municipal golf course. As a boy in Lufkin, Texas, Durham had learned the game while caddying at the whites-only country club; using hand-me-down clubs, he played the "shadow game," going around the club links when they were closed to members. In about 1958, Durham heard that Tyrrell Park was open to black golfers, and he began driving to Beaumont on weekends to play the municipal course. Later he moved to Port Arthur, commenced a machinist career at the Texaco refinery, and became a regular player at the Tyrrell course. For a long time he enjoyed a weekly game with three other black golfers: Joe Smith, a Beaumont schoolteacher; Duke Jackson, a Beaumont machinist; and A. T. Miller, the Port Arthur school principal who had played "the first round" at Tyrrell Park.[30]

In the beginning, Durham remembered, African Americans were not accepted as members in the Beaumont Golf Association or permitted to play their tournaments. Instead black golfers formed the Tri-City Golf Association, a group composed of players from Beaumont, Orange, and Port Arthur and one that hosted tournaments that drew other black golfers from Houston and Galveston. The Tri-City tournaments at Tyrrell Park were well organized, on some occasions with prizes and refreshments furnished by the local Budweiser beer distributor. At other times, when tournament rounds were complete, the players retired to the Appomattox Club on Harriot Street for food, fellowship, and awards ceremonies. Durham played the Tri-City tournaments many years, as did other Beaumont golfers, including Robert Gray, Curtis Linton, Ed Moore, Robert Williams, and Tom Stallings, as well as Booker Fayson, Joe Griffin, and Johnnie Ware. Among the last three, Durham recalled Joe Griffin as the most consistent player, often scoring in the mid-eighties. Griffin loved golf, including its etiquette, rituals, and ideals of self-discipline, traditions that he transmitted to his sons, Vernon, Tony, and

J. P. Jr., who learned the game while caddying for their father and his friends at the Tyrrell course. In addition Griffin taught the game to his wife Elizabeth, who became an avid and competent golfer. Durham remembers "Liz" Griffin as one of the first African American women in Beaumont to become a bona fide golfer.[31]

Judge Lamar Cecil lived only about eighteen months after handling the Lamar Tech litigation. He presided in his courtrooms in Beaumont and Jefferson, went to his clubs, and helped Mary take care of their family and social obligations. He consulted regularly with Dr. Jay C. Crager, a cardiologist, about his heart disease and hypertension, conditions that worsened and caused repeated episodes of fatigue and shortness of breath. In the mornings, he often stayed longer in bed, reading newspapers and drinking coffee. Frequently Dr. Julian Fertitta came to see and cheer him, climbing the stairs to his bedroom and sitting with him as they sipped coffee and talked privately. Lamar Cecil and Julian Fertitta were close friends, sharing a love for golf, cards, and the club life. Probably they told jokes and stories, making fun of themselves and everyone else. Perhaps Cecil told Fertitta inside stories about the golf course and Lamar Tech cases. Maybe he discussed his personal feelings about civil rights issues, about the African Americans who wanted to change the caste system, black leaders such as Dr. Ed Sprott, Jr., and Pauline Brackeen, black lawyers Theo Johns, Elmo Willard, and U. Simpson Tate, Johnnie Ware and the other black golfers, and Versie Jackson and the other black students. Maybe Cecil talked about Governor Shivers, Attorney General Shepperd, and other white leaders who defended the status quo.[32]

In his Beaumont and Jefferson courtrooms, Judge Cecil handled a variety of civil and criminal cases. Many of the civil cases involved oil companies, railroads, and insurance companies, corporations he recognized from his long experience as a defense attorney. Cecil also knew many of the attorneys who worked the cases in his court, as the big companies often retained the services of local law firms. Among the firms was Keith, Mehaffy, McNicholas & Weber, the group founded years earlier by Cecil, and among the local lawyers was James Mehaffy, the second man Cecil added to his fledgling organization. Jim Mehaffy, like Lamar Cecil, was a brilliant trial lawyer, James McNicholas recalled, but for some reason relations between the two men were less than perfect. Perhaps they differed over who should get credit for the all-important Eisenhower victory, the event that facilitated Cecil's appointment to the federal bench. Cecil had teamed with Jack Porter and other Republicans to help the general win the nomination, while Mehaffy had joined with Governor Shivers and other Democrats for Eisenhower to help Ike win the election. Or maybe they differed over the terms, financial or otherwise, of Cecil's withdrawal from the partnership. Whatever the reasons, the two men were often at swords' points, exchanging playful insults and verbal barbs.[33]

Judge Cecil handled at least one more civil rights case, this one in Deep East Texas, where large populations of black citizens had lived for generations under the constraints of the southern caste system. On July 1, 1957, Titus Edwards, an African American, sued the city of Marshall for desegregation of a municipal park and its swimming pool. Edwards, president of the Marshall Youth Conference, filed a class-action suit on behalf of himself and fellow African Americans. Styled *Titus Edwards v. Charles Spangler, Mayor, et al.,* the suit papers were drawn by William J. Durham and U. Simpson Tate, the NAACP lawyers headquartered in Dallas. Obviously Tate and some members of the Texas NAACP were still in business, despite efforts by Attorney General Shepperd to intimidate and shut them down.[34]

The Marshall swimming pool case was assigned to Judge Cecil's court in Jefferson, Texas. Marshall was the seat of Harrison County, while Jefferson, just twenty miles due north, was the seat of Marion County. The combined populations of the two contiguous counties amounted to about fifty-eight thousand, with African Americans comprising more than 52 percent of the total population. With a relatively large black population and strong traditions of the caste system, the town of Marshall and its swimming pool must have been a potentially dangerous target for Tate and the NAACP, especially in view of rising opposition from Governor Shivers, Attorney General Shepperd, various White Citizens Councils, and other segregationists. Perhaps it was cold calculation on the part of Tate, having won two cases in Judge Cecil's court in Beaumont and believing the judge would be favorable to him and his black clients even in a swimming pool case in Deep East Texas.[35]

In the Defendant's Answer, the city readily acknowledged its segregation policy at the municipal swimming pool but strongly urged its continuation. "Marshall is located in the heart of East Texas . . . where segregation of the races in public recreational facilities has always been practiced," the city's lawyer wrote. "The Negro population of the city is . . . in excess of 50% of the total. In addition . . . two major Negro educational institutions are located within . . . the city, and these institutions bring a large influx of non-resident Negro students to the city. . . . It is very important that officials of the city maintain good relations between the races," Marshall's attorney continued. The city warned against desegregation, stating that "to allow Negroes to swim in the city swimming pool at the same time that it is being used by members of the white race would result in violence, bloodshed and injuries to members of both races."[36]

Apparently the prospects of race violence were real. On July 31 Judge Cecil conducted a preliminary hearing in his Jefferson courtroom, listening to arguments from Tate, the plaintiff's attorney, and from Gaines Baldwin, the city's lawyer. In addition he took testimony from Edwards, the black plaintiff, as well as white city officials from Marshall. The city pleaded for additional time to work out the problem and warned against the danger of violence. The local police chief testified that trouble would erupt if Negroes were admitted to the pool, and trouble might result in bloodshed. Judge Cecil believed the law favored the black plaintiffs, but he took city officials at their word about the risk of violence. While setting the trial for November 4, he denied a request from the black lawyers for a temporary injunction that would have caused the immediate desegregation of swimming pool. "I feel sure there can be no proper defense by Marshall officials, but . . . for the present, the danger of violence outweighs the damage to the plaintiff and others of his race," said Judge Cecil. "I would as soon be hurt or killed myself as to sign an order which might result in someone else being hurt or killed."[37]

Refusing to order immediate desegregation of the swimming pool, Judge Cecil gave Marshall city officials ten months to work out an orderly transition. But city officials had other plans. Moving quickly, before the public trial, they carried out a privatization program to eliminate the prospect of desegregation. During October the city administration sold the park and its swimming pool to private interests, after winning voter approval for such action in a citywide election. In the November 4 trial, Judge Cecil conceded the results of the privatization program, ruling the desegregation question was now moot and dismissing the complaint of Titus Edwards and the other black plaintiffs. In this way, white officials used privatization of city facilities as a legal means to protect the caste system and avoid racial integration.[38]

While Judge Cecil was handling the Marshall swimming pool case in his Jefferson courtroom, controversies about desegregation provoked hot debate elsewhere in the Lone Star State. Gov. Price Daniel, offended by President Eisenhower's use of federal troops in the ongoing Little Rock school integration crisis, sought ways to defend state segregation laws against federal intervention. During November, 1957, Governor Daniel proposed new "troop-school" legislation that would close public schools threatened by federal military occupation and authorize the state attorney general to defend local school boards when challenged in federal courts. Others rejected such proposals and suggested that resistance to school desegregation was unwarranted and unproductive. Dr. Frederick Eby, retired University of Texas education professor, observed that "this integration is the law of the land" and urged Texas lawmakers to spend their time trying to improve "our total education system." Dr. Walter P. Webb, a University of Texas historian who spoke to the annual meeting of Southern Historical Association in Houston, echoed the sentiment. Segregation in education was "a cause already lost," he said, ruled unlawful by "the highest authority in the land." Webb urged fellow southerners to accept school desegregation and work instead on political and economic development in the South.[39]

After the Marshall swimming pool case, Judge Lamar Cecil had no more civil rights cases. During January and February of 1958, he handled an assortment of criminal and civil cases and carried out routine judicial duties in Beaumont. On Friday, February 14, he had a long and arduous day, presiding in his Beaumont courtroom, wearing his black robes, and sitting at his high bench. Beginning at ten o'clock in the morning, he spent the entire day listening to lengthy arguments in a products liability case: *Sylvian Sonnier v. Indemnity Insurance Company of North America*. The plaintiff,

Sonnier, claimed he had suffered disabling injuries caused by Funacin, a medicinal ointment. Sonnier was represented by A. W. Dycus, a Beaumont lawyer, while the insurance company was defended by several attorneys, including James Mehaffy, Judge Cecil's former associate and verbal sparring partner. Late in the afternoon, while listening to testimony, Judge Cecil suffered a catastrophic and fatal stroke. Mehaffy and the other lawyers heard him gasp and saw him collapse at his bench.[40]

Mehaffy and the other men carried Judge Cecil into his chambers and laid him gently on a long leather couch. They called an ambulance, hovered about as medical personnel administered oxygen, and watched as the barely conscious man lived out the last few minutes of his existence. In this instance, as with many others in his life, Cecil comported himself with aplomb and spoke words that became legendary among his friends. According to James McNicholas, the judge revived himself momentarily, opened his eyes, looked up at Mehaffy and the others, then uttered his famous last words: "Screw you, Mehaffy, get me a drink." Thus Lamar Cecil passed away, unpredictable and irreverent to the end, but leaving behind a notable judicial record in which he helped reshape race relations in southeast Texas and improve the lives of many black Texans.[41]

NOTES

Preface

1. Marshall quoted in Howard Ball, *A Defiant Life: Thurgood Marshall and the Persistence of Racism in America* (New York: Crown Publishers, Inc., 1998), 381–82. The progress achieved by African Americans since World War II is summarized in Henry J. Abraham and Barbara A. Perry, *Freedom and the Court: Civil Rights and Liberties in the United States*, 6th ed. (New York: Oxford University Press, 1994), 321–26.
2. Marshall quoted in Ball, *A Defiant Life*, 381–82.

Prologue

1. Beaumont City Council minutes, June 14, 1955, City Record 0016, Tyrrell Historical Library, Beaumont, Tex.
2. Ibid.; *Beaumont Journal*, June 14, 1955; *Beaumont Enterprise*, June 15, 1955.
3. Mayor Elmo Beard quoted in Beaumont City Council minutes, June 14, 1955.
4. Mayor Beard and Theodore Johns quoted in ibid.
5. Ibid. (The 1943 race riot is discussed in chapter 1.)
6. Ibid.

Chapter 1

1. United States, Bureau of the Census, *Census of Population, 1950: Seventeenth Census of the United States* (Washington, D.C.: Government Printing Office, 1952) (hereafter cited as *U.S. Census, 1950*). The 1950 census shows Beaumont's population to have been 94,014, with 29.4 percent nonwhite. The *Beaumont City Directory 1956* ([Dallas: Morrison & Fourmy Directory Company, 1956], ix) estimates Beaumont's 1955 population to have been 110,000, with 32,000 nonwhite.
2. *Beaumonter* (newsletter of the Beaumont Chamber of Commerce) 1, no. 1 (1955): 1–4 (all Beaumont Chamber of Commerce materials are located in the Beaumont Chamber of Commerce Collection, Tyrrell Historical Library, Beaumont, Tex.); *Beaumont City Directory 1956*, introduction, x–xi.

3. Elmo Reed Beard obituary, *Beaumont Enterprise,* Mar. 18, 1997.

4. *Beaumont City Directory 1956,* introduction, vii–xxiii; Beaumont Chamber of Commerce, *Come to Beaumont* (marketing brochure), ca. 1955.

5. *Beaumonter* 5, no. 2 (1958): 1–4; Beaumont Chamber of Commerce, *Annual Report,* 1954.

6. *Beaumont City Directory 1956,* Alphabetical List of Names, 104–105, 123–24. The city council service of Venza, an Italian American, and Cokinos, a Greek American, demonstrated the immigration and assimilation of various ethnic groups, not only Italian and Greek but also Acadian French, Mexican, Lebanese, Jewish, and others, as documented in *Portrait of a People: An Ethnic History of Beaumont, Texas* (Beaumont, Tex.: Beaumont Historical Landmark Commission, undated).

7. Beaumont Chamber of Commerce, *Come to Beaumont.*

8. Beaumont history is surveyed in Judith W. Linsley and Ellen W. Rienstra, *Beaumont: A Chronicle of Promise* (Woodland Hills, Calif.: Windsor Publications, 1982); also in John H. Walker and Gwendolyn Wingate, *Beaumont: A Pictorial History* (Norfolk, Va.: Donning Company, 1983). Slavery, secession, and antebellum conditions in Beaumont are covered in Robert J. Robertson, "Beaumont on the Eve of the Civil War, As Seen in the *Beaumont Banner," Texas Gulf Historical and Biographical Record* 30, no. 1 (1994): 8–26.

9. Slavery in Beaumont is covered in Robert J. Robertson, "Slavery and the Coming of the Civil War, As Seen in the *Beaumont Banner," East Texas Historical Journal* 34 (1996): 14–29. The African American experience in Beaumont during Reconstruction and "redemption" is covered briefly in Robert J. Robertson, *Her Majesty's Texans: Two English Immigrants in Reconstruction Texas* (College Station: Texas A&M University Press, 1998), 43–69.

10. The status of African Americans in the South during the 1950s is summarized in James T. Patterson, *Grand Expectations: The United States, 1945–1974* (New York: Oxford University Press, 1996), 380–84. The development of Jim Crow segregation in the South is discussed in Edward L. Ayers, *Southern Crossing: A History of the American South, 1877–1906* (New York: Oxford University Press, 1995), 40–41, 92–100, 263–64; John Hope Franklin, *From Slavery to Freedom: A History of Negro Americans,* 4th ed. (New York: Knopf, 1974), 267–76, 320–22; Stephan Thernstrom and Abigail Thernstrom, *America in Black and White: One Nation, Indivisible* (New York: Simon & Schuster, 1997), 25–52; and C. Vann Woodward, *The Strange Career of Jim Crow,* 2nd rev. ed. (New York: Oxford University Press, 1966), xvii, 5–10, 43–45, 65, 70–116. The development of Jim Crow segregation in Texas is discussed in Alwyn Barr, *Black Texans: A History of Negroes in Texas, 1528–1971* (Austin: Pemberton Press, 1973), 140–71; and W. Marvin Dulaney, "African Americans," in *The New Handbook of Texas,* ed. Ron C. Tyler (Austin:

Texas State Historical Association, 1996), 1:46-52. Jim Crow practices in Houston are discussed in Merline Pitre, *In Struggle against Jim Crow: Lulu B. White and the NAACP, 1900–1957* (College Station: Texas A&M University Press, 1999), 16–19. The initiation of Jim Crow regulations in Beaumont is discussed briefly in Paul Isaac, "Municipal Reform in Beaumont, Texas, 1902–1909," *Southwestern Historical Quarterly* 78, no. 4 (April, 1975): 409–32. The 1927 "Texas Ordinance for Segregation of Races" is found in *Vernon's Annotated Revised Civil Statutes of the State of Texas* (Kansas City, Mo.: Vernon Law Book Company, 1963), vol. 2, *Cities, Towns, and Villages*, 276–77.

11. Ayers, *Southern Crossing*, 263–64; David R. Goldfield, *Black, White, and Southern: Race Relations and Southern Culture, 1940 to the Present* (Baton Rouge and London: Louisiana State University Press, 1990), xiii–xv, 1–6; Judith W. Linsley, "Main House, Carriage House: African American Domestic Employees at the McFaddin-Ward House in Beaumont, Texas, 1900–1950," *Southwestern Historical Quarterly* 103, no. 1 (1999): 17–51.

12. Goldfield, *Black, White, and Southern*, 2–6; Linsley, "Main House, Carriage House," 18-19; Thernstrom and Thernstrom, *America in Black and White*, 31–44.

13. Marguerite Yourcenar, "Ah, Mon Beau Château," in *The Dark Brain of Piranesi and Other Essays* (New York: Farrar, Straus, Giroux, 1984), 58–63.

14. The main features of the southern caste system during the 1950s were common knowledge to all Beaumonters, white and black, including the author, who is white. Other whites who remember the caste system and were interviewed by the author and/or provided written comments include Johnnie B. Barlow (Oct. 18, 2000), Leonard Bruno (Mar. 8, 2002), Jimmie P. Cokinos (Apr. 23, 2002), Woodson E. Dryden (June 14, 2001), William T. Faucett (Jan. 28, 2002), Benny H. Hughes Jr. (Feb. 1, 2002), Tanner T. Hunt, Jr. (Jan. 22, 2002), Ednita Lane (Nov. 21, 2000), James D. McNicholas (May 11, 2003), Nancy Brooks Neild (Feb. 1, 2002), John Terry Smith, M.D. (July 30, 2001), Mrs. Connor Smith (Apr. 16, 2004), Jerry C. White (Feb. 16, 2002), and Mildred Campbell Yates (Jan. 24, 2002). Black Beaumonters who recall the caste system and were interviewed by the author and/or provided written comments include Johnnie Antoine (Aug. 15, 2001), Theodore R. Johns (Feb. 14, 2000), Ed Moore (Feb. 6, 2002), Elizabeth Mouton (Nov. 21, 2000), Cleveland Nisby (Jan. 27, 2002), and Pat Willard (Feb. 20, 2002). Interview notes, written comments, and other materials are in the author's collection.

15. *Beaumont City Directory 1956*, Alphabetical List of Names, 177.

16. Franklin, *From Slavery to Freedom*, 430.

17. *Beaumont City Directory 1956*, introduction, vii–xxiii.

18. Ibid., Alphabetical List of Names, 11, 37, 582. W. F. Graham and C. F. Graham, Jr., developers of the White House department store, sold financial control about 1951 to Jerome N. Ney, of Fort Smith, Arkansas,

who installed C. H. Happ as general manager. Tanner T. Hunt, Jr. (interview, Jan. 22, 2002), confirms that the *Beaumont Enterprise* refused to publish photographs of African Americans.

19. *Beaumont City Directory 1956,* Alphabetical List of Names, 177, 312, 403, 514, 564, 603; Nancy Brooks Neild, interview with author, Feb. 1, 2002; Jerry C. White interview, Feb. 16, 2002.

20. Mildred Campbell Yates interview, Jan. 24, 2002.

21. *Beaumont City Directory 1956,* Alphabetical List of Names, 267. Tanner T. Hunt, Jr. (interview, Jan. 22, 2002), recounts the story of Elmo Willard working in food service at Hotel Beaumont.

22. The existence of the brothels was common knowledge during the 1950s to Beaumonters, including the author, Cleveland Nisby (interview, Jan. 27, 2002), and Tanner Hunt (interview, Jan. 22, 2002). The prohibition of sexual relations and marriage between the races is covered in Ayers, *Southern Crossing,* 96; Barr, *Black Texans,* 141; Bruce A. Glasrud, "Black Texans, 1900–1930: A History" (Ph.D. diss., Texas Tech University, 1969), 186–87; and Thernstrom and Thernstrom, *America in Black and White,* 42. Segregation in southern brothels is mentioned in Woodward, *The Strange Career of Jim Crow,* 102.

23. *Beaumont City Directory 1956,* Alphabetical List of Names, 282; *Beaumont Enterprise,* June 15, 1955.

24. Pat Willard interview, Feb. 20, 2002.

25. John Terry Smith, M.D., interview, July 30, 2001.

26. *Beaumont City Directory 1956,* Classified Business Directory, 31; Mildred Yates oral interview, Jan. 24, 2002.

27. *Beaumont City Directory 1956,* Classified Business Directory, 31; John Terry Smith, M.D., interview, July 30, 2001; Pat Willard interview, Feb. 20, 2002.

28. *Beaumont City Directory 1956,* Classified Business Directory, 55–56. Segregation in the public schools and exclusion of African Americans from Lamar College was common knowledge to Beaumonters, including the author, Tanner T. Hunt, Jr. (interview, Jan. 22, 2002), and Cleveland Nisby (interview, Jan. 27, 2002). Racial discrimination in Texas in terms of salaries, libraries, and facilities is documented in William J. Brophy, "The Black Texan, 1900–1950: A Quantitative History" (Ph.D. diss., Vanderbilt University, 1974), 26–62; and Neil Gary Sapper, "A Survey of the History of the Black People of Texas, 1930–1954" (Ph.D. diss., Texas Tech University, 1972), 401–402. Many black citizens, including Cleveland Nisby and Ed Moore, believe that white administrators in Beaumont discriminated against black schools during the 1940s and 1950s, but the author has not searched budgetary and other financial sources to confirm such discrimination.

29. The development of African American churches is discussed in E. Franklin Frazier, *Black Bourgeoisie* (Glencoe, Ill.: Free Press, 1957), 87–90; and Barr, *Black Texans,* 165–67. The development of black churches in Beaumont during Reconstruction is covered briefly in

Robertson, *Her Majesty's Texans,* 94–96. See also *Beaumont City Directory 1956,* introduction, xvi, and Classified Business Directory, 13–15.

30. *Beaumont City Directory 1956,* introduction, xvii–xviii. Segregation in fraternal and civic organizations is covered in Ayers, *Southern Crossing,* 42–43; Barr, *Black Texans,* 167; and Frazier, *Black Bourgeoisie,* 90–94.

31. *Beaumont City Directory 1956,* Alphabetical List of Names, 472. Rotary membership and the weekly Rotary meeting were common knowledge to Beaumonters, including the author and John Terry Smith (interview, July 30, 2001). Activities of Hughes Murdock and his staff are recalled by former employee Johnnie Antoine (interview, Aug. 15, 2001).

32. *Beaumont City Directory 1956,* Classified Business List, 17. Memberships of Judge Lamar Cecil, Randolph Reed, and other Beaumont elites in the Beaumont Club, Beaumont Country Club, and Town Club are recorded in club rosters in the author's collection. Private club membership benefits such as "liquor-by-the-drink" and income tax deductibility of dues were well known to Beaumonters, including the author and Benny H. Hughes, Jr. (interview, Feb. 1, 2002).

33. Discrimination against women in the Beaumont Club, Beaumont Country Club, and other private clubs was common knowledge to club members, including the author, Benny H. Hughes, Jr. (interview, Feb. 1, 2002), and Mrs. Connor Smith (interview with author, Apr. 16, 2004).

34. The relationship of white members and black waiters was common knowledge to club members, including the author and Benny H. Hughes, Jr. (interview, Feb. 1, 2002).

35. Ibid. The symbiotic relationship between white employers and black domestic workers is discussed in Linsley, "Main House, Carriage House," 17–51.

36. Chamber of Commerce literature quoted in *Beaumont City Directory 1956,* introduction, xx; Tanner T. Hunt, Jr. (interview, Jan. 22, 2002). Early development of Stuart Stadium and the minor league baseball team is discussed in Ken Poston, "Stuart Stadium: A Tribute to Commitment," *Texas Gulf Historical and Biographical Record* 30, no. 1 (1994): 79–92. Subsequent development of the baseball team, including its eventual move to Austin, is discussed in Walker and Wingate, *Beaumont: A Pictorial History,* 165–69.

37. *Beaumont City Directory 1956,* Alphabetical List of Names, 15, 35, 96, 112, 217, 355, 367, 431, 454, 522, 560.

38. *Beaumont City Directory 1956,* Street Guide, 212. The friendship of Judge Cecil with James W. Mehaffy and others is confirmed by Mary Reed Cecil, interview with author, Mar. 16, 2001. Racial discrimination and segregation in housing is covered in Ayers, *Southern Crossing,* 40–41; Barr, *Black Texans,* 140–41; William H. Chafe, *Civilities and Civil Rights: Greensboro, North Carolina, and the Black Struggle for Freedom* (New York: Oxford University Press, 1980), 20–21; Glasrud, "Black

Texans, 1900–1930," 181–84; Barry J. Kaplan, "Race, Income, and Ethnicity: Residential Change in a Houston Community, 1920–1970," *Houston Review* 3 (1981): 185–86; and Woodward, *The Strange Career of Jim Crow,* 100–101.

39. *Beaumont City Directory 1956,* Classified Business List, 2, 12, 58. Segregation in transportation is covered in Ayers, *Southern Crossing,* 93–95; Barr, *Black Texans,* 140; Sapper, "Survey of the History of the Black People of Texas," 409–10; Thernstrom and Thernstrom, *America in Black and White,* 25–52; and Woodward, *The Strange Career of Jim Crow,* 9–10. Details of segregation in transportation in Beaumont, including the "White/Colored" signs on city buses, were recalled by Cleveland Nisby (interview, Jan. 27, 2002). Financial arrangements between Beaumont City Lines, Inc., and the city are documented in City of Beaumont, Tex., "Annual Budget, June 30, 1955," Tyrrell Historical Library, Beaumont, Tex.

40. See *Beaumont City Directory 1956,* introduction, xxi, on the appearance and operations of city hall; Naaman J. Woodland, "The Leadership of Mrs. Beeman Strong of the Beaumont Music Commission," *Texas Gulf Historical and Biographical Record* 34, no. 1 (1998): 35–47. Woodland, longtime member of the Beaumont Music Commission, did not recall seeing African Americans at music commission events during the 1950s (Woodland, interview with author, May 4, 2004).

41. City of Beaumont, Tex., "Annual Budget, June 30, 1955."

42. Ibid.

43. Discrimination in employment is discussed briefly in Thernstrom and Thernstrom, *America in Black and White,* 31–35, and documented thoroughly in Brophy, "The Black Texan," 99–127; see also *U.S. Census, 1950,* Income, Table 37. Differences between white and black Americans in occupation and income, as revealed in United States censuses, are discussed and detailed in Reynolds Farley and Walter Allen, *The Color Line and the Quality of Life in America* (New York: Russell Sage Foundation, 1987), 263–70, 280–81, 293–300, 313–14.

44. Occupational trends for African Americans between 1940 and 1960 are discussed and detailed in Jo Ann Pankratz Stiles, "The Changing Economic and Educational Status of Texas Negroes, 1940–1960" (master's thesis, University of Texas at Austin, 1966), 1–6, 21–26, 41–65, 150. The development of the all-black OCAW Local 229 is covered in Marcus Robbins, "Our Inalienable Right: A Brief History of Locals 229 and 243 Oil Workers International Union, Magnolia Refinery, 1937–1945," *Texas Gulf Historical and Biographical Record* 29, no. 1 (1993): 55–68. Activities of the black OCAW locals in Beaumont and Port Arthur refineries are discussed in Brophy, "The Black Texan," 163–66.

45. The early history of the NAACP, Negro Goodwill Council, and other local groups, as well as black leaders, is covered in Linsley and Rienstra, *Beaumont: Chronicle of Promise,* 98, 112–14; the leadership of

Reverend Graham and other black leaders is confirmed by Cleveland Nisby (interview, Jan. 27, 2002); *Beaumont Enterprise,* June 15, 1954.

46. *Beaumont Enterprise,* June 15, 1954; dedication of Wall Street library in Maurine Gray, *Beaumont Libraries: Then & Now* (Beaumont, Tex.: Friends of Beaumont Public Libraries, 1972), 26–27; City of Beaumont, Tex., "Annual Budget, June 30, 1955."

47. *Beaumont Journal,* June 14, 1954.

48. James Burran, "Violence in an 'Arsenal of Democracy': The Beaumont Race Riot, 1943," *East Texas Historical Journal* 14 (1976): 38–51; James Olson and Sharon Phair, "The Anatomy of a Race Riot: Beaumont, Texas, 1943," *Texana* 11 (1973): 64–72. See also Pitre, *In Struggle against Jim Crow,* 39–41. The Beaumont race riot is mentioned also in Barr, *Black Texans,* 189; Goldfield, *Black, White, and Southern,* 36; and David M. Kennedy, *Freedom from Fear: The American People in Depression and War, 1929–1945* (New York: Oxford University Press, 1999), 770.

Chapter 2

1. The existence of the black business districts during the 1950s was common knowledge to Beaumonters, including the author and Cleveland Nisby (interview, Jan. 27, 2002). The development of the black middle class and black business districts is discussed in detail in Frazier, *Black Bourgeoisie,* 20, 23–26, 47–53; Bart Landry, *The New Black Middle Class* (Berkeley: University of California Press, 1987), 2–8, 19–21, 41–57; and James M. SoRelle, "The Emergence of Black Business in Houston: A Study of Race and Ideology, 1919–1945," in *Black Dixie: Afro-Texan History and Culture in Houston,* ed. Howard Beeth and Cary D. Wintz (College Station: Texas A&M University Press, 1992), 103–15; William J. Brophy, "Black Business Development in Texas Cities, 1900–1950," *Red River Valley Historical Review* 6 (Spring, 1981): 46–47; and Brophy, "The Black Texan," 128–49, 207–208.

2. The black middle-class inhabitants of the Forsythe, Gladys, Irving, and Washington Boulevard districts are indicated in *Beaumont City Directory 1956,* Street and Avenue Guide, 90–92, 97–98, 122–23, 224–25. The black middle class in Beaumont is discussed in Amilcar Shabazz, "The Desegregation of Lamar State College of Technology: An Analysis of Race and Education in Southeast Texas" (master's thesis, Lamar University, 1990), 37–38, 46. Characteristics of the black middle class are discussed in Brophy, "The Black Texan," 207–208; Landry, *The New Black Middle Class,* 2–8, 19–21, 41–57; and Frazier, *Black Bourgeoisie,* 47–59, 86–95.

3. *Beaumont City Directory 1956,* Street and Avenue Guide, 90–91.

4. Business and professional inhabitants of the Forsythe district are listed in *Beaumont City Directory 1956,* Street and Avenue Guide, 57–60, 90–91, 125–26, 157–58, 215–16, and 221–22. See also Shabazz, "The Desegregation of Lamar State College of Technology," 44–45, for a discussion of the black business district on Forsythe.

5. *Beaumont City Directory 1956*, Alphabetical List of Names, 267, 299, and Buyers' Guide, 42. The development of rock-and-roll music and the role of black musicians are covered in Michael Ochs, *Rock Archives: A Photographic Journey through the First Two Decades of Rock and Roll* (Garden City, N.Y.: Doubleday, 1984), 34, 42, 92, 96.

6. *Beaumont City Directory 1956*, Alphabetical List of Names, 434, 520. Ray Pike's name is also shown as "Pigot" (*Beaumont Enterprise*, June 15, 19, 1955).

7. *Beaumont City Directory 1956*, Street Guide, 90–91, and Classified Business List, 58; Pat Willard interview, Feb. 20, 2002.

8. *Beaumont City Directory 1956*, Alphabetical List of Names, 38, 105, 153, 609–10.

9. *Beaumont Journal*, June 14, 20, 1954. The integration of the Texas League is covered in Bill O'Neal, *The Texas League, 1888–1987: A Century of Baseball* (Austin: Eakin Press, 1987), 108–109.

10. *Beaumont Enterprise*, Sept. 26, Oct. 18, 1954.

11. Ibid., Oct. 18, 1954. Congressman Brooks's career is outlined in Robert J. Robertson, "Congressman Jack Brooks, the Civil Rights Act of 1964, and Desegregation of Public Accommodations and Facilities in Southeast Texas: A Preliminary Inquiry," *Texas Gulf Historical and Biographical Record* 35, no. 1 (1999): 18–31.

12. The role of the black church is discussed in Franklin, *From Slavery to Freedom*, 425–26; Frazier, *Black Bourgeoisie*, 87–90; Barr, *Black Texans*, 165–67; and Brophy, "The Black Texan," 187–207. The development of black Catholic churches is covered briefly in Ada Simond, "A History of African-American Catholicism in Texas," in *Bricks without Straw: A Comprehensive History of African Americans in Texas*, ed. David A. Williams (Austin: Eakin Press, 1997), 309–22.

13. *Beaumont City Directory 1956*, Classified Business List, 12–15. The development of black churches in Beaumont during Reconstruction is discussed briefly in Robertson, *Her Majesty's Texans*, 94–96.

14. *Beaumont City Directory 1956*, Classified Business List, 21, 32–35, 47–48. African American life insurance companies and their agents are discussed in Frazier, *Black Bourgeoisie*, 58–59; Landry, *The New Black Middle Class*, 21, 41, 62–66; and Brophy, "Black Business Development in Texas Cities," 50–52.

15. *Beaumont City Directory 1956*, Alphabetical List of Names, 375; Dr. Melton quoted in *Beaumont Enterprise*, July 19, 1987.

16. *Beaumont City Directory 1956*, Alphabetical List of Names, 582–83; *Beaumont Enterprise*, Aug. 13, 1977, Sept. 7, 1986.

17. *Beaumont City Directory 1956*, Street Guide, 90. The dimensions and appearance of the White Building, virtually the only building of the black Forsythe district still standing, are estimated by the author.

18. *The Informer and Freeman* (Houston), May 22, 1954; *Beaumont Enterprise*, June 10, 1954. The litigation campaign of Dr. Lawrence Nixon against the all-white primary of the Texas Democratic Party is dis-

cussed in Richard Kluger, *Simple Justice: The History of* Brown v. Board of Education *and Black America's Struggle for Equality* (New York: Knopf, 1987), 137–38.

19. Pat Willard (interview, Feb. 20, 2002) recalls feeling slighted by a White House clerk, when the woman addressed a white customer as "*Mrs.* Jones" but addressed Mrs. Willard only as "Pat."

20. Phillips quoted in *Beaumont Enterprise,* Oct. 27, 1987; Oliver quoted in *Beaumont Enterprise,* Jan. 31, 1988.

21. *Beaumont Enterprise,* Jan. 31, 1988.

22. Ibid. White patronage of black barbecue restaurants was common knowledge to Beaumonters, including Jerry C. White (interview, Feb. 16, 2002).

23. The identity and names of the black business districts and neighborhoods were common knowledge to Beaumonters, including Cleveland Nisby (interview, Jan. 27, 2002) and Jerry C. White (interview, Feb. 16, 2002).

24. *Beaumont City Directory 1956,* Street Guide, 97–98. See also Shabazz, "The Desegregation of Lamar State College of Technology," 45. The presence and success of Italian American grocers, including their business practices, are recalled by Ed Moore (interview, Feb. 6, 2002). The prevalence of grocers of Italian, Greek, and Chinese heritage in Houston's black neighborhoods is noted in SoRelle, "The Emergence of Black Business in Houston," 107.

25. *Beaumont City Directory 1956,* Street Guide, 179–82, and Alphabetical List of Names, 223, 570, 581.

26. *U.S. Census, 1950,* Housing, General Characteristics, Tables 17, 18, 21. For a brief discussion of African American housing in Beaumont, see Shabazz, "The Desegregation of Lamar State College of Technology," 40.

27. *Beaumont City Directory 1956,* Street Guide, 122–23, and Alphabetical List of Names, 284, 400.

28. Leonard Bruno, interviews with author, Mar. 8, 9, 2002.

29. *Beaumont City Directory 1956,* Alphabetical List of Names, 281. See also Diana J. Kleiner, "Houston *Informer and Texas Freeman,*" and Richard Allen Burns, "Carter Walker Wesley," both in *The Handbook of Texas Online* (Austin: Texas State Historical Association, May 19, 2003), <www.tsha.utexas.edu/handbook/online/index.html>. While microfilm copies of the Houston *Informer* are available in the Metropolitan Research Center, Houston Public Library, Houston, Tex., no such collection of the Beaumont *Informer* has been located. A single copy (Jan. 12, 1935) of the Beaumont newspaper is on file at the Tyrrell Historical Library, Beaumont, Tex.

30. Franklin, *From Slavery to Freedom,* 424. The Charlton-Pollard annual, the *Rice Shock,* is on file at the Tyrrell Historical Library, Beaumont, Tex.

31. *Beaumont City Directory 1956,* Street Guide, 186; J. P. Griffin, Jr., letter to author, July 1, 2002.

32. *Beaumont City Directory 1956,* Alphabetical List of Names, 284, 400, and Street Guide, 122–23, 224–25.

33. *Beaumont City Directory 1956,* Alphabetical List of Names, 61, 177, 248, 332, 417, 579.

34. Outline information about the Appomattox Club and other local groups is found in Juanita Jackson and Jean Wallace, *A Directory of Black Businesses, Churches, Clubs, and Organizations in Beaumont, Texas,* a pamphlet issued by the Beaumont Public Library in 1981, and on file at Tyrrell Historical Library, Beaumont, Tex. The role of civic and fraternal groups is discussed in Franklin, *From Slavery to Freedom,* 428; Frazier, *Black Bourgeoisie,* 90–95; Landry, *The New Black Middle Class,* 59–60; Barr, *Black Texans,* 167; and Brophy, "The Black Texan," 209.

35. *Beaumont City Directory 1956,* Street Guide, 16, 118–19. The juxtaposition of black and white neighborhoods was common knowledge to Beaumonters, including the author, Ed Moore (interview, Feb. 6, 2002), and Cleveland Nisby (interview, Jan. 27, 2002).

36. *Beaumont City Directory 1956,* Street Guide, 48–49, 118–19, 198, 221.

37. NAACP (Beaumont, Tex.) Branch Files, 1951–56, Library of Congress, Washington, D.C. (hereafter cited as Beaumont NAACP Files). In these files are eighty-five letters between and among Beaumont NAACP, Texas State Conference of Branches of NAACP in Dallas, and national NAACP headquarters in New York, N.Y. See Sprott's letter of Apr. 22, 1952, and others. The leadership role of Sprott is discussed in Shabazz, "The Desegregation of Lamar State College of Technology," 53, 63.

38. Lucille Black, letter to Ben Rogers, Mar. 16, 1953, Beaumont NAACP Files.

39. Pauline Brackeen, letter to Lucille Black, membership secretary, NAACP, New York, June 12, 1952; see also Gloster B. Current, letter to Pauline Brackeen, Feb. 3, 1955, both in Beaumont NAACP Files.

Chapter 3

1. "Joe Doakes" and other such names are discussed in Stuart Berg Flexner, *I Hear America Talking* (New York: Van Nostrand Reinhold, 1976), 435; Marshall quoted in Ball, *A Defiant Life,* 181–83.

2. Dr. Lonnie Smith and other NAACP plaintiffs are covered in Kluger, *Simple Justice,* 236–37, 260–67, 280–84, 700–701.

3. The activities and risks of NAACP plaintiffs are discussed in Michael L. Gillette, "Heman Marion Sweatt: Civil Rights Plaintiff," in *Black Leaders: Texans for Their Times,* ed. Alwyn Barr and Robert A. Calvert (Austin: Texas State Historical Association, 1981), 157–59.

4. New Deal programs and Roosevelt's actions on behalf of African Americans are discussed in Richard Polenberg, *One Nation Divisible: Class, Race, and Ethnicity in the United States since 1938* (New York: Viking Press, 1980), 31–32; Harvard Sitkoff, *The Struggle for Black Equality,*

1954–1980 (New York: Hill and Wang, 1981), 10–11; and Harvard
Sitkoff, *A New Deal for Blacks: The Emergence of Civil Rights as a National
Issue* (New York: Oxford University Press, 1978), 326–33.

5. The impact of World War II on African Americans is discussed in
    Polenberg, *One Nation Divisible*, 31–32, 71–74; and Sitkoff, *The Struggle
    for Black Equality*, 11–13. African American employment in United
    States shipyards during World War II is discussed in Lester Rubin, *The
    Negro in the Shipbuilding Industry* (Philadelphia: Industrial Research
    Unit, Wharton School of Finance and Commerce, University of Penn-
    sylvania, 1970), 41–53. Experiences of black workers in Texas ship-
    yards during World War II, including the 1943 Beaumont race riot,
    are discussed in Ernest Obadele-Starks, *Black Unionism in the Industrial
    South* (College Station: Texas A&M University Press, 2000), 101–12.

6. Military service of African Americans during World War II is discussed
    in Polenberg, *One Nation Divisible*, 76–77; and Patterson, *Grand Expec-
    tations*, 385–86.

7. The impact on African Americans of the Truman administration,
    postwar expansion, and the Korea War is covered in Sitkoff, *The
    Struggle for Black Equality*, 14–16; and Polenberg, *One Nation Divisible*,
    99–101, 108, 113–14. For Earl White's service, see Joe Wolfcale, "Dis-
    ability Is Not a Handicap for Richmond Golfer," *Contra Costa Times*
    (Walnut Creek, Calif.), date unknown, clipping provided by Geraldine
    White.

8. Date of birth and other basic information about Fayson is recorded
    in his U.S. Army discharge papers, Dec. 3, 1945 (copies provided
    by county clerk's office, Jefferson County, Beaumont, Tex., now in
    author's collection). Other information provided by his widow, Mary
    Bell Fayson, interview with author, May 1, 2000, and Johnnie Barlow
    interview, Oct. 18, 2000.

9. *Beaumont Enterprise*, May 22, 1935.

10. Ibid., May 23, 1935.

11. Booker Fayson and Johnnie Mae Phillips, Marriage Records, Jefferson
    County Courthouse, Beaumont, Tex. Fayson's employment at Penn-
    sylvania Ship Yard is recorded in U.S. Army Separation Qualification
    Record (undated), provided by Mary Bell Fayson.

12. Fayson U.S. Army discharge papers. The role, including quantifica-
    tion, of African American troops in service and combat functions is
    covered in Ulysses Lee, *The Employment of Negro Troops* (Washington,
    D.C.: Office of the Chief of Military History, U.S. Army, 1966), 622–23;
    see also A. Russell Buchanan, *Black Americans in World War II* (Santa
    Barbara, Calif.: Clio Books, 1977), 97–98.

13. Eisenhower quoted in Lee, *The Employment of Negro Troops*, 623–27;
    the historian quoted is Lee (643).

14. Fayson's U.S. Army Separation Qualification Record and discharge
    papers; Erna Risch, *The Quartermaster Corps: Organization, Supply, and
    Services*, vol. 1, *The Technical Services: United States Army in World War II*

(Washington, D.C.: Office of the Chief of Military History, United States Army, 1953), 164–66; William F. Ross and Charles F. Romanus, *The Quartermaster Corps: Operations in the War against Germany, The Technical Services, United States Army in World War II* (Washington, D.C.: Office of the Chief of Military History, U.S. Army, 1965), 701–707.

15. Fayson's discharge papers show various campaigns in which he served and service medals he received.

16. Fayson's discharge papers.

17. *Beaumont City Directory 1947* (Dallas: Morrison & Fourmy Directory Company, 1947), Alphabetical List of Names, 196; also *Beaumont City Directory 1950* (Dallas: Morrison & Fourmy Directory Company, 1950), Alphabetical List of Names, 209.

18. *Beaumont City Directory 1949* (Dallas: Morrison & Fourmy Directory Company, 1949), Alphabetical List of Names, 204; also *Beaumont City Directory 1950,* Alphabetical List of Names, 209. Fayson's purchase of the Harriot Street property is recorded in Real Property Records, Office of the County Clerk, Jefferson County Courthouse, Beaumont, Tex. Fayson's attendance at Texas Southern University is confirmed in Norma A. Robinson, registrar, Texas Southern University, letter to author, May 24, 2000. Felicia Williams, insurance technician, Texas Department of Insurance, letter to author, May 30, 2000, confirms issuance of Fayson's local recording agent license. For information about the absence of racial discrimination in the Servicemen's Readjustment Act, more commonly known as the GI Bill of Rights, see Michael J. Bennett, *When Dreams Come True: The GI Bill and the Making of Modern America* (Washington, D.C.: Brassey's, 1996), 26–27.

19. *Beaumont City Directory 1952* (Dallas: Morrison & Fourmy Directory Company, 1952), Alphabetical List of Names, 150; also *Beaumont City Directory 1954* (Dallas: Morrison & Fourmy Directory Company, 1954), Alphabetical List of Names, 162. Fayson's purchase of the Washington Boulevard property is recorded in Real Property Records, Office of the County Clerk, Jefferson County Courthouse, Beaumont, Tex. Mary Bell Fayson furnished a photograph of Fayson in his insurance office, which shows furniture and related paraphernalia, and the business card.

20. Cleveland Nisby interview, Jan. 27, 2002; Mary Bell Fayson interviews with author, Apr. 28, May 22, 2002. Johnnie Fayson, Booker Fayson's second wife, died about 1958, and in 1965 he married Catherine Mary Bell Trahan Thomas.

21. Joseph P. Griffin, U.S. Army discharge papers, Office of the County Clerk, Jefferson County, Beaumont, Tex., copies in author's collection; J. P. Griffin, Jr., interviews with author, May 7, 10, 2002.

22. Joseph P. Griffin, U.S. Army discharge papers; also Application for Federal Employment, June 17, 1948, Office of Postmaster, U.S. Post Office, Beaumont, Tex. For a discussion of the venereal disease control program, see Buchanan, *Black Americans in World War II,* 72–73.

23. Joseph P. Griffin, U.S. Army discharge papers. Service of Griffin's 1863rd Engineer Aviation Battalion on Guam is recorded in John D. Silvera, *The Negro in World War II* (New York: Arno Press and the *New York Times,* 1969), appendix II, Middle Pacific (no pagination). The Guam race riot is reported in Morris J. MacGregor Jr., *Integration of the Armed Forces, 1940–1965* (Washington, D.C.: Center of Military History, U.S. Army, 1981), 92–93.

24. Employment history in Griffin, Application for Federal Employment, June 17, 1948; J. P. Griffin, Jr., interviews, May 7, 10, 2002.

25. Griffin, U.S. Army discharge papers; Griffin, Application for Federal Employment, June 17, 1948.

26. The ideals and history of civil service are discussed in Paul P. Van Riper, *History of the United States Civil Service* (Evanston, Ill.: Row, Peterson, 1958), 8–10, 158, 161–62, 241–42, 438–39. See also Samuel Krislov, *The Negro in Federal Employment: The Quest for Equal Opportunity* (Minneapolis: University of Minnesota Press, 1967), 5, 9, 22, 31–32.

27. For a discussion of African Americans in the postal department and protection afforded by civil service status, see Krislov, *The Negro in Federal Employment,* 135–37.

28. J. P. Griffin, Jr., interviews, May 7, 10, 2002.

29. Ibid.; J. P. Griffin, Jr., letter to author, July 1, 2002.

30. Johnnie R. Ware, Application for Federal Employment, Sept. 9, 1949, Office of Postmaster, U.S. Post Office, Beaumont, Tex.

31. Ernestine Strickland, registrar at Huston-Tillotson College in Austin, confirmed Ware's enrollment, course work, and other accomplishments at the college (Strickland, telephone interview with author, Nov. 28, 2000). Ware's marriage, family life, residences, church attendance, and so forth, were confirmed by his daughter, Linda Ware Kyle (interview with author, May 13, 2002). The history of Pioneer Presbyterian Church is mentioned in a pamphlet by Disa Marie Nelson, *A Brief History of Westminster Presbyterian Church of Beaumont* (Beaumont, Tex.: Westminster Presbyterian Church, 1980), 21.

32. Ware, Application for Federal Employment, Sept. 9, 1949; Hubert McCray confirms Ware's love of golf (McCray interview with author, Apr. 24, 2002).

33. *Beaumont City Directory 1950,* Alphabetical List of Names, 573; Ed Moore, interview with author, Nov. 20, 2000; Hubert McCray interview, Apr. 24, 2002.

34. Outline of Parker's postal career confirmed by Sharon Dunigan, U.S. Postal Service, Beaumont, Tex., interview with author, June 18, 2001. The employment of Thomas and Albertine Parker by the McFaddin family is discussed in detail in Linsley, "Main House, Carriage House," 17–51.

35. For a discussion of racism, segregation, and paternalism, see Linsley, "Main House, Carriage House," 18–19, 51. Judith W. Linsley confirmed

details of Thomas Parker, Jr.'s, service with the McFaddin family (Linsley interview with author, May 15, 2002).

36. Details of Tom Parker's personal life confirmed by Albertine Simpson Simon (Parker's daughter), telephone interview with author, May 13, 2002. Information about Parker's inheritance and attendance at Tuskegee, and other information about his life at the McFaddin house, is confirmed in Albertine Parker (Parker's mother), oral interview, Feb. 17, 1988, Tape #32, 2–24, McFaddin-Ward House Museum, Beaumont, Tex.

37. Laura Narcisse, interview with author, Mar. 22, 2002; Charles Narcisse (brother of William), interviews with author, Apr. 8, 2002, May 13, 2002, and May 19, 2004; William Narcisse military discharge papers, Feb. 25, 1946, Office of the County Clerk, Jefferson County Courthouse, Beaumont, Tex.

38. *Beaumont City Directory 1949*, Alphabetical List of Names, 404, and subsequent issues. Narcisse's lifestyle and church attendance confirmed in Charles Narcisse interviews, Apr. 8, May 13, 2002.

39. Interviews with author: Henry Durham, May 22, 2003; Ruby White Harris, June 25, 2003; Louis White, June 27, 2003.

40. Earl White's life is outlined in Wolfcale, "Disability Is Not a Handicap for Richmond Golfer." Other personal information furnished by White's wife, Geraldine White, interview with author, Sept. 9, 2000.

41. Earl White, U.S. Army retirement papers, Oct. 31, 1952, Office of County Clerk, Jefferson County Courthouse, Beaumont, Tex.

42. *Beaumont City Directory 1950*, Alphabetical List of Names, 583. Other information provided in Geraldine White interview, Sept. 9, 2000.

Chapter 4

1. *Encyclopedia Britannica*, 15th ed., *s.v.* "golf."

2. Development of country clubs and golf is covered in Kenneth T. Jackson, *Crabgrass Frontier: The Suburbanization of the United States* (New York: Oxford University Press, 1985), 97–99; and Benjamin G. Rader, *American Sports: From the Age of Folk Games to the Age of Televised Sports*, 2nd ed. (Englewood Cliffs, N.J.: Prentice Hall, 1990), 92–94, 194–200.

3. Herbert Warren Wind, *The Story of American Golf: Its Champions and Its Championships*, 3rd rev. ed. (New York: Knopf, 1975), 351–90.

4. Ibid.; golfing statistics supplied by Judy Thompson, National Golf Foundation, Jupiter, Fla., e-mails to author, June 14, 28, 2002.

5. The "shadow people" and other service workers are described in Peter McDaniel, *Uneven Lies: The Heroic Story of African-Americans in Golf* (Greenwich, Conn.: American Golfer, 2000), 34–46. The author estimates the number of service workers at one for every twenty golfers and the number of "shadow players" at one for every twenty service workers.

6. The history and role of caddies are covered in Geoffrey Cousins, *Golf in Britain: A Social History from the Beginnings to the Present Day* (London: Routledge & Kegan Paul, 1975), 101–104; and Charles Price, *The World of Golf: A Panorama of Six Centuries of the Game's History* (New York: Random House, 1962), 28–30. The caddying careers of Ben Hogan, Byron Nelson, and others are mentioned in numerous places, including J. C. King and Frances G. Trimble, "Golf," in *The New Handbook of Texas,* 3:204–205. Author Pete McDaniel recounts his own caddying experiences in *Uneven Lies,* 10–13. The role and experiences of black caddies are also detailed in Calvin H. Sinnette, *Forbidden Fairways: African Americans and the Game of Golf* (Chelsea, Mich.: Sleeping Bear Press, 1998), 35–50.

7. Discrimination against black golfers is discussed in Marvin P. Dawkins and Graham C. Kinloch, *African American Golfers during the Jim Crow Era* (Westport, Conn.: Praeger, 2000), 3–10.

8. The development of black golf clubs is detailed in Dawkins and Kinloch, *African American Golfers during the Jim Crow Era,* 21–34; and McDaniel, *Uneven Lies,* 59–76.

9. The PGA exclusion of black golfers as well as the history of the UGA and its players are covered in Dawkins and Kinloch, *African American Golfers during the Jim Crow Era,* 35–64; and McDaniel, *Uneven Lies,* 47–48.

10. The desegregation efforts of Joe Louis, Teddy Rhodes, Charles Sifford, Bill Spiller, and others are covered in Dawkins and Kinloch, *African American Golfers during the Jim Crow Era,* 62–63, 65–84; McDaniel, *Uneven Lies,* 85–91, 101–17; John H. Kennedy, *A Course of Their Own: A History of African American Golfers* (Kansas City, Mo.: Andrews McMeel, 2000), 49–89; and Sinnette, *Forbidden Fairways,* 121–35. The groundbreaking appearance of Joe Louis in the San Diego Open was covered in the Houston *Informer,* Jan. 19, 1952.

11. The litigation campaign is discussed in Dawkins and Kinloch, *African American Golfers during the Jim Crow Era,* 137–52; McDaniel, *Uneven Lies,* 91–96; and Sinnette, *Forbidden Fairways,* 135–36, where the author reports thirty–three instances between 1945 and 1966 in which black golfers employed legal action to advance their cause.

12. An overview of Texas golf is provided in King and Trimble, "Golf," 3:204–205. Private and public courses are described in Kevin Newberry, *Texas Golf: The Best of the Lone Star State* (Houston: Gulf Publishing, 1998), 260–63; and Doug Mitchell, "Golf in the Lone Star State: Texas' Oldest Courses," *Texas Golfer Magazine* 1, no. 7 (Jan., 2001): 4–5.

13. Public golf is covered in Newberry, *Texas Golf,* 260–63; and Doug Mitchell, "Golf in the Lone Star State: Municipal Golf Takes Off," *Texas Golfer Magazine* 1, no. 8 (Feb., 2001): 8–9. Golfing facilities in state parks are listed in *Texas Almanac, 1956–1957* (Dallas: Belo Corp., 1957), 500–505. Municipal and daily-fee courses are listed in various city directories, such as *Houston City Directory 1952* (Houston: Morrison & Fourmy Publishing, 1952), Classified Business List, 1911.

14. Bill Penn, former TGA executive director, interviews with author, July 20, 23, 2002. Information about the development of the Texas Golf Association (TGA) and its tournaments is found on the TGA Internet website <www.txga.org>; Texas tournaments are covered in Newberry, *Texas Golf,* 240–45.

15. The Texas Negro Golf Association and various chapters are mentioned in the Houston *Informer,* June 26, 1954. The First Annual Southwestern Golf Open (Negro) in 1941 is mentioned in Brophy, "The Black Texan," 204, and the Texas Negro Golf Championship is covered in Sapper, "Survey of the History of the Black People of Texas," 423–24. The Lee Elder victory in Dallas in 1952 and the 1955 Lone Star Tournament in Houston are covered in the Houston *Informer,* Jan. 26, 1952, and June 18, 1955, respectively.

16. Quotations from Houston *Informer,* June 26, 1954.

17. Ibid., July 7, 1954.

18. *Law v. Mayor and City Council of Baltimore, et al.,* Civil Action 3837, June 18, 1948, cited as 78 F. Supp. 346.

19. *Beaumont City Directory 1952,* Street and Avenue List, 155; *Beaumont City Directory 1954,* Street and Avenue List, 175; opening of Beaumont Country Club covered in *Beaumont Enterprise,* Oct. 27, 1907.

20. *Beaumont Enterprise,* June 15, 1954.

21. Ibid., May 4, 5, 1946.

22. Ibid., Apr. 6, 1953.

23. Ibid., Apr. 16, 19, 1954, and Apr. 18, 1955. The *Beaumont Enterprise,* May 27, 28, 1964, provides details of Althea Gibson's entry in the tournament, and its issue of May 20, 1965, confirms the relocation of the tournament to Bayou Den Golf Club. The controversy about Althea Gibson was recalled by the author and others, including Kyle Wheelus, Jr. (interview with author, Mar. 29, 2004), and was discussed in detail in the *Beaumont Enterprise,* Sept. 30, 2003.

24. The opening of Beaumont's first municipal course is noted by Mayor Austin J. Barnes, Beaumont City Council minutes, Apr. 11, 1928. The employment of white and black caddies and the "longest drive" legend are reported by Johnnie Barlow (interview, Oct. 18, 2000). The "longest drive" legend was common knowledge to Beaumonters, including the author, and was confirmed by Kyle Wheelus, Jr. (interview with author, May 7, 2004).

25. The donation and development of Tyrrell Park and its golf course are covered in the *Beaumont Enterprise,* Feb. 8, 1987. See also Carolyn S. Smith, letter to author, July 5, 2002 (author's collection); Smith is currently preparing a biographical manuscript on W. C. Tyrrell.

26. *Beaumont Enterprise,* Nov. 9, 1980, Mar. 15, 1981, Oct. 25, 1990.

27. For information about Booker Fayson and other Beaumont golfers playing in Houston, see Beaumont City Council minutes, June 14, 1955. The Houston golf course desegregation campaign is discussed in Sapper, "Survey of the History of the Black People of Texas," 423–26,

and covered in detail in the "Segregation—Houston" microfiche file of newspaper articles, especially *Houston Chronicle,* May 26, 1954, Texas Room, Houston Metropolitan Research Center, Houston Public Library, Houston, Tex.

28. *Houston Post,* Jan. 25, 1950. Biographical materials about Houston lawyers Herman Wright and Ben N. Ramey, including State Bar of Texas membership registration cards and obituary notices (author's collection), furnished by Jeffrey C. Adams, State Bar of Texas, Austin, Tex., in letter to author, Aug. 8, 2002. The association of Mandell & Wright with labor, liberal, and NAACP causes is covered in Pitre, *In Struggle Against Jim Crow,* 72–73.

29. *Beal, et al., v. Holcombe, Mayor of City of Houston, et al.,* Civil Action No. 5407, filed Jan. 14, 1950, U.S. District Court, Southern District of Texas, Houston Division (cited hereafter as *Beal v. Holcombe,* Civil Action No. 5407). The *Beal v. Holcombe* case papers that the author studied include the Complaint, Defendants' Answer, Plaintiffs' Brief, Defendants' Brief, Plaintiffs' Supplemental Brief, Transcription of Evidence, Trial Brief, Stipulation, Findings of Fact and Conclusions of Law, and Final Judgment. See also *Beal v. Holcombe,* Civil Action No. 13562, filed Dec. 20, 1951, when *Beal v. Holcombe* was appealed from the U.S. District Court, Southern District of Texas, Houston, to the United States Court of Appeals for the Fifth Circuit, New Orleans, Louisiana. Case papers studied include Brief for Appellees, Petition for Rehearing, Brief for Appellants, and Final Judgment. (Copies of original documents, from the National Archives and Records Administration, Southwest Division, Fort Worth, Tex., are in the author's collection.)

30. For discussion of the parks, see *Beal v. Holcombe,* Civil Action No. 5407, Defendants' Answer, 3–5; for Ramey's remarks, see *Houston Chronicle,* July 19, 1950.

31. For Kennerly's statement, see *Beal v. Holcombe,* Civil Action No. 5407, Findings of Fact and Conclusions of Law, 5.

32. *Beal v. Holcombe,* Civil Action No. 13562, Final Judgment, Mar. 22, 1952.

33. *Houston Chronicle,* May 24, 25, 1954.

34. Ibid. See also *Houston Chronicle,* May 26, 1954, June 2, 3, 1954; Houston *Informer,* June 5, 1954.

35. *Beaumont Enterprise,* June 15, 1954.

36. Ibid., June 3, 15, 1954.

37. Ibid., June 15, 1954.

38. The history and activities of the United Racial Council are related and discussed in detail by editor Robert W. Akers in the *Beaumont Enterprise,* Sept. 25, 26, 1954. The URC mission statement is set forth in *Beaumont Enterprise,* July 1, 1954, and council members are mentioned in *Beaumont Enterprise,* Sept. 18, 1954. The author's interviews with Richard Price (Aug. 1, 2002) and Myrtle Sprott DePlanter (Aug. 2, 2002) indi-

cate that Archie L. Price was the Price who served as vice chairman of the URC.

39. Eisenhower quoted in Houston *Informer,* June 26, 1954.

40. Houston *Informer,* June 26, 1954. See also Akers, *Beaumont Enterprise,* Sept. 25, 26, 1954.

41. Mission statement quoted in *Beaumont Enterprise,* July 1, 1954.

42. See Akers, *Beaumont Enterprise,* Sept. 25, 26, 1954.

43. *Dallas Express,* July 10, 1954.

44. *Beaumont Enterprise,* Aug. 7, 1954.

45. Ibid., Aug. 10, 1954.

46. Ibid., Sept. 18, 1954.

Chapter 5

1. Terry Wallace, "Elmo Willard," *Beaumont Enterprise,* Feb. 20, 1985.

2. Information about Prairie View A&M College is in the *Texas Almanac* (Dallas: Belo Corp., 1947), 368–76. For biographical information about Theodore R. Johns, see the printed program, *Black History Recognition Celebration,* Ministers' Conference of Port Arthur, Tex., Feb. 18, 1989; Theodore Johns, interview with Judith Linsley and Jo Ann Stiles, Feb. 26, 1998, transcript, Oral History Collection, 2004-076 (both documents at Tyrrell Historical Library, Beaumont, Tex.).

3. Johns interview with Linsley and Stiles.

4. Ibid.

5. Ibid.

6. Ibid.

7. Ibid.

8. Ibid.; also, Johns, interview with author, Feb. 14, 2000.

9. Johns interview with Linsley and Stiles.

10. Ibid.

11. Pat Willard, interview with author, Aug. 29, 2002; Bill Deevy, "Elmo Willard," *Metropolitan Beaumont* (Beaumont Chamber of Commerce magazine), May/June, 1989, 40–43; Elmo R. Willard III, Fisk University Application for Admission, Jan. 19, 1947, Ms. 109, Elmo Willard Collection, Tyrrell Historical Library, Beaumont, Tex.

12. Willard, Fisk University Application for Admission, Jan. 19, 1947.

13. Pat Willard interview, Aug. 29, 2002.

14. Ibid.

15. Ibid.; A. S. Arnold, letter to George M. Johnson, May 24, 1951, Ms. 109, Elmo Willard Collection.

16. Pat Willard interview, Aug. 29, 2002.

17. Ibid. See also Deevy, "Elmo Willard," 40–43.

18. Pat Willard interview, Aug. 29, 2002.

19. Howard University law school and its role in civil rights litigation are discussed in Kluger, *Simple Justice,* 123–131; and Rayford W. Logan, *Howard University: The First Hundred Years, 1867–1967* (New York: New

York University Press, 1969), 375–78, 431–32. Howard University law school curriculum and faculty are outlined in *Howard University Bulletin, General Catalogue,* published annually, 1948–49 and subsequent years. The careers of Theo Johns and Elmo Willard at Howard University law school are discussed in Shabazz, "The Desegregation of Lamar State College of Technology," 60–61.

20. Kluger, *Simple Justice,* 123–31. The participation of Johns and Willard in moot court sessions is mentioned in Johns, interview with Linsley and Stiles; and in Deevy, "Elmo Willard," 40–43, respectively.

21. The biracial composition of the NAACP and the Legal Defense and Education Fund is described in Kluger, *Simple Justice,* 101–102, 133–38, and 436–40. The role of the NAACP and the Legal Defense Fund in the civil rights litigation campaign is discussed in Patterson, *Grand Expectations,* 385–89.

22. The career of Thurgood Marshall is sketched briefly in Patterson, *Grand Expectations,* 386–88, and covered in detail in Kluger, *Simple Justice,* with Marshall's education being described on pages 173–94. Marshall is the subject of numerous biographies, including Ball, *A Defiant Life;* Roger Goldman and David Gallen, *Thurgood Marshall: Justice for All* (New York: Carroll & Graf, 1992); Randall W. Bland, *Private Pressure on Public Law: The Legal Career of Justice Thurgood Marshall, 1934–1991,* rev. ed. (Lanham, Md.: University Press of America, 1993); Juan Williams, *Thurgood Marshall: American Revolutionary* (New York: Times Books, 1998), and others.

23. Selected Supreme Court cases are discussed in Kluger, *Simple Justice,* as follows: *Mitchell v. United States,* 220; *Henderson v. United States,* 277–78; *Shelley v. Kraemer,* 248–55; *Smith v. Allright,* 234–37; *Sweatt v. Painter,* 256–84; and *McLaurin v. Oklahoma State Regents,* 267–84. *Smith v. Allright* and *Beal v. Holcombe* (the Houston golf desegregation case) are discussed in Charles L. Zelden, *Justice Lies in the District: The United States District Court, Southern District of Texas, 1902–1960* (College Station: Texas A&M University Press, 1993). The cases are also outlined in Georgiana F. Rathbun, ed., *Revolution in Civil Rights,* 4th ed. (Washington, D.C.: Congressional Quarterly, 1968), 6–9; and discussed in Abraham and Perry, *Freedom and the Court,* 338–41. The *Sweatt v. Painter* case is covered in detail in Gillette, "Heman Marion Sweatt," 157–88; and both the *Sweatt* and *McLaurin* cases are discussed in detail in Michael L. Gillette, "The NAACP in Texas, 1937–1957" (Ph.D. diss., University of Texas at Austin, 1984), 41–90. The active role of Professor James Nabrit, Jr., in *Sweatt v. Painter* and other litigation is described in Kluger, *Simple Justice,* 262–63, 272, 274, 291–92.

24. *Brown v. Board of Education* is summarized in Rathbun ed., *Revolution in Civil Rights,* 6–7; described briefly in Patterson, *Grand Expectations,* 387–95; and Abraham and Perry, *Freedom and the Court,* 341–46; and discussed at length in Kluger, *Simple Justice,* 315–778. See also Robyn Duff Ladino, *Desegregating Texas Schools: Eisenhower, Shivers, and the*

Crisis at Mansfield High School (Austin: University of Texas Press, 1996), 16–21. See also Ball, *A Defiant Life,* 114–40. The roles of professors James M. Nabrit, Jr., and George E. C. Hayes in the *Brown* cases are mentioned in Kluger, *Simple Justice,* 578–79, and Goldman and Gallen, *Thurgood Marshall,* 93–94.

25. The conclusion and meaning of *Brown v. Board of Education* is covered briefly in Patterson, *Grand Expectations,* 387–94, and detailed in Kluger, *Simple Justice,* 700–46. Apparently the wider implications of the *Brown* decision and its application to other public facilities were perceived rapidly by Texas lawyers, as exemplified by Will Sears, Houston city attorney, and Charles Smith, who chaired the Beaumont Chamber of Commerce committee on race relations.

26. Beaumont City Council minutes, June 14, 1955.

27. *Beaumont Journal,* June 20, 1955; *Beaumont Enterprise,* June 21, 1955; Johnnie Barlow, interview with author, July 1, 2001.

28. *Beaumont Enterprise,* June 21, 1955; *Fayson, et al., v. Beard, et al.,* Civil Action No. 2920, filed June 23, 1955, U.S. District Court, Eastern District of Texas, Beaumont Division (cited hereafter as *Fayson v. Beard*). The *Fayson v. Beard* case papers that the author studied include Complaint, Defendants' Answer, Verification, Request for Admission, Defendants' Response to Request for Admissions, Stipulation, Plaintiffs' Memorandum of Points and Authorities, Memorandum Brief in Behalf of Defendants, Motion to Allow Oral Argument, Memorandum Decision, and Order. (Copies of original documents, from the National Archives and Records Administration, Southwest Division, Fort Worth, Tex., are in the author's collection.)

29. *Fayson v. Beard,* case papers.

30. Information about the Beaumont branch of the NAACP, its officers and membership, and its relationship to the Texas State Conference of Branches and the national headquarters in New York is found in the Beaumont NAACP Files, with copies in the author's collection. For a history of the Beaumont branch of the NAACP, see Nancy Dailey, "History of the Beaumont, Texas, Chapter of the National Association for the Advancement of Colored People, 1918–1970" (master's thesis, Lamar University, 1971). The Texas State Conference of Branches, its leaders, and activities are covered in detail in Gillette, "The NAACP in Texas, 1937–1957," vii–viii, 1, 6–7, 10, 19–20, 31, 137–38, 161. For the career of Lulu B. White, see Pitre, *In Struggle against Jim Crow,* 37–38, 111–13, 128.

31. The vital role of the State Conference "as the principal vehicle for civil rights activism" is discussed and summarized in Gillette, "The NAACP in Texas, 1937–1957," 352–56 (quoted text, 352). Tate's relationship to Marshall and his wide-ranging legal activities with the Texas State Conference are covered in Gillette, "The NAACP in Texas, 1937–1957," vii, 137–38, 161, 207, and for golf course desegregation in Houston, Fort Worth, and Beaumont, see 222–24. For the legal ac-

tivities of the Texas State Conference, see also Melvin J. Banks, "The Pursuit of Equality: The Movement for First Class Citizenship among Negroes in Texas, 1920–1950" (Ph.D. diss., Syracuse University, 1962), 188–92, 408–409. Information about Tate's activities, including his efforts to reduce employment discrimination at Sheffield Steel Company, is found in "Report of U. Simpson Tate, Regional Counsel, NAACP Legal Defense and Educational Fund, Inc., Southwest Region, Sept., 1955," NAACP II, Series C, Box 232 (six folders, 1947–1955), Manuscript Division, Library of Congress, Washington, D.C. (cited hereafter as "Report of U. Simpson Tate, Sept., 1955)."

32. *Fayson v. Beard,* Complaint, 3.

33. Ibid.; John D. Rienstra obituary, *Beaumont Enterprise,* Nov. 21, 1977.

34. *Fayson v. Beard,* Complaint, 1–7.

35. *Fayson v. Beard,* Defendants' Answer, 4. Article 1015b, "Ordinance for segregation of races," is set forth in *Vernon's Annotated Revised Civil Statutes of the State of Texas,* 2:276–77.

36. *Beaumont Journal,* Aug. 1, 1955; *Fayson v. Beard,* Request for Admission, 1–2, Defendants' Response to Request for Admissions, 1–3, and Stipulation, 1–3.

37. *Beaumont Enterprise,* Aug. 24, 1955.

38. Ibid., Aug. 25, 1955.

39. *Beaumont Enterprise,* samplings of front-page stories from the summer of 1955: July 24 (Tate's call for desegregating schools; establishment of Kilgore Citizens' Council), July 28 (admission of black students to Texas Western College), Aug. 2 (Governor Shivers's statement), Aug. 10 (petition for desegregating Lubbock schools), Aug. 13 (petition for desegregating Orange schools), Aug. 18 (petition for desegregating Waco schools), and Aug. 27 (petition for desegregating Big Spring schools).

40. *Fayson v. Beard,* Memorandum of Points and Authorities, 1–6, Memorandum Brief in Behalf of Defendants, 1–5.

41. *Fayson v. Beard,* Memorandum Brief in Behalf of Defendants, 1–5.

42. *Fayson v. Beard,* Memorandum of Points and Authorities; "Report of U. Simpson Tate, Sept., 1955," 1–6.

43. *Fayson v. Beard,* Motion to Allow Oral Argument.

Chapter 6

1. Lamar J. R. Cecil obituary, *Beaumont Enterprise,* Feb. 15, 1958; Lamar H. Cecil obituary, *Houston Post,* Jan. 27, 1939. Information about Lamar J. R. Cecil's career at Saint Charles College was furnished, with permission from Grayson Cecil, by Jesuit Father William Huette, interview with author, Dec. 19, 2002.

2. Edith Cecil Flynn, interview with author, Feb. 3, 2003.

3. Lamar J. R. Cecil academic records, furnished with the permission of Grayson Cecil, by Shirley A. Lake, Registrar's Office, Catholic Univer-

sity of America, letter to author, Dec. 16, 2002. Information about Cecil's Paulist seminarian career at Saint Paul's College provided, with permission from Grayson Cecil, by Paulist Father John E. Lynch, e-mails to author, Dec. 9, 11, 2002.

4. Lamar J. R. Cecil academic records, Catholic University, Dec. 16, 2002; Edith Cecil Flynn interview, Nov. 13, 2002.

5. Mary Cecil interview, Mar. 16, 2001; Edith Cecil Flynn, interview with author, Dec. 16, 2002.

6. Lamar J. R. Cecil academic records furnished, with permission from Grayson Cecil, by Jerry Montag, Registrar, Rice University, letter to author, Nov. 1, 2002. For the "Slime" parade and other elements of Rice Institute campus life, see the Rice student newspaper, *The Thresher*, Sept. 28, 1923.

7. Cecil academic records, Rice University Registrar, Nov. 1, 2002. Academic course content is described in *The Rice Institute Catalogue, 1922–1923* (Houston: Rice Institute, 1922). Cecil and other graduates listed and pictured in university annual *Campanile 1923* (Houston: Rein Printing, 1923).

8. Lamar J. R. Cecil law school records, furnished with permission from Grayson Cecil, by Margo Iwanski, Office of the Vice President, University of Texas at Austin, in letter to author, Dec. 10, 2002; law school program, faculty, and students, in *Catalogue of the University of Texas, 1927–1928* (Austin: University of Texas, 1927), 293–300, 344–45; Edith Cecil Flynn interview, Dec. 16, 2002.

9. Edith Cecil Flynn interview with author, Nov. 2, 2002.

10. *Catalogue of the University of Texas, 1927–1928*, 344–45.

11. Mary Cecil interview, Mar. 16, 2001; Cecil office and residence locations recorded in *Beaumont City Directory 1929* (Houston: Morrison & Fourmy, 1929), Alphabetical List of Names, 172, and subsequent issues.

12. *Beaumont Journal,* Sept. 15, 1930; *Beaumont Enterprise,* Sept. 16, 1930.

13. Mary Cecil interview, Mar. 16, 2001; Grayson Cecil, interview with author, Jan. 2, 2003.

14. Cecil's law affiliations, partnerships, and associations are recorded in *Beaumont City Directory 1929,* 172, and subsequent issues; James D. McNicholas, interview with author, Mar. 28, 2001.

15. Cecil's career is outlined in Major T. Bell, "Lamar Cecil: The Days That Were His," *Texas Gulf Historical and Biographical Record* 12, no. 1 (1976): 20–24; James D. McNicholas interview, Mar. 28, 2001.

16. Mary Cecil interview, Mar. 16, 2001; James D. McNicholas interview, Mar. 28, 2001.

17. For Stein's "lost generation," see Ernest Hemingway, *A Moveable Feast* (New York: Charles Scribner's Sons, 1964), 29; F. Scott Fitzgerald, *This Side of Paradise* (New York: Charles Scribner's Sons, 1920), 255; William E. Leuchtenburg, *The Perils of Prosperity, 1914–1932* (Chicago and London: University of Chicago Press, 1958), 7–8, 142–43, 155.

See also Michael E. Parrish, *Anxious Decades: America in Prosperity and Depression, 1920–1941* (New York and London: Norton, 1992), 183–84, 187–88, 194–96.

18. Leuchtenburg, *The Perils of Prosperity*, 158–74; Parrish, *Anxious Decades*, 417–20. See also Loren Baritz, ed., *The Culture of the Twenties* (Indianapolis and New York: Bobbs-Merrill, 1970), xxxv–xxxvii, and F. Scott Fitzgerald, "History's Most Expensive Orgy," in Baritz, ed., *The Culture of the Twenties*, 413–24.

19. Norman H. Clark, *Deliver Us from Evil: An Interpretation of American Prohibition* (New York: Norton, 1976), 211–13.

20. Ibid., 213–14.

21. Mary Cecil interview, Mar. 16, 2001; James D. McNicholas interview, Mar. 28, 2001. Cecil's long acquaintance with Johnnie Ware was confirmed by Tanner T. Hunt, Jr. (interview, Jan. 22, 2002).

22. Locker-room nicknames, jokes, and aphorisms between Cecil and his friends were common knowledge to people who knew them, including the author, James D. McNicholas (interview, Mar. 18, 2001), and Tanner T. Hunt, Jr. (interview, Jan. 22, 2002). H. L. Mencken is quoted in Parrish, *Anxious Decades*, 196–200 (Religion, Puritanism, and Conscience); and Leuchtenburg, *The Perils of Prosperity*, 152–53 (Love).

23. Leuchtenburg, *The Perils of Prosperity*, 153–54; Mary Cecil interview, Mar. 16, 2001; Grayson Cecil interview, Jan. 2, 2003; *Beaumont Enterprise*, Jan. 15, 1950; Kenneth E. Ruddy, interview with author, Apr. 7, 2002. The exclusion of young African American women from the Neches River Festival was common knowledge to Beaumonters, including Tanner T. Hunt, Jr. (interview, Jan. 22, 2002).

24. Lamar Cecil, Jr., interview with author, Mar. 21, 2003.

25. Grayson Cecil interview, Jan. 2, 2003.

26. Ibid.

27. The sympathectomy procedure is discussed in Donna Hoel, with Robert B. Howard, M.D., "Hypertension: Stalking the Silent Killer," *Postgraduate Medicine* 101, no. 2 (Feb., 1997) <www.postgradmed.com>; Grayson Cecil interview, Jan. 2, 2003.

Chapter 7

1. Edith Cecil Flynn, interviews with author, Jan. 4, Feb. 3, 2003.

2. George N. Green, "Martin Dies," and Robert Wooster, "Jesse Martin Combs," biographical sketches, *The Handbook of Texas Online*, Jan. 10, 2003. See also George Norris Green, *The Establishment in Texas Politics: The Primitive Years, 1938–1957* (Westport, Conn., and London: Greenwood Press, 1979), 69–75. Cecil's retort was recalled by Edith Cecil Flynn (interview, Jan. 4, 2003).

3. Benckenstein's career is detailed in his obituary, *Beaumont Enterprise*, Oct. 20, 1966.

4. The Republican side of the 1944 election in Texas is covered in Paul Casdorph, *A History of the Republican Party in Texas, 1865–1965* (Austin: Pemberton Press, 1965), 156–60, and Roger Olien, *From Token to Triumph: The Texas Republicans since 1920* (Dallas: SMU Press, 1982), 83–87.

5. Benckenstein quote and other information from *Beaumont Enterprise,* Oct. 20, 22, 1944, respectively.

6. Tyson quoted in *Beaumont Enterprise,* Nov. 3, 1944.

7. Texas election results are reported in Casdorph, *A History of the Republican Party in Texas,* 160; Jefferson County votes are reported in the *Beaumont Enterprise,* Nov. 8, 1944. Ed Edson's remarks about the 1944 election results were recalled by Mary Cecil (interview, Mar. 16, 2001).

8. Information about R. B. Creager, Henry Zweifel, Jack Porter, L. J. Benckenstein, and their leadership of the Texas Republican Party is contained in Casdorph, *A History of the Republican Party in Texas,* 118–97, and Olien, *From Token to Triumph,* 58–138. See also Carl H. Moneyhon, "Republican Party," *The Handbook of Texas Online,* Jan. 10, 2003.

9. Casdorph, *A History of the Republican Party in Texas,* 176–97; Olien, *From Token to Triumph,* 112–38. See also O. Douglas Weeks, *Texas Presidential Politics in 1952* (Austin: Institute of Public Affairs, University of Texas, 1953), 50–68; Herbert S. Parmet, *Eisenhower and the American Crusades* (New York: Macmillan, 1972), 73–82; and Seth Shepard McKay, *Texas and the Fair Deal, 1945–1952* (San Antonio: Naylor, 1954), 356–424.

10. Hobart K. McDowell, letter to H. J. Porter, Dec. 17, 1951, Jack Porter Papers, courtesy Mike Porter, Blanco, Tex.

11. Randolph C. Reed obituary, *Beaumont Enterprise,* Feb. 19, 1987.

12. *Beaumont Enterprise,* May 4, 1952.

13. Ibid.; also, Olien, *From Token to Triumph,* 120.

14. Casdorph, *A History of the Republican Party in Texas,* 181–83; Olien, *From Token to Triumph,* 119–22; Weeks, *Texas Presidential Politics in 1952,* 53–56. See also Paul T. David, Malcolm Moos, and Ralph M. Goldman, *Presidential Nominating Politics in 1952* (Baltimore: Johns Hopkins Press, 1954), 3:319–21.

15. Casdorph, *A History of the Republican Party in Texas,* 179–82; Olien, *From Token to Triumph,* 121–22; Weeks, *Texas Presidential Politics in 1952,* 50–53.

16. *Beaumont Enterprise,* May 7, 1952.

17. Ibid.

18. Ibid.

19. Ibid., May 6, 1952. Mehaffy's disqualification was confirmed by Bobby T. Cowart (interview with author, Feb. 4, 2003).

20. Casdorph, *A History of the Republican Party in Texas,* 183–86; Olien, *From Token to Triumph,* 125; Weeks, *Texas Presidential Politics in 1952,* 60–66; David, Moos, and Goldman, *Presidential Nominating Politics in 1952,* 3:322–24.

21. Casdorph, *A History of the Republican Party in Texas*, 183–84; Olien, *From Token to Triumph*, 125; Weeks, *Texas Presidential Politics in 1952*, 60–62.

22. Mary E. Montgomery affidavit, June 17, 1952 ("Zweifel brief"), Jack Porter Papers; Lane quoted in Weeks, *Texas Presidential Politics in 1952*, 63.

23. Casdorph, *A History of the Republican Party in Texas*, 185; Olien, *From Token to Triumph*, 125; Weeks, *Texas Presidential Politics in 1952*, 63–64.

24. Casdorph, *A History of the Republican Party in Texas*, 185; Olien, *From Token to Triumph*, 125; Weeks, *Texas Presidential Politics in 1952*, 64, 69–70. According to Weeks, the official Taft delegation was an uninstructed group with thirty for Taft, four for Eisenhower, and four for MacArthur, while the Eisenhower delegation had thirty-three instructed for Eisenhower and five instructed for Taft.

25. Weeks, *Texas Presidential Politics in 1952*, 64.

26. Casdorph, *A History of the Republican Party in Texas*, 184–85; Olien, *From Token to Triumph*, 125–28; Weeks, *Texas Presidential Politics in 1952*, 65–68 (Eisenhower remark, 67); *Beaumont Enterprise*, May 28, 1952 (Lodge quote).

27. Casdorph, *A History of the Republican Party in Texas*, 188; Olien, *From Token to Triumph*, 128; Weeks, *Texas Presidential Politics in 1952*, 71–72.

28. Casdorph, *A History of the Republican Party in Texas*, 188–89; David, Moos, and Goldman, *Presidential Nominating Politics in 1952*, 1:68–70, 72; Weeks, *Texas Presidential Politics in 1952*, 71–72.

29. Casdorph, *A History of the Republican Party in Texas*, 189; David, Moos, and Goldman, *Presidential Nominating Politics in 1952*, 1:70–71; Weeks, *Texas Presidential Politics in 1952*, 72–73.

30. David, Moos, and Goldman, *Presidential Nominating Politics in 1952*, 3:327–28; Weeks, *Texas Presidential Politics in 1952*, 73–74.

31. David, Moos, and Goldman, *Presidential Nominating Politics in 1952*, 1:70, 1:76–77, 3:327–28; Weeks, *Texas Presidential Politics in 1952*, 72–74.

32. Edith Cecil Flynn interview, Feb. 3, 2003; *Houston Post*, July 10, 1952; *New York Times*, July 10, 1952.

33. David, Moos, and Goldman, *Presidential Nominating Politics in 1952*, 1:78–79; Weeks, *Texas Presidential Politics in 1952*, 74; Parmet, *Eisenhower and the American Crusades*, 91.

34. David, Moos, and Goldman, *Presidential Nominating Politics in 1952*, 3:328–29; Weeks, *Texas Presidential Politics in 1952*, 74–75; Parmet, *Eisenhower and the American Crusades*, 91; *Beaumont Enterprise*, July 10, 1952.

35. Casdorph, *A History of the Republican Party in Texas*, 194; *Beaumont Enterprise*, July 10, 1952.

36. Mary Cecil interview, Mar. 16, 2001; Weeks, *Texas Presidential Politics in 1952*, 71.

37. David, Moos, and Goldman, *Presidential Nominating Politics in 1952*, 1:90; *Houston Post*, July 10, 1952; *New York Times*, July 10, 1952; *Beaumont Enterprise*, July 11, 1952.

38. *New York Times,* July 10, 1952; David, Moos, and Goldman, *Presidential Nominating Politics in 1952,* 1:90; Parmet, *Eisenhower and the American Crusades,* 98; McKay, *Texas and the Fair Deal,* 393–95.

39. David, Moos, and Goldman, *Presidential Nominating Politics in 1952,* 1:90. *Presidential Nominating Politics in 1952* contains five volumes: (1) *The National Story,* (2) *The Northeast,* (3) *The South,* (4) *The Middle West,* and (5) *The West,* all prepared under the auspices of the American Political Science Association, with the cooperation of the Brookings Institution, and published in 1954 by Johns Hopkins Press.

40. David, Moos, and Goldman, *Presidential Nominating Politics in 1952,* 3:331–32; Olien, *From Token to Triumph,* 133; Weeks, *Texas Presidential Politics in 1952,* 74–75.

41. Casdorph, *A History of the Republican Party in Texas,* 194; Olien, *From Token to Triumph,* 137–38; Weeks, *Texas Presidential Politics in 1952,* 91–94.

42. Weeks, *Texas Presidential Politics in 1952,* 95–96; Olien, *From Token to Triumph,* 137–38.

43. *Beaumont Enterprise,* Nov. 1, 2, 1952.

44. Ibid., Nov. 3, 1952.

45. Ibid., Nov. 4, 1952.

46. National election results reported in Patterson, *Grand Expectations,* 260. For state, county, and urban center results, see Casdorph, *A History of the Republican Party in Texas,* 196–97; Olien, *From Token to Triumph,* 138; Weeks, *Texas Presidential Politics in 1952,* 97–106.

47. Weeks, *Texas Presidential Politics in 1952,* 106–108; *Beaumont Enterprise,* Nov. 5, 1952.

48. Lamar Cecil, letter to Dwight Eisenhower, Nov. 7, 1952, Box 559, White House Central Files, Dwight D. Eisenhower Presidential Library, Abilene, Kans.

49. Dwight D. Eisenhower, letter to Lamar Cecil, Nov. 20, 1952, Box 559, White House Central Files, Eisenhower Presidential Library.

Chapter 8

1. Lamar Cecil, letter to William P. Rogers, June 3, 1953, Box 301, White House Central Files, Eisenhower Presidential Library.

2. *Beaumont Enterprise,* Feb. 11, 1954. The history and particulars of the Eastern District of Texas and the Fifth Circuit are set forth on the Federal Judicial Center website, <www.fjc.gov>, Apr. 13, 2004 .

3. For details on the Eastern District and its judges, see Federal Judicial Center website, <www.fjc.gov>. Population numbers, including racial factors in the Eastern District of Texas, are found in *Texas Almanac, 1954–1955* (Dallas: Belo Corp., 1955), 100–102.

4. The Feb. 17, 1954, letter from Jack Porter to Attorney General Herbert Brownell, Jr., and other letters documenting Cecil's campaign for the judicial nomination are found in the Lamar Cecil nomination file now in the possession of Grayson Cecil and used with her permis-

sion. For the process of nominating federal judges during the Eisenhower administration, see Harold W. Chase, *Federal Judges: The Appointing Process* (Minneapolis: University of Minnesota, 1972), 89–119,
and Sheldon Goldman, *Picking Federal Judges: Lower Court Selection
from Roosevelt through Reagan* (New Haven and London: Yale University Press, 1997), 190–253.

5. For evidence of Cecil's trip to Washington, D.C., see Lamar Cecil,
letter to Gen. W. B. Persons, Apr. 19, 1954, Box 662, White House
Central Files, Eisenhower Presidential Library. Wilton B. Persons's and
Robert Cutler's ties to President Eisenhower are discussed in Parmet,
Eisenhower and the American Crusades, 151 (Persons), 191 (Cutler).

6. Cecil to Persons, Apr. 19, 1954.

7. Wilton B. Persons, letter to Lamar Cecil, Apr. 30, 1954, Box 117, White
House Central Files, Eisenhower Presidential Library.

8. On the judicial commission for Judge Joe M. Ingraham, see Federal
Judicial Center website, <www.fjc.gov>. For the nomination and rec-
ommendation of Cecil, see William P. Rogers, letter to Charles F.
Willis, Assistant, White House, Apr. 13, 1954, and Herbert Brownell,
Jr., letter to President Eisenhower, Apr. 13, 1954, both in Box 376,
White House Central Files, Eisenhower Presidential Library.

9. For Constitutional provisions, "senatorial courtesy," and other aspects
of the judicial nominating procedures, see Neil D. McFeely, *Appointment of Judges: The Johnson Presidency* (Austin: University of Texas
Press, 1987), 1–3; see also Robert A. Carp and Ronald Stidham, *Judicial
Process in America,* 5th ed. (Washington, D.C.: Congressional Quarterly Press, 2001), 229–38.

10. *Beaumont Enterprise,* Aug. 20, 1954. The letter in which Dillon Anderson recommended Lamar Cecil's nomination (letter to Robert Cutler,
Feb. 3, 1954, Lamar Cecil judicial nomination file, courtesy Grayson Cecil) mentioned his annual income from private practice, an
amount that far exceeded a judge's annual salary.

11. For documentation of Cecil's recess commission, see William J. Hopkins, White House internal memorandum to Sherman Adams, Aug. 26,
1954, over-marked with pencil notation showing commission, signed
Aug. 31, 1954, Box 376, White House Central Files, Eisenhower Presidential Library. For Cecil's Senate confirmation hearing, see Transcript
of Judiciary Committee Hearings, Consideration of Nominations,
Nov. 19, 1954, Committee on the Judiciary, U.S. Senate, 83rd Cong.,
Record Group 46, 23–26, National Archives and Records Administration, Washington, D.C. For discussion of "recess appointments," see
Carp and Stidham, *Judicial Process in America,* 230.

12. Transcript of Judiciary Committee Hearings, Nov. 19, 1954, 23–26;
Goldman, *Picking Federal Judges,* 109–24, 129.

13. Transcript of Judiciary Committee Hearings, Nov. 19, 1954, 23–26.

14. Chase, *Federal Judges,* 110–33; Goldman, *Picking Federal Judges,* 152. Patronage jobs given by the Eisenhower administration to Texas

Republicans and Democrats for Eisenhower are discussed in Olien, *From Token to Triumph,* 152–58.

15. *Beaumont Enterprise,* Sept. 9, 1954. The oath of office for United States judges is found under Title 28, Section 453, and Title 5, Section 3331, United States Code, with copy furnished by Dave Maland, Clerk, United States District Court, Eastern District of Texas, Tyler, Tex., in letter to author, Jan. 27, 2003.
16. *Beaumont Enterprise,* Sept. 18, 1954.
17. Ibid., Sept. 10, 1954.
18. Lamar Cecil, letter to President Eisenhower, Sept. 10, 1954; and Thomas E. Stephens, Secretary to the President, letter to Lamar Cecil, Sept. 15, 1954, both in Box 376, White House Central Files, Eisenhower Presidential Library.
19. Interviews with author: Rhoda Carter, former secretary to Lamar Cecil, Mar. 26, 2001; Andrew Cokinos, Nov. 15, 2002.
20. An overview and quantification of Judge Cecil's cases as well as litigant names are found in Record Group 21, U.S. District Court Minutes, Eastern District of Texas, Beaumont Division, Minutes (Sept. 10, 1954–Aug. 30, 1955), Entry E48E001A, National Archives and Records Administration, Southwest Division, Fort Worth, Tex. The fumbled introduction of Judge Cecil by Cokinos was recalled by Grayson Cecil (interview with author, Dec. 12, 2002).
21. Judge Cecil's docket for August, 1955, was reflected in Minutes, Eastern District of Texas, Beaumont, cited above in note 20. See also *Fayson v. Beard,* Civil Action 2920, case papers.
22. "Significance and History," architectural description of the Jack Brooks Federal Building, Beaumont, Tex., furnished by Keith Andreucci, Government Services Administration, Fort Worth, Tex., Jan. 15, 2002.
23. *Beaumont Enterprise,* Sept. 2, 1955.
24. Ibid.
25. *Fayson v. Beard,* Civil Action 2920, Memorandum Decision, Sept. 7, 1955, 1–2.
26. Ibid., 2–4.
27. Ibid., 4–5.
28. Ibid., 5–6.
29. Ibid., 9.
30. *Beaumont Enterprise,* Sept. 8, 1955. Cecil's ruling was cited in *City of Montgomery, et al., v. Gilmore,* Apr. 15, 1960; *F. L. Shuttlesworth, et al., v. Gaylord,* Nov. 8, 1961; *Bohler v. Lane,* March, 1962; *L. A. Watson, Jr., et al., v. City of Memphis, et al.,* May 27, 1963; *Lagarde, et al., v. City of Baton Rouge,* May 18, 1964; and *Hazel Palmer, et al., v. Allen C. Thompson, et al.,* June 14, 1971.
31. *Beaumont Enterprise,* Sept. 13, 15, 1955; Linda Ware Kyle interview, May 13, 2002.
32. *Beaumont Enterprise,* Sept. 13, 15, 1955.
33. *Fayson v. Beard,* Civil Action No. 2920, Final Order, Sept. 13, 1955.

34. *Beaumont Enterprise,* Sept. 16, 1955; Johnnie Barlow, interview, Oct. 18, 2000. Junius Dautrive and A. T. Miller are listed in *Worley's Port Arthur City Directory, 1956* (Dallas: John F. Worley Directory Company, 1956), Alphabetical List of Names, 111, 316. For Miller's background and accomplishments, see Amilcar Shabazz, *Advancing Democracy: African Americans and the Struggle for Access and Equity in Higher Education in Texas* (Chapel Hill and London: University of North Carolina Press, 2004), 161–63.

35. Johnnie Barlow interview, Oct. 18, 2000; "show of force" response by black golfers mentioned by Harry Kowalski, Beaumont City Council minutes, Sept. 20, 1955.

36. *Beaumont Enterprise,* Sept. 13, 1955; Beaumont City Council minutes, Sept. 20, 1955.

37. *Beaumont Enterprise,* Sept. 16, 1955.

38. Ibid.

39. Grayson Cecil interview, Mar. 31, 2003.

Epilogue

1. The whites-only provision is shown in *Mrs. Versie Jackson and James Anthony Cormier v. F. L. McDonald, President, Lamar State College of Technology, et al.,* Civil Action No. 3172, filed Mar. 14, 1956, U.S. District Court, Eastern District of Texas, Beaumont Division (cited hereafter as *Jackson v. McDonald*). (Copies of original documents, from the National Archives and Records Administration, Southwest Division, Fort Worth, Tex., are in the author's collection.) For the early history of Lamar University, see John W. Storey, "The Origins and Formative Years of Lamar University, 1921–1942: The Pietzsch-Bingman Era," *Texas Gulf Historical and Biographical Record* 33, no. 1 (1997): 12–27.

2. Shabazz, *Advancing Democracy,* 168–80. For early efforts to desegregate Lamar College and initiation of the three-step litigation program in 1955, see Shabazz, "The Desegregation of Lamar State College of Technology," 73–82, 84–86. For Lamar board of regents meeting, see *Beaumont Enterprise,* Aug. 24, 1955.

3. Dailey, "History of the Beaumont, Texas, Chapter of the National Association for the Advancement of Colored People," 56–59; Shabazz, "The Desegregation of Lamar State College of Technology," 84–87; and Gillette, "The NAACP in Texas, 1937–1957," 236–38.

4. *Jackson v. McDonald,* case papers. For Theo Johns's recollections, see Johns interview with Linsley and Stiles.

5. See *Jackson v. McDonald,* case papers; Edith Cecil Flynn, interview with author, May 3, 2003.

6. *Jackson v. McDonald,* Defendants' Answer, 3–4. For information about Attorney General Shepperd and his campaign against the NAACP, see George E. Christian, "John Ben Shepperd," *The Handbook of Texas Online,* May 1, 2003.

7. *Jackson vs. McDonald,* Defendants' Answer, 2–3.

8. *Jackson v. McDonald,* Plaintiff's Motion to Strike Redundant and Scandalous Materials, 1–3.

9. For the desegregation of Texas Western College and North Texas State College by federal court order, see Dailey, "History of the Beaumont, Texas, Chapter of the National Association of Colored People," 59–60; see also Vanderbilt University School of Law, *Race Relations Law Reporter* (Nashville: Vanderbilt University, 1956), 1:323–25; Gillette, "The NAACP in Texas, 1937–1957," 235–36. For referendum and results, see *Beaumont Enterprise,* July 30, 1956.

10. *Beaumont Enterprise,* July 31, 1956. For a discussion of the Lamar Tech case, see Warren Breed, *Beaumont, Texas: College Desegregation without Popular Support* (New York: Anti-Defamation League of B'nai B'rith, 1957), 5–7.

11. *Beaumont Enterprise,* July 31, 1956.

12. *Jackson vs. McDonald,* Findings of Fact and Conclusions of Law, and Final Order.

13. Breed, *Beaumont, Texas: College Desegregation without Popular Support,* 5–7; Shabazz, "The Desegregation of Lamar State College of Technology," 97–109.

14. *Beaumont Enterprise,* Sept. 21, 22, 1956. The Texas attorney general's campaign against the NAACP was repeated in Alabama, Mississippi, Florida, Georgia, and other southern states, as described in Ball, *A Defiant Life,* 146–47. The attorney general's campaign against the NAACP in Texas is covered in detail in Gillette, "The NAACP in Texas, 1937–1957," 288–332.

15. *Beaumont Enterprise,* July 31, 1956.

16. Ibid., Sept. 21, 1956.

17. Ibid., Sept. 24, 25, 1956.

18. Ibid., Sept. 25, 1956.

19. Dailey, "History of the Beaumont, Texas, Chapter of the National Association for the Advancement of Colored People," 62–63.

20. *Beaumont Enterprise,* Oct. 2, 3, 4, 1956.

21. Ibid., Oct. 3, 1956.

22. Ibid., Oct. 2, 1956.

23. Ibid., Oct. 3, 1956.

24. Ibid., Oct. 5, 1956.

25. Ibid.; Jimmie P. Cokinos, interview with author, June 10, 2003. Lamar Cecil, Jr. (interview with author, June 6, 2004), remembered receiving word from the FBI about a threat of violence against the family residence and moving out for a brief time.

26. *Beaumont Enterprise,* Oct. 16, 17, 18, 1956.

27. Ibid., Oct. 5, 6, 1956.

28. See *Jackson v. McDonald,* Appeal for Dismissal, May 17, 1957, and Gillette, "The NAACP in Texas, 1937–1957," 328–32, 341–52, for discussion of Attorney General Shepperd's attack on the NAACP and its impact on the organization's activities statewide. For later activities of

the Beaumont NAACP, see Dailey, "History of the Beaumont, Texas, Chapter of the National Association for the Advancement of Colored People," 63–67, 71–76.

29. For the life of Earl White in California, see Wolfcale, "Disability Is Not a Handicap for Richmond Golfer"; Geraldine White, interview with author, May 26, 2003.

30. Henry Durham interview, May 22, 2003.

31. Ibid.; J. P. Griffin, Jr., interview with author, May 27, 2003. Other Beaumont golfers were recalled by Ed Moore (interview with author, June 9, 2004).

32. Mary Cecil interview, Mar. 16, 2001.

33. James McNicholas interview, May 11, 2003.

34. Racial segregation in East Texas is described in Pitre, *In Struggle Against Jim Crow*, 5–7; *Titus Edwards v. Charles Spangler, Mayor, et al.*, Civil Action No. 638, filed July 15, 1957, U.S. District Court, Eastern District of Texas, Jefferson Division (cited hereafter as *Edwards v. Spangler*). (Copies of original documents, from the National Archives and Records Administration, Southwest Division, Fort Worth, Tex., are in the author's collection.)

35. For demographic and other information about Jefferson and Marshall, Tex., see *Texas Almanac, 1954–1955*, 561, 584.

36. *Edwards v. Spangler*, Defendant's Answer, 4–5.

37. *Tyler Morning Telegraph*, Aug. 1, 1957.

38. Ibid.; *Tyler Courier-Times*, Nov. 5, 1957.

39. For discussion of the Little Rock school crisis, see Patterson, *Grand Expectations*, 413–16; for the "troop-school" legislation proposed by Gov. Price Daniel (Daniel succeeded Allan Shivers as governor on Jan. 15, 1957), see *Beaumont Enterprise*, Nov. 7, 8, 9, 10, 12, 20, and 23, 1957; Frederick Eby quoted in *Beaumont Enterprise*, Nov. 19, 1957; Walter P. Webb quoted in *Beaumont Enterprise*, Nov. 8, 1957.

40. Judge Lamar Cecil, Record Group 21, U.S. District Court Minutes, Eastern District of Texas, Beaumont Division, Minutes (Feb. 14, 1958), Entry E48E001A; see also Lamar Cecil's obituary, *Beaumont Enterprise*, Feb. 15, 1958.

41. *Beaumont Enterprise*, Feb. 15, 1958; James McNicholas interview, Mar. 28, 2001.

BIBLIOGRAPHY

* *

Archival Materials

Beaumont Chamber of Commerce Collection. Tyrrell Historical Library, Beaumont, Tex.

Beaumont, Tex. City Council minutes, 1954–56. Tyrrell Historical Library, Beaumont, Tex.

Beaumont, Tex. City of. "Annual Budget, June 30, 1955." Tyrrell Historical Library, Beaumont, Tex.

Cecil, Lamar J. R. Correspondence. White House Central Files. Dwight D. Eisenhower Presidential Library, Abilene, Kans.

Jefferson County, Tex. Marriage and Real Property Records. Jefferson County Courthouse, Beaumont, Tex.

Johns, Theodore R. Oral interview with Judith W. Linsley and Jo Ann Stiles, February 26, 1989 (transcription). Tyrrell Historical Library, Beaumont, Tex.

NAACP (Beaumont, Texas) Branch Files, 1951–56. Library of Congress, Washington, D.C.

NAACP II, 1947–55. Series C, Box 232. (6 folders, 1947–55). Manuscript Division, Library of Congress, Washington, D.C.

Parker, Albertine. Oral interview with Judith Linsely. February 17, 1988. Tape 32. McFaddin-Ward House Museum, Beaumont, Tex.

U.S. District Court, Eastern District of Texas, Beaumont Division. Record Group 21, Minutes (1954–56), Boxes 1 and 2, Entry E48E001A. National Archives and Records Administration, Southwest Division, Fort Worth, Tex.

U.S. Senate. Judiciary Committee. Transcript, Judiciary Committee Hearings, Consideration of Nominations, November 19, 1954, 83rd Cong. Record Group 46. National Archives and Records Administration, Washington, D.C.

Books, Articles, Theses, and Dissertations

Abraham, Henry J., and Barbara A. Perry. *Freedom and the Court: Civil Rights and Liberties in the United States.* 6th ed. New York: Oxford University Press, 1994.

Ayers, Edward L. *Southern Crossing: A History of the American South, 1877–1906.* New York: Oxford University Press, 1995.

Ball, Howard. *A Defiant Life: Thurgood Marshall and the Persistence of Racism in America.* New York: Crown Publishers, 1998.

Banks, Melvin J. "The Pursuit of Equality: The Movement for First Class Citizenship among Negroes in Texas, 1920–1950." Ph.D. dissertation, Syracuse University, 1962.

Baritz, Loren, ed. *The Culture of the Twenties.* Indianapolis and New York: Bobbs-Merrill, 1970.

Barr, Alwyn. *Black Texans: A History of Negroes in Texas, 1528–1971.* Austin: Pemberton Press, 1973.

Beaumont City Directory. Dallas: Morrison & Fourmy Directory Company, 1947, 1949, 1950, 1952, 1954, 1956.

Beaumont City Directory. Houston: Morrison & Fourmy, 1929.

Bell, Major T. "Lamar Cecil: The Days That Were His." *Texas Gulf Historical and Biographical Record* 12, no. 1 (1976): 20–24.

Bennett, Michael J. *When Dreams Came True: The GI Bill and the Making of Modern America.* Washington, D.C.: Brassey's, 1996.

Black History Recognition Celebration (pamphlet). Ministers' Conference of Port Arthur, Tex., Feb. 18, 1989.

Breed, Warren. *Beaumont, Texas: College Desegregation without Popular Support.* New York: Anti-Defamation League of B'nai B'rith, 1957.

Brophy, William J. "Black Business Development in Texas Cities, 1900–1950." *Red River Valley Historical Review* 6 (Spring, 1981): 46–47.

———. "The Black Texan, 1900–1950: A Quantitative History." Ph.D. dissertation, Vanderbilt University, 1974.

Buchanan, A. Russell. *Black Americans in World War II.* Santa Barbara, Calif.: Clio Books, 1977.

Burran, James. "Violence in an 'Arsenal of Democracy': The Beaumont Race Riot, 1943." *East Texas Historical Journal* 14 (1976): 38–51.

Campanile 1923 (Rice Institute yearbook). Houston: Rein Printing, 1923.

Carp, Robert A., and Ronald Stidham. *Judicial Process in America.* 5th ed. Washington, D.C.: Congressional Quarterly Press, 2001.

Casdorph, Paul. *A History of the Republican Party in Texas, 1865–1965.* Austin: Pemberton Press, 1965.

Catalogue of the University of Texas, 1927–1928. Austin: University of Texas, 1927.

Chafe, William H. *Civilities and Civil Rights: Greensboro, North Carolina, and the Black Struggle for Freedom.* New York: Oxford University Press, 1980.

Chase, Harold W. *Federal Judges: The Appointing Process.* Minneapolis: University of Minnesota Press, 1972.

Clark, Norman H. *Deliver Us from Evil: An Interpretation of American Prohibition.* New York: Norton, 1976.

Cousins, Geoffrey. *Golf in Britain: A Social History from the Beginnings to the Present Day.* London: Routledge & Kegan Paul, 1975.

Dailey, Nancy. "History of the Beaumont, Texas, Chapter of the National

Association for the Advancement of Colored People, 1918–1970."
Master's thesis, Lamar University, 1971.

David, Paul T., Malcolm Moos, and Ralph M. Goldman. *Presidential Nominating Politics in 1952*. 5 vols. Baltimore: Johns Hopkins Press, 1954.

Dawkins, Marvin P., and Graham C. Kinloch. *African American Golfers during the Jim Crow Era*. Westport, Conn.: Praeger, 2000.

Deevy, Bill. "Elmo Willard." *Metropolitan Beaumont* (Beaumont Chamber of Commerce magazine), May/June, 1989, 40–43.

Dulaney, W. Marvin. "African Americans." In *The New Handbook of Texas*, edited by Ron C. Tyler. Austin: Texas State Historical Association, 1996.

Farley, Reynolds, and Walter R. Allen. *The Color Line and the Quality of Life in America*. New York: Russell Sage Foundation, 1987.

Flexner, Stuart Berg. *I Hear America Talking: An Illustrated Treasury of American Words and Phrases*. New York: Van Nostrand Reinhold, 1976.

Franklin, John Hope. *From Slavery to Freedom: A History of Negro Americans*. 4th ed. New York: Knopf, 1974.

Frazier, E. Franklin. *Black Bourgeoisie*. Glencoe, Ill.: Free Press, 1957.

Gillette, Michael L. "Heman Marion Sweatt: Civil Rights Plaintiff." In *Black Leaders: Texans for Their Times*, edited by Alwyn Barr and Robert A. Calvert. Austin: Texas State Historical Association, 1981.

———. "The NAACP in Texas, 1937–1957." Ph.D. dissertation, University of Texas at Austin, 1984.

Glasrud, Bruce A. "Black Texans, 1900–1930: A History." Ph.D. dissertation, Texas Tech University, 1969.

Goldfield, David R. *Black, White, and Southern: Race Relations and Southern Culture, 1940 to the Present*. Baton Rouge and London: Louisiana State University Press, 1990.

Goldman, Roger, and David Gallen. *Thurgood Marshall: Justice for All*. New York: Carroll & Graf, 1992.

Goldman, Sheldon. *Picking Federal Judges: Lower Court Selection from Roosevelt through Reagan*. New Haven and London: Yale University Press, 1997.

Gray, Maurine. *Beaumont Libraries: Then & Now*. Beaumont, Tex.: Friends of Beaumont Public Libraries, 1972.

Green, George Norris. *The Establishment in Texas Politics: The Primitive Years, 1938–1957*. Westport, Conn., and London: Greenwood Press, 1979.

Hoel, Donna, with Robert B. Howard, M.D. "Hypertension: Stalking the Silent Killer." *Postgraduate Medicine* 101, no. 2 (February, 1997) (available at <www.postgradmed.com>).

Houston City Directory, 1952. Dallas: Morrison & Fourmy Publishing, 1952.

Howard University Bulletin, General Catalogue, 1948–1949. Washington, D.C.: Howard University, 1948.

Isaac, Paul. "Municipal Reform in Beaumont, Texas, 1902–1909." *Southwestern Historical Quarterly* 78, no. 4 (April, 1975): 409–32.

Jackson, Juanita, and Jean Wallace. *A Directory of Black Businesses*,

Churches, Clubs, and Organizations in Beaumont, Texas. Beaumont, Tex.: Beaumont Public Library, 1981.

Jackson, Kenneth T. *Crabgrass Frontier: The Suburbanization of the United States.* New York: Oxford University Press, 1985.

Kaplan, Barry J. "Race, Income, and Ethnicity: Residential Change in a Houston Community, 1920–1970." *Houston Review* 3 (1981): 185–86.

Kennedy, David M. *Freedom from Fear: The American People in Depression and War, 1929–1945.* New York: Oxford University Press, 1999.

Kennedy, John H. *A Course of Their Own: A History of African American Golfers.* Kansas City, Mo.: Andrews McMeel, 2000.

Kluger, Richard. *Simple Justice: The History of* Brown v. Board of Education *and Black America's Struggle for Equality.* New York: Knopf, 1987.

Krislov, Samuel. *The Negro in Federal Employment: The Quest for Equal Opportunity.* Minneapolis: University of Minnesota Press, 1967.

Ladino, Robyn Duff. *Desegregating Texas Schools: Eisenhower, Shivers, and the Crisis at Mansfield High.* Austin: University of Texas Press, 1996.

Landry, Bart. *The New Black Middle Class.* Berkeley: University of California Press, 1987.

Lee, Ulysses. *The Employment of Negro Troops.* Washington, D.C.: Office of the Chief of Military History, U.S. Army, 1966.

Leuchtenburg, William E. *The Perils of Prosperity, 1914–1932.* Chicago and London: University of Chicago Press, 1958.

Linsley, Judith W. "Main House, Carriage House: African American Domestic Employees at the McFaddin-Ward House in Beaumont, Texas, 1900–1950." *Southwestern Historical Quarterly* 103 (July, 1999): 17–51.

Linsley, Judith W., and Ellen W. Rienstra. *Beaumont: A Chronicle of Promise.* Woodland Hills, Calif.: Windsor Publications, 1982.

Logan, Rayford W. *Howard University: The First Hundred Years, 1867–1967.* New York: New York University Press, 1969.

MacGregor, Morris J., Jr. *Integration of the Armed Forces, 1940–1965.* Washington, D.C.: Center of Military History, U.S. Army, 1981.

McDaniel, Pete. *Uneven Lies: The Heroic Story of African-Americans in Golf.* Greenwich, Conn.: American Golfer, 2000.

McFeely, Neil D. *Appointment of Judges: The Johnson Presidency.* Austin: University of Texas Press, 1987.

McKay, Seth Shepard. *Texas and the Fair Deal, 1945–1952.* San Antonio: Naylor, 1954.

Mitchell, Doug. "Golf in the Lone Star State: Municipal Golf Takes Off." *Texas Golfer Magazine* (February, 2001): 8–12.

———. "Golf in the Lone Star State: Texas' Oldest Courses." *Texas Golfer Magazine* 1, no. 7 (January, 2001): 4–5.

Nelson, Disa Marie. *A Brief History of Westminster Presbyterian Church of Beaumont* (pamphlet). Beaumont: Westminster Presbyterian Church, 1980.

Newberry, Kevin. *Texas Golf: The Best of the Lone Star State.* Houston: Gulf Publishing, 1998.

Nösner, Ellen Susanna. *Clearview, America's Course: The Autobiography of William J. Powell*. Haslette, Mich.: Foxsong Publishing, 2000.

Obadele-Starks, Ernest. *Black Unionism in the Industrial South*. College Station: Texas A&M University Press, 2000.

Ochs, Michael. *Rock Archives: A Photographic Journey through the First Two Decades of Rock and Roll*. Garden City, N.Y.: Doubleday, 1984.

Olien, Roger. *From Token to Triumph: The Texas Republicans since 1920*. Dallas: SMU Press, 1982.

Olson, James, and Sharon Phair. "The Anatomy of a Race Riot: Beaumont, Texas, 1943." *Texana* 11 (1973): 64–72.

O'Neal, Bill. *The Texas League, 1888–1987: A Century of Baseball*. Austin: Eakin Press, 1987.

Parmet, Herbert S. *Eisenhower and the American Crusades*. New York: Macmillan, 1972.

Parrish, Michael E. *Anxious Decades: America in Prosperity and Depression, 1920–1941*. New York and London: Norton, 1992.

Patterson, James T. *Grand Expectations: The United States, 1945–1974*. New York: Oxford University Press, 1996.

Pitre, Merline. *In Struggle against Jim Crow: Lulu B. White and the NAACP, 1900–1957*. College Station: Texas A&M University Press, 1999.

Polenberg, Richard. *One Nation Divisible: Class, Race, and Ethnicity in the United States since 1938*. New York: Viking Press, 1980.

Portrait of a People: An Ethnic History of Beaumont, Texas. Beaumont, Tex.: Beaumont Historical Landmark Commission, undated.

Posten, Ken. "Stuart Stadium: A Tribute to Commitment." *Texas Gulf Historical and Biographical Record* 30, no. 1 (1994): 79–92.

Price, Charles. *The World of Golf: A Panorama of Six Centuries of the Game's History*. New York: Random House, 1962.

Rader, Benjamin G. *American Sports: From the Age of Folk Games to the Age of Televised Sports*. 2nd ed. Englewood Cliffs, N.J.: Prentice Hall, 1990.

Rathbun, Georgiana F., ed. *Revolution in Civil Rights*. 4th ed. Washington, D.C.: Congressional Quarterly, 1968.

The Rice Institute Catalogue, 1922–1923. Houston: Rice Institute, 1922.

Rice Shock (Charlton-Pollard High School yearbook). Beaumont, Tex.: Beaumont Independent School District, 1955.

Risch, Erna. *The Quartermaster Corps: Organization, Supply and Services*. Vol. 1, *The Technical Services: United States Army in World War II*. Washington, D.C.: Office of the Chief of Military History, U.S. Army, 1953.

Robertson, Robert J. "Beaumont on the Eve of the Civil War, As Seen in the *Beaumont Banner*." *Texas Gulf Historical and Biographical Record* 30, no. 1 (1994): 8–26.

———. "Congressman Jack Brooks, the Civil Rights Act of 1964, and the Desegregation of Public Accommodations and Facilities in Southeast Texas: A Preliminary Inquiry." *Texas Gulf Historical and Biographical Record* 35, no. 1 (1999): 18–31.

————. *Her Majesty's Texans: Two English Immigrants in Reconstruction Texas.* College Station: Texas A&M University Press, 1998.

————. "Slavery and the Coming of the Civil War, As Seen in the *Beaumont Banner.*" *East Texas Historical Journal* 34 (1996): 14–29.

Robbins, Marcus. "Our Inalienable Right: A Brief History of Locals 229 and 243 of Oil Workers International Union, Magnolia Refinery, 1937–1945." *Texas Gulf Historical and Biographical Record* 29, no. 1 (1993): 55–68.

Ross, William F., and Charles F. Romanus. *The Quartermaster Corps: Operations in the War against Germany, The Technical Services, United States Army in World War II.* Washington, D.C.: Office of the Chief of Military History, U.S. Army, 1965.

Rubin, Lester. *The Negro in the Shipbuilding Industry.* Philadelphia: Industrial Research Unit, Wharton School of Finance and Commerce, University of Pennsylvania, 1970.

Sapper, Neil Gary. "A Survey of the History of the Black People of Texas, 1930–1954." Ph.D. dissertation, Texas Tech University, 1972.

Shabazz, Amilcar. *Advancing Democracy: African Americans and the Struggle for Access and Equity in Higher Education in Texas.* Chapel Hill and London: University of North Carolina Press, 2004.

————. "The Desegregation of Lamar State College of Technology: An Analysis of Race and Education in Southeast Texas." Master's thesis, Lamar University, 1990.

Silvera, John D. *The Negro in World War II.* New York: Arno Press and the *New York Times,* 1969.

Simond, Ada. "A History of African-American Catholicism in Texas." In *Bricks without Straw: A Comprehensive History of African Americans in Texas,* edited by David A. Williams. Austin: Eakin Press, 1997.

Sinnette, Calvin H. *Forbidden Fairways: African Americans and the Game of Golf.* Chelsea, Mich.: Sleeping Bear Press, 1998.

Sitkoff, Harvard. *A New Deal for Blacks: The Emergence of Civil Rights as a National Issue.* New York: Oxford University Press, 1978.

————. *The Struggle for Black Equality, 1954–1980.* New York: Hill and Wang, 1981.

SoRelle, James M. "The Emergence of Black Business in Houston: A Study of Race and Ideology, 1919–1945." In *Black Dixie: Afro-Texan History and Culture in Houston,* edited by Howard Beeth, Howard and Cary D. Wintz. College Station: Texas A&M University Press, 1992.

Stiles, Jo Ann Pankratz. "The Changing Economic and Educational Status of Texas Negroes, 1940–1960." Master's thesis, University of Texas at Austin, 1966.

Storey, John W. "The Origins and Formative Years of Lamar University, 1921–1942: The Pietzsch-Bingman Era." *Texas Gulf Historical and Biographical Record* 33, no. 1 (1997): 12–27.

Texas Almanac. Dallas: Belo Corporation, 1947, 1955, 1957.

Thernstrom, Stephan, and Abigail Thernstrom. *America in Black and White: One Nation, Indivisible*. New York: Simon & Schuster, 1997.

Tyler, Ron C., et al., eds. *The New Handbook of Texas*. 6 vols. Austin: Texas State Historical Association, 1996.

United States. Bureau of the Census. *Census of Population, 1950: Seventeenth Census of the United States*. Washington, D.C.: Government Printing Office, 1952.

Vanderbilt University School of Law. *Race Relations Law Reporter*. Nashville, Tenn.: Vanderbilt University, 1956.

Van Riper, Paul P. *History of the United States Civil Service*. Evanston, Ill.: Row, Peterson, 1958.

Vernon's Annotated Revised Civil Statutes of the State of Texas. Kansas City, Mo.: Vernon Law Book Company, 1963.

Walker, John H., and Gwendolyn Wingate. *Beaumont: A Pictorial History*. Norfolk, Va.: Donning Company, 1983.

Weeks, O. Douglas. *Texas Presidential Politics in 1952*. Austin: Institute of Public Affairs, University of Texas, 1953.

Wind, Herbert Warren. *The Story of American Golf: Its Champions and Its Championships*. 3rd ed. rev. New York: Knopf, 1975.

Woodland, Naaman J. "The Leadership of Mrs. Beeman Strong of the Beaumont Music Commission." *Texas Gulf Historical and Biographical Record* 34, no. 1 (1998): 35–47.

Woodward, C. Vann. *The Strange Career of Jim Crow*. 2nd rev. ed. New York: Oxford University Press, 1966.

Worley's Port Arthur City Directory, 1956. Dallas: John F. Worley Directory Company, 1956.

Yourcenar, Marguerite. "Ah, Mon Beau Château." In *The Dark Brain of Piranesi and Other Essays*. New York: Farrar, Straus, Giroux, 1984.

Zelden, Charles L. *Justice Lies in the District: The United States District Court, Southern District of Texas, 1902–1960*. College Station: Texas A&M University Press, 1993.

INDEX

• •

INDEX